UNIVERSITY OF NORTH CAROLINA AT CHAPEL HILL
DEPARTMENT OF ROMANCE LANGUAGES

NORTH CAROLINA STUDIES
IN THE ROMANCE LANGUAGES AND LITERATURES

Founder: URBAN TIGNER HOLMES

Distributed by:

UNIVERSITY OF NORTH CAROLINA PRESS
CHAPEL HILL
North Carolina 27514
U.S.A.

NORTH CAROLINA STUDIES IN THE
ROMANCE LANGUAGES AND LITERATURES
Number 198

A BAHIAN HERITAGE

A BAHIAN HERITAGE

An Ethnolinguistic Study of African Influences on Bahian Portuguese

BY

WILLIAM W. MEGENNEY

CHAPEL HILL

NORTH CAROLINA STUDIES IN THE ROMANCE
LANGUAGES AND LITERATURES
U.N.C. DEPARTMENT OF ROMANCE LANGUAGES
1978

Library of Congress Cataloging in Publication Data

Megenney, William W.
  A Bahian heritage.

  (North Carolina studies in the Romance languages and literatures; no. 198)
  Bibliography: p.
  Includes index.
  1. Portuguese language—Dialects—Brazil—Bahia (State). 2. Portuguese language—Foreign elements—African. I. Title. II. Series.

PC5447.B3M4   469'.798'4   78-7710
ISBN 0-8078-9198-3

I. S. B. N. 0-8078-9198-3

DEPÓSITO LEGAL: V. 1.492 - 1978   I. S. B. N. 84-399-8373-5
ARTES GRÁFICAS SOLER, S. A. - JÁVEA, 28 - VALENCIA (8) - 1978

PREFACE

Since this monograph is destined principally for speakers of English, the author has translated into English quotations which appear in foreign languages.

To give the Negro an appreciation of his past is to endow him with the confidence in his own position in this country and in the world which he must have, and which he can best attain when he has available a foundation of scientific fact concerning the ancestral cultures of Africa and the survivals of Africanisms in the New World. And it must again be emphasized that when such a body of fact, solidly grounded, is established, a ferment must follow which, when this information is diffused over the population as a whole, will influence opinion in general concerning Negro abilities and potentialities, and thus contribute to a lessening of interracial tensions.

MELVILLE J. HERSKOVITS

ACKNOWLEDGEMENTS

I wish to express my sincere gratitude to Professors Guilherme and Yêda Pessoa de Castro, to Juana Elbein and Deoscóredes M. dos Santos, to all of my Bahian informants who supplied valuable Afro-Bahian chants and expressions, and to my African informants, who all contributed invaluable information for the compilation of this study.

I owe a special indebtedness to Professor William E. Welmers of the Department of Linguistics at UCLA for making many helpful suggestions on a draft, especially in Chapter IV.

I am also grateful to the University of California for having provided me with financial assistance, through the Committee on Research of the Riverside Campus, for the typing of the manuscript and for some African native informants.

*To my Mother and Father
and to my wife, Ruth*

CONTENTS

	Page
INTRODUCTION	19

CHAPTER

		Page
I.	PREVIOUS STUDIES OF AFRO-BRAZILIAN AND AFRO-BAHIAN LINGUISTICS	23
II.	ORIGINS OF THE AFRICAN TRIBES TAKEN TO BAHIA	61
III.	ETHNOLINGUISTIC DATA GATHERED IN THE "CANDOMBLÉS" OF THE CITY OF SALVADOR	87
IV.	LEXICAL AFRICANISMS IN BAHIAN PORTUGUESE	115
V.	THE BAHIAN PEOPLE AND THEIR LANGUAGE IN DIFFERENT LEVELS OF SOCIETY	163

APPENDIX

		Page
I.	A Small Vocabulary of Yoruba, Gathered in Bahia by Dr. Oscar de Carvalho in 1900	193
II.	"Ewe" Material	195
III.	"Yoruba" Material	200
IV.	"Ijesha," "Angola" and Portuguese Material	212
V.	Additional Words Recorded as Part of The Passive Vocabulary in Bahia	217

	Page
A SELECTED BIBLIOGRAPHY	218
A LIST OF BAHIAN WORDS OF AFRICAN ORIGIN DEFINED IN CHAPTER IV	229

LIST OF FIGURES

		Page
1.	Sub-Saharan Africa, Indicating the Major Regions from Which the Portuguese Imported Slaves to Brazil	64
2.	Classification of West African Languages According to Joseph H. Greenberg	75

LIST OF TABLES

	Page

1. Symbols for Vowel Phones   29
2. Symbols for Consonant Phones   30
3. Popular Colloquial Words Used in Salvador and Tentatively Identified as Being of African Origin, Selected from Edison Carneiro's List   46
4. Numbers of Sudanese and Bantu Slaves in Bahia Between the Years 1741 and 1799   82

INTRODUCTION

The purpose of investigating the African linguistic vestiges in the city of Salvador da Bahia, capital of the state of Bahia, Brazil, is to discover ethnolinguistic data which will provide valuable information concerning the impact that the African languages and cultures have had on contemporary Bahian Portuguese. It is important to gather vocabulary items of non-Romance origin and determine which have African roots, in order to locate, within Bahian society, different types of African cultural remains. Such investigative activities will lead to a better understanding of the socio-economic relationships among the various levels of Bahian society and of the processes of linguistic borrowing reflected by these relationships.

Since the greatest concentration of western African peoples that were brought to Bahia is found in the cult organizations (*candomblé*), which still retain some of their original languages, members of these vestigial nuclei are helpful sources for research in this area of African penetration into Bahian life.

Problems of African influences in Brazil are centered in Bahia because it was here that the most important focal point of slavery existed. Salvador was, in colonial and imperial times, and continues to be in the contemporary republican era, the center of ethnic activities stemming from sub-Saharan Africa. It is understandable, then, that inquiries concerning the African heritage in Brazil should begin and develop in Bahia.

The population of the city of Salvador, and even of the entire state of Bahia, is perhaps unique when compared to most other areas of the country [1] in that it, ever since the early days of its captaincy

---

[1] The area in and around the state of Guanabara also has a history of large black importations from Africa.

status, has always had a preponderant number of black people, and in that this number has gradually contributed to the development of a growing miscegenation which, in turn, has had a direct effect on socio-economic structures in as much as they reflect the racial components of the society. The linguistic changes brought about in Bahian Portuguese, then, stem from this ethno-demographic phenomenon of large percentages of blacks finding ways and means of incorporating some of their cultural heritage into the life styles of the Portuguese population in Bahia.

A review of previous Afro-Brazilian studies indicates that there were three main phases of investigation. The first phase was an evolutionary one primarily concerned with general anthropological questions. The second was one of revision of initial studies with an emphasis on cultural traits. The third, which represents today's labors, is a period of a much more rigorously empirical methodology oriented toward modern techniques of descriptive linguistics.

Chapter I of this study deals with previous work done in the field of Afro-Brazilian linguistics from its beginnings in 1900 to the present day. A critical analysis of these publications provides greater insights into past and present studies of slaves imported to Bahia, and of how these slaves are related to contemporary social and ethnolinguistic problems. This chapter also helps us to distinguish between the speculation and the empirical recording and interpretation of data. Chapter II examines the problem of determining the origins of slaves brought to Bahia. An understanding of the geographical sources of Portuguese slave activities in Africa along with approximate estimates of the numbers of members from each tribe or area will aid in discovering which languages the blacks implanted in Bahia, and of these languages, which ones predominated. The third chapter presents a collection of valuable samples of archaic African languages which are a part of the Afro-Bahian subculture. Some of these samples can be used to determine the amount of influence the African tongues have had on Bahian Portuguese. In Chapter IV the data gathered in my own interviews and that of a carefully selected group of competent authors in the field are combined for a more complete interpretation of the penetrations which these imported African languages have had on the lexicon of the Portuguese spoken in Salvador. The final chapter relates the findings of the preceding discussion to the three main socio-economic levels in the city of Bahia. This connection between the linguistic and socio-historical aspects of the problem points out important relationships in current usages of Portuguese among Bahians.

Chapter I

PREVIOUS STUDIES OF AFRO-BRAZILIAN AND AFRO-BAHIAN LINGUISTICS

There are a considerable number of studies in Afro-Bahian and Afro-Brazilian linguistics and ethnolinguistics which have been compiled and published during the twentieth century. Materials dealing with this subject before 1900, however, are practically non-existent. This chapter will review the twentieth-century publications, considered chronologically, in this area of study.

The first noteworthy study is a collection of 114 Yoruba words with their corresponding Portuguese meanings, gathered by Dr. Oscar de Carvalho in Bahia in 1900. The list was lent to me by Yêda Pessoa de Castro, who has it on file in her office at the University of Bahia. The words on the list are written according to the Portuguese system of orthography, and therefore their exact pronunciation cannot be determined.[1]

More than thirty years elapsed before the appearance of the next study in Afro-Brazilian linguistics, which was written by Jacques Raimundo and published in 1933. It contains a brief discussion of the origins of the various tribes taken captive by the Portuguese and held as slaves in Brazil and includes a description of some features of the Yoruba language.

In is interesting to note that in this study the author comments about the effort put forth on the part of the Negro and his master to understand one another. The matter is only mentioned, but allusion is made to the idea that, because of such mutual exertion for

---

[1] See Appendix I. Oscar de Carvalho, "Pequeno Vocabulário de Língua Nagô," 1900. Unpublished MS.

communication, a kind of Pidgin Portuguese developed which was instrumental in catalyzing a reciprocal exchange of lexical elements between Portuguese and the West African languages. As a result of this linguistic interchange, the Portuguese language was highly enriched with a host of vocabulary items, especially in the culinary arts and in religious activities.

Curiously, many scholars believe that a Portuguese-based pidgin language existed along the African coast by the time the slave trade to the New World began. This language was undoubtedly transmitted to Brazil. It probably expanded there, and at some point may have become a creole. In this case, present day Bahian Portuguese, particularly among the lower classes, may well be a "post-creole" by increasing conformity to Portuguese.

Jacques Raimundo's study concludes with a long list of Yoruba words written with Portuguese orthography. Each word is defined and explained meticulously.

In 1934 João Ribeiro published *O Elemento Negro*.[2] It begins with a discussion of a classification of the languages of "Black Africa," followed by a section treating some Portuguese dialects in Africa. Further speculative discussion, concerning morphological borrowings from "some African dialects" into Portuguese, is followed by a general outline of sources for Brazil's African vocabulary.

A series of works concerning Afro-Brazilian ethnolinguistics was published under one cover in conjunction with the first Afro-Brazilian Congress held in 1934.[3] One of these papers is titled "O Negro no Folklore e na Literatura do Brasil" by Renato Mendonça. The folklore section is especially interesting since it elaborates on many of the musical instruments and songs of African origin. The other paper dealing directly with African influence in Brazil is a list of Yoruba words, in Portuguese orthography, with a translation into Portuguese for each word. The list is interrupted in one section by some general statements about Yoruba grammar and some songs concerning Yoruba saints, translated into Portuguese from an oral rendition of Yoruba.

---

[2] (Rio de Janeiro, Record: 1934).

[3] *Estudos Afro-Brasileiros* (Trabalhos apresentados *ao Primeiro Congresso Afro-Brasileiro reunido no Recife em 1934*) (Rio de Janeiro, Ariel Editôra Ltda.: 1935).

Nina Rodrigues' study, *Os Africanos no Brasil*,[4] begins with an enumeration of the names and origins of the various tribes brought from western Africa to the state of Bahia. Among others, the Yoruba, Ewe, Mina, Hausa, Tapas, Gurunxis (variant forms of spelling are found among different authors), Fulahs, Mandingas and Bantu are discussed in some detail. In addition to their origin, the author theorizes about the number of slaves shipped to Bahia, the proportion of male to female members of each tribe in Bahia, and the personality of each tribe, as a whole.

Chapter V, titled "African Survivals — the Language and the Fine-Arts in the Black Colonies," is of special importance since here the author devotes about seventy-five pages to the problems of the various languages and dialects of African Origin influencing Portuguese, the lack of interest in such matters in Brazil, and the importance of certain languages, namely Yoruba, Ewe, Hausa, Bornun, Tapa, Grunci, Tshi, Mandinga, Fula, Felupio, Wolof, and the Bantu languages as a group. Nina Rodrigues states that Yoruba was used as a *língua geral* and explains some points of its grammatical structure. This chapter also contains a number of vocabularies of African languages still spoken during the 19th century in Brazil.

Nina Rodrigues believes that the Yoruba had a numerical preponderance and a cultural and religious dominance which caused them to overshadow the other "nations" in Bahia, to preserve themselves intact and to be the dominant people from Africa in Bahia during the nineteenth century. The author reminds us that other peoples were as numerous, such as the ones from Angola (referring here to all of the major places where slaves were brought), but were not as domineering as the Yoruba in the areas of culture and especially religion.

While discussing the positive existence of six Sudanese languages which were taken to Brazil, Nina Rodrigues states that the Viscount of Pôrto Seguro had noted that the Yoruba language was used as a *língua geral* in Bahia. Nina Rodrigues says that this would have been possible since the slaves who had established the most fame for themselves in Brazil were the ones that came from the Mina Coast, and they were more numerous in Bahia than in any other part of

---

[4] 2nd ed. (São Paulo, Companhia Editôra Nacional: 1935).

Brazil. Here in Bahia, the slaves spoke Yoruba among themselves, and were slow to learn Portuguese.

The author of *Os Africanos no Brasil* informs us that Elisée Réclus, in his book *Estados Unidos do Brasil*, refers to the Yoruba as having used their own language for purposes of celebrating all their religious rituals. The use of this language for this purpose was spread among the other African slaves who lived in Bahia.

In the same book Nina Rodrigues writes that the Ewe language comes from the same parent tongue as Yoruba and that its grammar is almost identical with that of the *Nagô*. This, of course, would explain the Yoruba-Ewe complex which was formed in Bahia, for if their languages were so similar, the Yoruba and the Ewe should have found very little difficulty in combining themselves together under one religious roof in a land which was alien to both.

Throughout this entire volume, Nina Rodrigues reiterates his belief that the Yoruba were numerically greater and culturally dominant especially in the state of Bahia. He mentions the fact that there were other "nations" taken to Brazil as slaves, such as the Tapas, the Nifês, and the various peoples from the Bantu-speaking area, but that all of them spoke Yoruba as well as their native tongues. If this is true, as the author states, does it mean that Yoruba was indeed the *lingua franca* of Brazil, or at least of Bahia? Nina Rodrigues would seem to indicate this as he writes on page 232 of the edition cited that the Hausa, as an example, were very numerous in Bahia during the first half of the nineteenth century. They were intelligent people, knowing how to read and write in Arabic, and yet the Yoruba were able to dominate them and to impose their language in this area as a *lingua franca*. Nevertheless, the author questions his own findings and sees no reason to discredit the possibility of finding Hausa to have been the *lingua geral* in Bahia. According to Nina Rodrigues, Hausa, Kanuri, Tapa, and Grunce were spoken in Bahia even at the time of writing the book. The Mandês or Mandingas were also numerous in this north-central coastal region of Brazil and the author poses the question of their having been the chief proponents of a *lingua geral* which served as a means of general communication among the blacks at some point in time during the three centuries of slave traffic in Brazil.

Nina Rodrigues presents a list of vocabulary items on pages 236-239 (edition previously cited) and says that his reason for doing this is simply to prove that these languages were spoken in Bahia during the nineteenth century. The lexical items cited belong to the following languages: Grunce, *Gêge* (Ewe), Hausa, Kanuri, and Tapa.

Gilberto Freire, one of the foremost authorities on the life and growth of the Brazilian people, discusses at great length the formation of the Brazilian slave-holding, hybrid society in his well-known book *Casa Grande e Senzala,* published in 1936. Two of the five chapters in the work are entitled "O Escravo Negro na Vida Sexual e de Família do Brasileiro" (The Negro Slave in the Sexual and Family Life of the Brazilian). In these chapters, the Brazilian sociologist informs us of the important role the Negro has played in the development of Brazilian Portuguese.

Freire presents observations of the linguistic influence on Brazilian children prompted by the black females serving colonial families. According to Freire, the language of the younger members of the family grew softer through contact with the Negro nurse. Certain words, he writes, that today are harsh or sharp-sounding when pronounced by the European Portuguese, are much smoother in Brazil, because of the influence of the African. Many of Freire's descriptions are impressionistic and non-scientific; but they do, in their own way, approach a faithful delineation of what actually has happened.

The priests, who served as schoolmasters, and the plantation chaplains, who, after the Jesuits had withdrawn, became the main factors responsible for the education of Brazilian children, attempted to react against the overwhelming Negro influence that was constantly growing in all levels of society. They were not able to overcome so strong a force, however: for example, the modifications of certain words, which are attributed to Negro influence and recorded during the early days of contact between the Portuguese and the Africans, are still maintained today. Father Miguel do Sacramento Lopes Gama transcribed words and utterances in 1832 which he stated had been perverted by Negro slaves. Freire tells us the following about Frei Miguel do Sacramento Lopes Gama:

> ...era um dos que se indignavam quando ouvia "meninas galantes" dizerem "mandá, buscá, e comê" em vez de "mandar, buscar, e comer," "mi espere, ti faço, ou mi deixa," em vez de "espere-me, faço-te ou deixe-me"; quando diziam "muler" por "mulher," ou "coler" por "colher," ou usavam

tais expressões como "le pediu" por "lhe pediu" ou "cadê êle" por "onde está êle." [5]

(... he was one of those who became angry whenever he heard "nice young ladies" say "*mandá, buscá,* and *comê*" instead of "*mandar, buscar,* and *comer*," "*Mi espere, ti faço,* or *mi deixa,*" instead of "*espere-me, faço-te* or *deixe-me*"; when they would say "*muler*" for "*mulher,*" or "*coler*" for "*colher,*" or use such expressions as "*le pediu*" for "*lhe pediu*" or "*cadê êle*" for "*onde está êle.*")

The peculiar pronunciation and syntactical constructions represented in Frei Miguel's orthography are extremely common in present-day Bahia. The following utterances, transcribed from contemporary oral speech, will serve as examples: [mãn'da], [bus'ka], [ku'me] ~ [ko'me], [mi ɛs'pɛri], [či 'fasu], [mi 'deyši], [mu'le] ~ [mu'lex], [ku'le] ~ [ko'le] ~ [ku'lex] ~ [ko'lex], [li pɛ'jyu], [ka'de 'Ili]. (See Tables 1 and 2 for description of symbols.)

My phonetic transcription differs from Frei Miguel's orthographical reproduction because the Brazilian priest's system of writing is, by its very nature (Portuguese spelling system and not phonetic symbols), not accurate and therefore liable to misrepresentation and misinterpretation. However, a general knowledge of the orthographical system of Portuguese suffices for a correct understanding of the sound shifts that Frei Miguel was attempting to reproduce in writing.

Several chapters in Arthur Ramos' book *As Culturas Negras no Nôvo Mundo* [6] are particularly interesting in connection with the introduction of the Yoruba and Ewe languages in Brazil. One of the first topics alluded to is the formation of a *língua geral* in Bahia, which Ramos regards as a variant of Yoruba. Without citing any names, he asserts that several authors have noted that the Negro slaves brought to Bahia were able to understand one another with relative ease in Yoruba. The accuracy of these statements cannot be verified simply because there are no historical data attesting a *língua*

---

[5] Padre Miguel do Sacramento Lopes Gama, *O Carapuceiro* (Recife: 1832, 1834, 1837, 1943, 1947), cited in *Casa Grande e Senzala*, p. 245.

The phonetic changes involved here are the following: omission of word final [r]; [λ] > [l]; [e] or [ə] > [i]. The syntactical changes are: the placement of the direct and indirect object pronouns before the imperative form of the verb instead of after it.

[6] (Rio de Janeiro, Civilização Brasileira, S. A. Editôra: 1937).

TABLE I

SYMBOLS FOR VOWEL PHONES

		front		central			back
		unrounded		unrounded			rounded
high	closed	i					u
	open	I					ʊ
mid	closed	e		ə			o
	open	ɛ		ɐ			
low	closed	æ					ɔ
	open	a		a			

Nasal vowels are marked by superscript ~.
Lengthened vowels are marked by superscript · .
[y] and [w] are the glide forms of [i] and [u], respectively.

TABLE 2

SYMBOLS FOR CONSONANT PHONES

Manner of Articulation		Point of Articulation bilabial	lab-dent.	alveolar	alveopal.	palatal	velar	post-vel.	glottal
stops									
unaspirated	vl.	p		t	ṭ		k	k̠	
	vd.	b		d			g		
affricated	vl.				č				
	vd.				ǰ				
fricatives									
flat	vl.	f̣	f						h
	vd.	β̇	v						
grooved	vd.			s	š	ẓ̌	x		
				z	ǰ				
frictionless									
nasal	vd.	m		n	ñ		ŋ		
lateral	vd.			l	λ				
vibrants									
flapped				r					
semivowels	vd.	w				y			

vl. - voiceless; vd. - voiced.
[w] and [y] are non-syllabic, in contrast to syllabic [u] and [i], respectively.
[gb] is listed separately as a unit phone in parts of the data because of its frequency of occurrence.
Stress is indicated by the placement of ' before the syllable receiving primary stress.
˜ indicates free variation.
Lengthened consonants are indicated by superscript · .

geral. Ramos believes that one of the reasons for Yoruba dominance over the other African languages was the overwhelming numerical majority of its speakers. This may be true, though historical documents indicate that large numbers of both Yoruba and Ewe peoples were not brought to Bahia until 1800-1850; no exact figures for either tribe are given for this time period, merely statistical accounts of the slaves taken from the Gold Coast. However, a large amount of African cultural and linguistic vestiges found in Bahia today are of Yoruba origin. In effect, the statement that Ramos makes about the predominance of Yoruba at the time his work was written is credible in as much as the same is true today. He states: "A língua nagô é, de fato muito falada na Bahia, seja por quase todos os velhos africanos das diferentes nacionalidades, seja por grande número de crioulos e mulatos." [7] (The Nago language is, in fact, spoken very much in Bahia, both by almost all of the old Africans of the various nationalities, and by the larger number of creoles and mulattoes.)

The idea of the dominance of Yoruba people in Bahia must have been impressive in the past. Reviewing a number of historical events related in *As Culturas Negras no Nôvo Mundo,* one is surprised at the misconceptions regarding Yoruba penetration in Bahia. One of these events concerns the arrival of some Catholic missionaries who had come from Africa to the city of Bahia to distribute religious literature and preach to the people. They were told that they should address themselves to the Negro population in Yoruba if they expected to be understood. The missionaries, not wanting any of their message to be lost, followed the advice of those who had informed them of the language situation in Bahia. On the fourth of January, 1899, Father Coquard preached a sermon completely in Yoruba to the slave population in the Igreja da Sé. The sermon was a total failure. No one understood what had been said. The reason for such complete incomprehension can easily be demonstrated. The language used in the sermon was pure African Yoruba. The Yoruba spoken by the Bahian slaves was a language which, evidently, by 1899, had been so radically altered by influence from the Portuguese, that it was no longer identifiable with its African parent in terms of mutual intelligibility.

---

[7] *As Culturas,* p. 311.

An indication of Yoruba dominance over the other African tribes brought to Bahia may be noted in what Ramos calls the "cultural superiority" of this "nation." This cultural superiority may have exerted an even greater force in the process of subduing and absorbing the other African peoples in Bahia than that of mere numerical preponderance. [8]

Sousa Carneiro, in his book entitled *Os Mitos Africanos no Brasil*, brings out three fundamental stages in the development of Brazilian Portuguese. The second of these, the African *língua geral*, which many Portuguese believed to be based on Kimbundu, one of the languages of Angola, interests us most in this study. Concerning this, Carneiro states that Yoruba and Ewe had an important part in helping to mold New World Portuguese:

> ... com firmeza invejável, o nagô ou iorubês, mais conhecido por língua iorubana ou iorubá, que, ao inverso do que pensaram os portuguêses tornando geral a língua de Angola, fêz-se, na sede da Colónia, em harmonia com o gêge, o dominador dos termos dos cultos fetiches, e, sem perder a preponderância nos termos da culinária, destarte fartou-se, com essa língua, de vencer o quimbundo e intervir na adopção quase integral de seus vocábulos. [9]

> (... with enviable firmness, Nago or Yoruba, better known as the Yoruba language, which contrary to what the Portuguese thought (that the language of Angola had become generalized), became, in the heart of the colony, along with Ewe, the common denominator of fetish cult terms, and, without losing its preponderance in the area of the culinary arts, overcame Kimbundu influences and prevented the adoption of all but a few vocabulary items from this language.)

This statement is a plausible one, especially applicable to Bahia. In this city, the preponderance of *candomblé* houses in which Yoruba is used for songs and exorcisms would indicate a cultural and linguistic dominance of this language over the other African tongues spoken here, at least in the nineteenth century.

Carneiro makes the important observation that changes were induced in the African languages brought to Brazil because of the new

---

[8] Pedro McGregor, in his book, *The Moon and Two Mountains*, would tend to agree with these statements, as we shall see in a later chapter.
[9] *Os Mitos*, p. 22.

and different linguistic contacts experienced there. The author notes that many of the members of the African tribes in Brazil mingled with one another. This may be attested today by the fact that present-day *candomblé* houses manifest definite evidence of tribal intermixture in the common use of certain songs, spirits and words among the various "nations."

Carneiro's recognition of the marked differences between the African dialects in Brazil and their parent dialects in Africa demonstrates an acute perception of linguistic features. These differences were studied in greater detail and substantiated in a very recent work which will be discussed shortly.[10] Both studies noted that existing divergences between Afro-Brazilian dialects and those of Africa were caused not only by external linguistic influences, but also by an internal factor of conservatism among the tongues brought to Brazil, which seems to have become established some time after the period of separation.

Nelson de Senna published a study in 1938 on the African influence in Brazil.[11] The first part of the work discusses the *língua geral*, which de Senna claims is a New World development of the Kimbundu language from Angola. According to this interpretation, the *língua geral* was formed from bits and pieces of various African languages which had been borrowed into Kimbundu because of the high degree of intermixing of Negro tribes in the slave markets throughout Brazil. De Senna proposes, then, that practically all of the African vocabulary existent in Brazilian Portuguese was filtered through Kimbundu, since, according to him, this language served as a kind of *koinē* among the Negro slaves in most of Brazil. This observation may not be too far from the truth, since an appreciable amount of lexical items found in Bahia today probably stem from Kimbundu, as we shall see in Chapter IV.

In 1940 a Second Afro-Brazilian Congress was held in the city of Salvador da Bahia. The papers presented at this congress were

---

[10] See Deoscóredes M. dos Santos, "West African Sacred Art and Rituals in Brazil" (Nigeria, Monograph, Institute of African Studies, University of Ibadan: 1967).

[11] *Africanos no Brasil* (Belo Horizonte, Oficinas Gráficas Queiroz Breyner, Ltda.: 1938).

published under one title and provide only general information on Afro-Brazilian studies. [12]

Jacques Raimundo published another book in 1941 dealing with the influence of African languages on Brazilian Portuguese. [13] The first part of his study consists of African words from several different tribes, mainly of the Bantu family. According to Raimundo, all of these words are an integral part of every Brazilian's active vocabulary. From my own personal research in the city of Bahia, however, I found that many of the words on this list are not even in the general passive vocabulary of the inhabitants of that city. Only about 20 % of these words were recognized and identified by Bahian informants. My own observations would tend to indicate, then, that the author either exaggerated the widespread usage of the words or misinterpreted their significance, believing that all of the words on his list were, in effect, nationally current, whereas they could possibly represent a compendium of regional vocabularies.

Arthur Ramos, [14] in a study concerning cultural elements introduced into Brazil from Africa, states that African culinary arts, which are most abundant along the north-eastern coast of Brazil, were brought from Sudanese territory. This general locale is then specified when the author concludes that the names given to Afro-Brazilian foods and cooking utensils are of Yoruba and Ewe origin. Very few of these culinary vocabulary items are regarded by him as deriving from Kimbundu. This is in direct contrast to de Senna's study, which claims that most of Brazil's African vocabulary stems from the Kimbundu language. Conflicting opinions such as these can be found in many of the studies of Afro-Brazilian linguistics and culture. Such incongruencies weaken many of the hypotheses proposed concerning the origin and development of African elements in Brazil.

One important observation made by Ramos in this study is that a great many of the foods having African names were initially designed to serve in the religious ceremonies, as part of the offerings to the gods and saints of the various cults. In the Bahian *candomblés,* for

---

[12] Arthur Ramos et al, *O Negro no Brasil, Trabalhos apresentados ao 2º Congresso Afro-Brasileiro,* Bahia (Rio de Janeiro, Biblioteca de Divulgação Scientífica, Civilização Brasileira, S. A. Editôra, 1940).

[13] *A Lingua Portuguêsa no Brasil* (Rio de Janeiro, Imprensa Nacional: 1941).

[14] *A Aculturação Negra no Brasil* (São Paulo, Companhia Editôra Nacional: 1942).

example, the anger or unfavorable disposition of the "saints" were appeased, as they are today, by sacrificing such animals as a rooster, a hen, a goat or a ram. The blood from these sacrificed animals was used for the purpose of casting evil spells on enemies or for initiating those seeking membership into the *candomblé* organizations. The meat of the sacrificial offerings was prepared in many different ways and served to the initiated members of the religious groups, as well as to those invited to watch the ceremony. Most of the Afro-Brazilian dishes eaten in Bahia stem directly from these African *candomblés*.

In 1945, Mário Marroquim made a regional dialect study of Brazil's Northeast.[15] The results were not gratifying, however, since nothing of any cultural or linguistic value was achieved.

A critical study of an 18th century work by Antônio da Costa Peixoto dealing with the *língua geral* was published in 1945.[16] The study begins with a list of the vowel, semivowel and consonant sounds of the *língua geral de Mina* (a kind of lingua franca from Mina). It represents an improvement over previous studies of this kind, since the sounds are well described phonetically and modern phonetic symbols are used to represent each sound discussed.

The essence of Peixoto's publication is the assertion that a variety of Fon or Dahomey, which is classified as a dialect of Ewe,[17] was the *língua geral*. This the author denominates as *língua geral de Mina,* and states that it was used mainly in 17th century Brazil among the slaves. This dialect, termed *Ogunu, Gunu* or *Gu,* was supposed to have been spoken by the slaves captured along the *Costa da Mina*. These slaves were shipped principally to Bahia.

Some vestiges of the Ewe language can be found in present-day Brazil. A few words of Ewe origin can be found in the everyday speech of practically any Bahian[18] — words which have become such

---

[15] *A Língua do Nordeste* (São Paulo, Cia Editôra Nacional: 1945).

[16] *Temas Lusiadas: Obra Nova de Língua Geral de Mina de Antônio da Costa Peixoto* (Lisboa, Manuscrito da Biblioteca Pública de Évora e da Biblioteca Nacional de Lisboa, publicado e apresentado por Luis Silveira e acompanhado de comentário filológico de Edmundo Correia Lopes, Agência Geral das Colônias: 1945).

[17] See Greenberg's classification (in Chapter II), Figure 2.

[18] Many African words used in Bahia have not yet been identified etymologically. Many of the linguists in Bahia working on this problem, however, believe that they may be either Yoruba or Ewe.

an integral part of the Portuguese language that the average Bahian is completely unaware that they are of African origin.

At the same time, many Ewe elements have become confused with those of other African languages, especially Yoruba. It is a known fact that the Ewe and Yoruba *candomblé* cults mixed, as they also incorporated some religious elements of Tupi-Guarani and Roman Catholic practices. This religious syncretism, to which Nina Rodrigues referred in the early part of the 20th century, is still operative today. [19]

According to Luis Silveira, Ewe cults (called *candomblé de gêge* in Brazil) date from an early time in Brazilian history. As an example of one, Silveira cites a cult house in the village of Rosário da Cachoeira, in the state of Bahia, which was founded in 1765 by the black brothers of the *Irmandade do Bom Jesus* under special invocation of *O Senhor dos Martírios*. The name of the founding organization, as well as the invocation, indicate that the Ewe cults in Bahia had already adopted many Christian practices by the middle of the 18th century. In spite of the fact that Catholicism had become a meaningful part of the lives of many Afro-Brazilian slaves, or perhaps because of this fact, the ecclesiastical authorities of the time were strongly opposed to the establishment of any such African heresies. Nevertheless, the cult was officially organized and legally set into operation.

In one section of his book, Silveira reproduces some songs that he gathered in an Ewe *candomblé* house in the state of Maranhão with the help of Maria Andresa, a *mãe de santo*, or religious leader, of the house. The language used in the songs is supposed to be Fon, an Ewe dialect.

Silveira mentions the fact that he found it difficult to obtain satisfactory translations for the songs, a problem which I encountered also in my field work experiences. He was told by Maria Andresa that the initiated members of the *candomblé* should "feel" the meaning of the words without having to translate them.

Silveira informs us that the meanings of many of the religious songs in this cult house in Maranhão have been forgotten. In some cases he reports that the *mãe de santo* said that she was not sure to which African spirit the songs belonged. The loss of so much of the

---

[19] For detailed information, see P. McGregor, *The Moon and Two Mountains*.

substance of the Afro-Brazilian religious organizations may be attributed, among other causes, to the complete severing of contact between African Negroes and those taken to Brazil, as well as to an ever increasing lack of interest on the part of the Brazilian blacks in carrying on the traditions and beliefs of their fore-fathers — a lack which was fomented by the separation from Africa and by the influence of the Roman Catholic religion.

Concerning his experiences among the *candomblé* houses of Bahia, the author reports that he visited some which he describes as being almost pure Ewe, others as being a mixture of Yoruba and Ewe, and still others as Yoruba with slight touches of Ewe. One of the houses which the author calls "almost pure Ewe" was studied in some detail, and a report on some of the Ewe words and expressions used there was published in 1942. [20] Silveira writes that the members of this house knew few utterances in Ewe and that most of the songs and shouts used during the *candomblé* ceremony were in Portuguese.

Among the interesting points which Silveira makes in his book, one is of particular historical importance. He writes that Costa Peixoto, in his study, included a religious form which he registered as *legba* and translated as *demónio* (devil). Silveira claims that the word is of Yoruba origin and that its presence in Peixoto's study of the Ewe language, a study that was done two centuries ago, proves the existence of a Yoruba-Ewe synthesis in Brazil as early as the first half of the 18th century, a synthesis which Silveira believes had already taken place in Africa. [21]

The remaining portions of Silveira's book contain general discussions concerning some of the linguistic descriptions used by Costa Peixoto in his *Obra Nova de Língua Geral de Mina*. Peixoto's work is certainly no linguistic landmark, but it does provide some vocabulary items which were in use in Ewe *candomblé* houses in 18th century Brazil and which may be used as a basis for comparison in present-day investigative activities. A feature noted by Peixoto is the

---

[20] "Exéquias no Bôgum de Salvador" in *O Mundo Português*, X, 1942, pp. 559-565.
[21] The word légbà is, in fact, Yoruba, and it means "paralytic" (demon possessed, by extension?). I could find no similar Ewe word in any of the dictionaries consulted.
Professor Diedrich Westermann lists gbɔgbɔ́ vɔ and gbetsi vɔ́ for "demon," and abosám for "devil" in his *Gbesela Yeye,* pages 93 and 96 respectively.

phenomenon of vowel nasalizations in Brazilian Ewe. Costa Peixoto noticed that many of the final vowels of Ewe words tended to become strongly nasalized. He attributed this to the influence of the nasal vowels in Portuguese. But there is no way of proving that Portuguese had such a modifying effect on Ewe; and, when one considers that Ewe had nasal vowels of its own, Peixoto's theory becomes even less tenable. Dr. Ernst Henrici informs us that "di Vokale a, e, *e*, i, *o*, u kommen auch schwach nasaliert vor, doch ist der Nasal, bezeichnet durch ˜ über dem Vokal (ã, ẽ, u.s.w.) viel schwächer als im französischen und portugiesischen so dass fast nur eine leichte Dehnung des Vokales hörbar wird." [22] (the vowels a, e, *e*, i, *o*, u also occur strongly nasalized. The mark ˜ over the vowel indicates nasalization (ã, ẽ, and so forth). This nasal sound is much stronger than [the nasal sound] in French or Portuguese, so that almost no perceptible lengthening of the vowels can be heard.) Considering this, it is not likely that Portuguese nasality influenced Ewe.

Gladstone Chaves de Melo completed and published *A Língua do Brasil* in 1946. About half of this book treats the popular or spoken dialects of the middle, lower-middle and lower social classes in Brazil. There is also a section devoted to African influences on Brazilian Portuguese.

Given over to speculation, Chaves de Melo states that the African tongues influenced Portuguese most notably in its morphology. This may be observed in the use of singular forms with plural meanings in such expressions as *Os home tá i; as prima já chegaro; êle brigo c'os fujo; êsses minino são endiabrado (ou é endiabrado)*. [23] It is true that these forms are very common in Brazil, especially among the lower levels of society, but there is no evidence to indicate that African dialects were responsible for such linguistic variations.

Luis Vianna Filho published a book [24] in 1946 dealing with the slave traffic from Africa to Brazil. The book also treats the social

---

[22] *Lehrbuch der Ephe-Sprache* (Stuttgart und Berlin, W. Spemann: 1891), p. 12.

It is important to consult this study because it supplies us with information about the Ewe of the 19th century slave period.

[23] *A Língua do Brasil* (Rio de Janeiro, Livraria AGIR Editôra: 1946), p. 63. The common forms of these examples would be: *Os homens estão ahi; as primas já chegaram; êle brigou com os fujos; êsses meninos são endiabrados.*

[24] *O Negro na Bahia* (São Paulo, Coleção Documentos Brasileiros, Livraria José Olympio Editôra: 1946).

and economic development of the Negro in Brazilian life, which we will study in a later chapter in connection with the socio-linguistic structure of Bahian society.

Renato Mendonça touched upon the African element present in Brazilian Portuguese in a chapter devoted to this subject in his book *O Português do Brasil*, published in 1936. Twelve years later, after having investigated the same material more thoroughly, Mendonça published *A Influência Africana no Português do Brasil*. The book is divided into various topics relating to the main theme.

A chapter about linguistic change in Portuguese is followed by one on Afro-Brazilian folklore. One song, reproduced in this chapter, shows a mixture of Yoruba and Portuguese — a phenomenon that I found to be common in my own field work among Bahian *candomblés*. This little song was recorded in Bahia:

Ocú babá	(Ocú babá
Ocú gêlê	Ocú gêlê
Negro nagô	A Yoruban Negro
Virou Saruê [25]	Turned into a Saruê)

(Note that the Yoruba has no translation. I have translated only the Portuguese into English.)

Serafim da Silva Neto wrote a more accurate account of Brazilian Portuguese in 1951 in a book entitled *Introdução ao Estudo da Língua Portuguêsa no Brasil*. Since da Silva Neto's observations are relatively trustworthy and therefore can be used as a point of comparison for data examined in another chapter of this study, many of his observations will be discussed here.

According to da Silva Neto, the Negroes living along the Guinea Coast in the 15th, 16th and 17th centuries probably already spoke a Creole-Portuguese dialect of some sort, since they had ample contact with the Portuguese people during those centuries. Unfortunately, no written record of this language exists today, and it is even doubtful if any of it was ever put into writing. At any rate, it is believed that a *koinē* language, very similar to the one spoken in Africa, was used in Brazil.

---

[25] *A influência Africana*, quoted from M. Morais Filho, *Festas e Tradições Populares do Brasil*, p. 333.

There is only one text which da Silva Neto believes to be an imitation of a Negro speaking Portuguese in Brazil; it may date to the late 16th or 17th century. It is the speech of a Negro character, Matheus, who appears in a type of play called a *reisado*.[26] This source, entitled "Reisado do Cavallo Marinho e Bumba-meu-boi," was recorded in Pernambuco. Part of the Negro's speech is the following:

> Matheus: —O' boio, dare de banda
> Xipaia esse gente,
> Dare p'ra trage,
> E dare p'ra frente...
> Vem mai p'ra baxo,
> Roxando no chão
> E dá pai Fidére,
> Xipanta Bastião...
> Vem p'ra meu banda
> Bem difacarinha,
> Vai mettendo a testa
> No Cavallo-narinha.
> O, ô, meu boio,
> Desce d'essa casa,
> Dança bem bonito
> No meio da praça...
> Toca esse viola,
> Pondo bem miudo;
> Minha boio sabe
> Dançá bem graudo.[27]

---

[26] The definition of a *reisado* given by Sílvio Romero, the author of the book in which it appears, is the following:

> Os Reisados são folganças muito variadas. O característico d'elles é terem sempre no fim de várias cantigas e danças, o brinquedo — Bumba-meu-Boi. Ordinàriamente nos Reisados cantam-se xacaras antigas, velhos romances, novas canções satyricas, chulas, etc.

(*Cantos Populares do Brasil*, Segunda Edição Melhorada, Rio de Janeiro, Livraria Francisco Alves: 1897).

> (The *Reisados* are frolics of varied sorts. A principal characteristic of them is that they always include, at the end of several songs and dances, the game called Bumba-meu-Boi. [This is a traditional dance and pageant in northeastern Brazil.] Generally, old songs and satirical melodies are sung during the *Reisados*.)

[27] *Cantos Populares*, pp. 183-184. The translation of this passage into English would serve no practical purpose and has therefore been deemed unnecessary.

A few points of linguistic interest can be noted in this short dialogue. An "empty" syllable is added to words ending in "r" and "z": *dare, traze, trage*.[28] Final "s" is dropped: *mai* for *mais*. The intervocalic voiced grooved palatal fricative [j] becomes unvoiced: *rojando* > *roxando*. Intervocalic "l" and "r" are interchanged: *Fidélis* > *Fidére*. Intervocalic voiced [v] and [g] become voiceless [f] and [k]: *devagarinha* > *difacarinha*.

Concord in gender of possessive and demonstrative adjectives with the nouns they modify is not carried out:[29] *esse gente; meu banda; esse casa; esse viola; minha boio*. The word *bói* receives an extra vowel: *boio*.

It must be remembered that many of the Negroes brought from Africa did not know any Portuguese at all, not even a creolized form. Father Fernão Guerreiro,[30] a Portuguese priest who went to Brazil in 1603, noticed that many Negroes from Angola and from the Guinea Coast could not converse with the Portuguese in any manner of speech. As late as 1840, Gardner[31] reported that he found twenty Negro boys between the ages of ten and fifteen who had been shipped to Paraíba and who could neither speak nor understand any Portuguese.

Many of the rubber, sugar and coffee plantations had large numbers of black slaves who either spoke a creolized version of Por-

---

[28] The word *trage* represents two changes: 1) the archaizing retention of a final "e" and 2) the alveopalatal slit fricative [z] > [j], a palatal grooved fricative.

[29] Melville J. Herskovits, in *The Mythh of the Negro Past* (New York: 1941), states the following, on page 80:

> The Congo tribes are all Bantu speaking, and though there are considerable differences between the Sudanic and Bantu stocks, resemblances also exist which, under mutual contact with Indo-European tongues, would loom large. The system of classifying forms which is the primary mark of the Bantu languages could not, in any case, be carried over into Indo-European speech, but other traits, such as the absence of sex gender, and those "vocal images," "onomatopoetic words," and "descriptive adverbs," noted as of equal importance in the Sudanic and Bantu languages could readily be employed by English-, French-, Spanish-, and Portuguese-speaking New World Negroes, whatever their African linguistic background.

[30] Relação Annual, I, 379, quoted in Serafim da Silva Neto, *Introdução ao Estudo da Língua Portuguêsa no Brasil* (Rio de Janeiro, Departamento de Imprensa Nacional: 1951), p. 45.

[31] George Gardner, *Travels in the Interior of Brazil, 1836-1841* (London: 1849).

tuguese or none at all. Isolated groups of slaves were formed in the *senzalas* or slave quarters, where only a gallimaufry of Portuguese and African tongues could exist. Since almost all of the white masters' children became part of these groups as they played with the Negro children, a great deal of linguistic interchange readily took place between the *casa-grande*, or master's house, and the intimate group of the *senzalas*. The black and the white children, who easily and quickly acquire the peculiar characteristics of each other's speech at all linguistic levels (phonetic, phonemic, morphological, syntactic and lexical), served as the medium through which these mutual influences occurred.

Much of what was transmitted from the Negro speech to the Portuguese became permanent in the linguistic habits of the white slave owners, for many of them did not have the opportunity to receive any formal education that would impose the speech habits of European Portuguese on them as it suppressed the "undesired" kind which had a relatively strong Negro flavor. Silva Neto tells us that "nas fazendas, pequenos mundos isolados, os meninos brancos viviam intimamente ligados aos negrinhos, sem a possibilidade de, mais tarde, freqüentar as escolas." [32] (on the plantations, small isolated worlds, the white children lived intimately with the Negro children, without having the possibility of attending school.)

In 16th and 17th century Brazil, according to Silva Neto, there were three distinct levels of spoken Portuguese: 1) a "pure" type, spoken primarily by Portuguese recently arrived from Europe and by their immediate descendants; 2) a "half-corrupted" one, which the author calls *crioulo*, used by mestizos and most commonly characterized by incomplete conjugations; 3) a "completely corrupted" kind, current among mestizos, blacks and Indians, showing a complete lack of conjugated forms.

Da Silva Neto believes that the Portuguese spoken in present-day Africa and Asia is very similar to the *crioulo* type of Brazilian colonial times. He cites no studies to support his view but merely alludes in a general way to observations of modern rural dialects made in Africa and Asia which show strong evidence of similarities in the formative process with 16th and 17th century Brazilian Portuguese.

---

[32] *Introdução ao Estudo*, p. 45.

Since no bibliography accompanies his work, there is no way of ascertaining the source of his information. However, a more recent study supports the idea that modern Portuguese as spoken in Africa is similar to what colonial Portuguese in Brazil may have been. Because it provides some evidence bearing on this problem, a parenthetical review of the relevant data from this research project is in order at this point.[33]

The article was written by various researchers, all members of the faculty of the Universidade Federal da Bahia. Among the principal investigators were Guilherme Sousa de Castro and Yêda Pessoa de Castro, professors of linguistics at the Centro de Estudos Afro-Orientais of the university.

The study is the result of a one-year linguistics research project, conducted in 1962-1963, among the members of the so-called Brazilian community of Lagos, Nigeria, in West Africa. After justifying the fact that the Portuguese spoken in West Africa has been kept unchanged for almost 100 years, the authors discuss three of the answers to their 2,983 questions, obtained through a linguistic questionnaire in the Portuguese language; their purpose is to show the importance of such studies for the Brazilian culture throughout West African countries, where Brazilian Portuguese is still spoken by African-Brazilian descendants. The first examples, *fístula* and *caranguejo*, meaning "scar," indicate that the colloquial Portuguese as spoken in Bahia is an archaic one, for both these forms, very frequent in Bahia, are not found in recent Portuguese dictionaries with the meaning of "scar"; they occur in only the oldest dictionary, Padre Rafael Bluteau's *Vocabulário Português e Latino*.[34] This material is followed by a lullaby, obviously of Portuguese origin but with remarkable African influence, and by a children's game, "the Blind Goat," whose final part has been completely forgotten in Brazil.

Returning now to da Silva Neto's study, we see that before discussing many of the linguistic peculiarities of rural and low-class Brazilian Portuguese, the author proposes his theory concerning the language situation in colonial Brazil. In the variegated colonial Bra-

---

[33] Guilherme de Sousa Castro and Yêda Pessoa de Castro, "Estudo da Língua Portuguêsa numa comunidade brasileira em Lagos, Nigéria," in *Afro-Asia* (Salvador, Publicação Semestral do Centro de Estudos Afro-Orientais da Universidade da Bahia, Dezembro, No. 1, 1965).

[34] (Coimbra, Colégio das Artes da Companhia de Jesus: 1712).

zilian society, the pinnacle of the social pyramid was exposed to many influences of the lower classes, as it is to a certain extent today. The sociological factor which da Silva Neto terms "inverted influence" was highly operative, with the lower classes displaying more sway over the upper than vice versa. Under these circumstances, the black, forming well over three-fourths of the lower class population, especially in Bahia, would effect social and linguistic modifications in the ruling élite.

Da Silva Neto ends his study with a discussion about the differences between urban and rural Portuguese. His conclusions, which may or may not follow logical premises, are that the urban language is much more apt to change than the rural, because in the cities education and international exchange of all sorts are constantly at work to produce changes which tend to eliminate many slangy expressions and mispronunciations that are uncouth according to the language academies and similar institutions. The country is not favored with such cultural advantages; therefore, it does not experience these rapid changes but, rather, is much more conservative in all aspects of living. This observation should be kept in mind when studying any socio-cultural or linguistic problems in Brazil.

Recent studies, such as one done in the state of Bahia by a group of 25 students from the Universidade Federal da Bahia under the direction and supervision of Nelson Rossi, have proven that definite phonetic, morphological, syntactic, lexical and semantic differences exist between rural and urban speech. The project, conducted by Rossi, was completed in 1964, but has not yet been published.[35] It is one of the most efficient and well-structured linguistic field studies that has ever been carried out in Bahia. A well-planned questionnaire was used to elicit specific answers in personal interviews. The best results were obtained in the area of vocabulary (lexical and semantic problems). Categories used for testing were: a) agriculture, b) cattle raising, c) human anatomy and physiology, d) foods, e) geography and astronomy. It is hoped that studies similar to this one, and perhaps broader in scope, will be conducted and published in the future.

In 1951, Edison Carneiro compiled *A Linguagem Popular da Bahia*.[36] It is a comprehensive study, which includes many of the

---

[35] The manuscript form of this project was lent to me by Nelson Rossi.
[36] (Salvador, Publicações do Museu do Estado: 1951).

popular or colloquial words and expressions of everyday Bahian speech. Etymologies are not given. Because of recent investigative efforts carried out by members of the faculty at the Universidade Federal da Bahia, a few of the words from Carneiro's list have been tentatively identified as to their origin. Words of supposed African origin have been sorted out accordingly and are presented in Table 3 with the definition they have in Bahia. Exact etymologies (i.e., whether they are from Yoruba, Ewe, Bantu, etc.) for many of the words have not yet been demonstrated since they were determined by the process of elimination alone; that is, if a word could be proven with a reasonable degree of certainty not to be either Portuguese or Indian, it would be assumed to be African.[37] In reality, the problem of specific origin for non-Portuguese words has been a very difficult and very delicate one ever since scholars began to investigate it. Intensive research is now being carried on by professors of linguistics and history at the Universidade Federal da Bahia in an attempt to solve some of the pending etymological dilemmas.

Arthur Ramos, in his *O Folklore Negro do Brasil*,[38] says that certain gestures which accompany speech are of African origin. The hypothesis, though interesting, tends to be mere fanciful speculation. Other descriptions of Afro-Brazilian folkloric customs are presented in a colorful way but offer no linguistic information.

---

[37] All of the words in this list except *assa, biringa, brongo, jabá,* and *xodó* are examined as to their possible origin, in Chapter IV. The five words above could not be positively identified as having African etymologies.

[38] (2a edição, Rio de Janeiro: 1954, no publication date).

TABLE 3

POPULAR COLLOQUIAL WORDS USED IN SALVADOR AND TENTATIVELY IDENTIFIED BY BRAZILIAN LINGUISTS IN BAHIA AS BEING OF AFRICAN ORIGIN, SELECTED FROM CARNEIRO'S LIST

afòxé [39] rancho de negros no carnaval, o maracatu [40] (group of Negroes performing at carnival time, also called *maracatu*)

aguxó tipo de penteado de mulher (a kind of woman's hairdo)

assa (more commonly spelled *aça*) albino (an albino)

banguéla sem dentes (having no teeth)

banzé barulho (noise)

bimbinha o membro viril, em linguagem de crianças (the masculine sex organ, in the language of children)

binga pênis de criança (a child's penis)

biringa boceta de rapé (snuff box)

(*boneco de*) *alôdê* prêto retinto, de pele lustrosa (a very dark Negro, with shiny skin)

brongo lugar atrasado (a backward area)

bunda nádegas de mulher, quando muito largas e amplas em comparação com o tronco (a woman's buttocks, especially when very wide and full, in comparison to the rest of the body)

cacumbu 1) faca sem cabo; 2) pessoa adulta de pequena estatura (1) a knife without a handle; 2) a short adult person)

cafuné estalo que se dá com as unhas dos polegares na cabeça de outrem, entre os cabêlos, para provocar o sono (the noise made when snapping the fingernails of one's thubs on the head of another, in the hair, to lull to sleep)

cafuringa menino de estatura reduzida (a small boy)

chibungo pederasta passivo (a passive male homosexual)

combóça amante de homem casado ou amizado que está em bens termos ou reside sob o mesmo teto com a outra mulher (the lover of a married or "engaged" man)

fuxico 1) intriga; 2) remendo [com agulha e linha] (1) intrigue; 2) a mended place in a piece of cloth)

jabá xarque, carne do sertão (meat eaten in the Brazilian backlands)

mabaça gêmeo (twin)

quenga prostituta (prostitute)

quiabada comida (food)

quiabo pessoa alta e espigada (a tall, slender person)

xodó 1) agarramento [especialmente de fundo sexual]; 2) amante pre-

---

[39] No indication is given concerning accent marks. My own personal experience with oral renditions of the words, however, would lead me to interpret them as following the Portuguese system of written accents, i.e.,

⟨ ′ ⟩ primary stress on open vowel;

⟨ ` ⟩ secondary stress on closed or open vowel;

⟨ ^ ⟩ primary stress on closed vowel.

[40] The name given to street dancers at carnival time.

ferido (1) seizure [especially in a sexual context]; 2) a favorite lover)	zumbi pessoa que anda ou que gosta de andar no escuro (a person who likes to wander around in the dark)
zanzar andar distraído e absorto (to wander around absentmindedly)	

In 1961, Sílvio Elia compiled *O Problema da Língua Brasileira*,[41] which includes some of the better studies of Brazilian Portuguese that have been done in Brazil. Among those containing information concerning African influence on Portuguese, Elia cites Renato Mendonça, *O Português do Brasil*, Gladstone Chaves de Melo, *A Língua do Brasil* and Serafim da Silva Neto, *Introdução ao Estudo da Língua Portuguêsa no Brasil*. Other works discussed deal mainly with Brazilian dialectology.

As the most recent study to be reviewed here, Deoscóredes M. dos Santos and Juana Elbein published a monograph in 1967 entitled *West African Sacred Art and Rituals in Brazil*.[42] A large portion of this study is concerned with African and Afro-Brazilian artifacts, paintings and ritualistic figurines. The part devoted to the linguistic aspects of African and Afro-Bahian culture, however, is what interests us most.

Both dos Santos, who is a direct descendant of a Yoruba king and *pai de santo* of the *terreiro Axé Ôpô Afonjá*[43] in Salvador da Bahia, and Juana Elbein, a student of African and Afro-Brazilian culture from Buenos Aires, Argentina, who now resides in Bahia, made a trip to West Africa to visit dos Santos' family and learn more about the connection between life and culture in the Benin Bay area of Africa and that of Brazil in general and Bahia in particular. They traveled to many areas in Nigeria and Dahomey but focused most of their attention on those places which Bahian tradition indicated as being directly related to its own cultural heritage. The ancient kingdom of Ketu was investigated with careful attention and was found to have many cultural and linguistic elements in common with the Ketu *terreiros* of Bahia.

---

[41] (Rio de Janeiro, Instituto Nacional do Livro, Ministério da Educação e Cultura: 1961).

[42] This is a comparative study made possible under a contract between UNESCO and the Centro de Estudos Afro-Orientais da Universidade da Bahia. The monograph was produced with the assistance of the university at Ibadan, Nigeria. It was translated into English by Juana Elbein.

[43] *Terreiro* is the name given to all *candomblé* houses. It is derived from *terra*, meaning "earth" or "soil." All of the *terreiros* have dirt floors.

Illustrative of the kinds of cultural and linguistic materials that were gathered is a section of an article written by dos Santos for a local Bahian newspaper after his return from Africa, in which he describes his trip through the villages. One episode in the kingdom of Ketu is of special interest, since it shows some types of relationships that exist between African Yoruba and its Brazilian offshoot:

> Pierre Verger a quem todos conhecem em tôda região por Babalawô Fatunbi e que já conhecia o Rei, fêz a nossa apresentação. ... conversa vai conversa vem, eu disse ao Rei que era descendente da terra de Ketu. Êle muito espantado com o meu Nagô-Yorubá, mandou que eu desse prova do que tinha dito. E assim foi que cantei algumas cantigas enaltecendo a terra, o Rei e a riqueza do seu povo.
>
> O Rei, todos seus ministros e as demais pessoas que lá se encontravam na ocasião ficaram surpresos e me escutavam emocionados, pois êles nunca tinham imaginado antes de que, do outro lado do Oceano, pudesse ainda existir pessoas como eu, capazes de cantar os cânticos tradicionais da terra que eram cantados pelos nossos antepassados.
>
> Quando terminei de cantar o Rei bastante emocionado, passou a mostrar a coroa que estava usando e traduzindo uma das cantigas que nos disse que não era aquela coroa a que a cantiga se referia e sim a outra com a qual são consagrados os reis....
>
> Enquanto isso, Juana se lembrou do caso da família real e me perguntou porque não aproveitava o momento para recitar o Oriki ou Orilé de minha família, o que eu chamo de brasão oral...
>
> Tive que dizer as seguintes palavras em Nagô: Asipá borogun elesé kan gongôô. Quando terminei só vimos o Rei de repente exclamar ha! Asipá! e levantando-se da cadeira aonde estava sentado apontou para um lado do palácio dizendo: —a sua família mora ali! ... Logo nos levaram ao ojubó ódé, lugar de adoração a Oxóssi, nos mostrando aonde estava "assentado" enterrado o Axé da casa e foram chamar uma das pessoas mais velhas do bairro, pertencente à família, a fim de nos fornecer as informações precisas. E assim foi que ficamos sabendo de que tudo o que minha mãe e as pessoas mais velhas falavam na Bahia, era verdade. Independente da linhagem real a nossa família foi uma das 7 principais famílias que fundaram o reino de Ketu.[44]

---

[44] "Un Negro Baiano em Ketu," in *A Tarde*, Sábado, 30 de maio de 1968, secção "Suplemento," p. 3.

(Pierre Verger, whom everyone knows everywhere as Babalawô Fatunbi [Yoruba] and who already knew the king, introduced us.... As we were conversing, I told the king that I had descended from the Ketu nation. He was very much surprised by my Nago-Yoruba, and said he would like to have some proof of what I said. So, I sang some songs praising the land, the king and the richness of the people.

The King, along with all of his ministers and other people who were present, were surprised and listened very carefully. They had never before imagined that anyone like myself could exist on the other side of the ocean — anyone capable of singing the traditional songs of the land which had been sung by our ancestors.

After I finished singing, the King, highly excited, showed me the crown he was wearing and, while explaining one of the songs which he repeated for us, indicated that the song did not refer to that particular crown, but rather to another one which is used when consecrating kings....

While this was happening, Juana remembered the case of the royal family and asked me why I did not take advantage of the moment to recite the Oriki or Orilé of my family, that which I call the oral coat of arms...

I had to say the following words in Nago: Asipá borogun elesé kan gongôô. When I finished, the King suddenly exclaimed, ha! Asipá! and getting up from his chair, pointed to one side of the palace, saying: —your family lives there!... Then they took us to the ojubó ódé, the place where the god Oxóssi is honored, showed us the place where the Axé of the house was buried, and called one of the oldest members of the district, who was a member of the family, in order to supply us with some exact information. And so it was that we found out that everything about which my mother and the oldest persons of Bahia spoke, was true. Independent of the royal lineage, our family was one of the seven principal families which founded the kingdom of Ketu.)

Before continuing with the materials found in the Yoruba country, dos Santos supplies us with some important data concerning the African and his cultural habits in Brazil, with special emphasis on Bahia. He states:

> Thirty-five per cent of the total population of Brazil is of African descent, and this proportion rises to 70 per cent in the state of Bahia. This population of African descent preserves a large part of its original culture in varying de-

grees of acculturation, depending on how much or little has been retained of African roots and models, and on the sociohistorical circumstances of the various regions where these populations have settled.[45]

He indicated that, once the slave traffic had ceased and commercial relations with the West African coast had stopped, the Brazilian black began to lose all contact with his origins, as we have previously commented. There are many factors which contribute to the difficulties of identifying precisely the origin of any one Afro-Brazilian subculture. The total disappearance of the habits and customs of the first African slaves brought to Brazil, and of the first two or three generations of their descendants, the racial intermixture, and the complete disuse of the original African tongues for purposes of daily communication — all these factors make it difficult to understand fully the Yoruba which was preserved as a ritual language and is used today in the religious cults in Bahia.

Turning specifically to Bahia, dos Santos informs us that the Yoruba culture influenced all the others (for reasons not well understood) and survived with a structure of its own. The cult houses are excellent examples of present-day depositories of this ethnolinguistic phenomenon. Four of the most important of these houses, we are told, are thought to be directly descended from Ketu. Another survival is the *Gêge* cult, whose features resemble those of the Fon culture of Africa. Since the Fon were strongly dominated by the Yoruba for some time, they were strongly influenced by the *Nagô*, especially in religious and aesthetic matters.[46] At the same time, the

---

[45] *West African*, p. 6.

[46] Deoscóredes M. dos Santos, in *West African Sacred Art and Rituals in Brazil*, states the following on page 55: "... Thus as the Fon perhaps Jéje culture was itself the result of an active process of contacts with these various peoples, accompanied by strong Yorubá influence in religion and aesthetics, it was not difficult for the two cultures to combine in Bahia, since furthermore the Yorubá elements, just as had happened in Africa, dominated and exerted a strong influence over all the others."

I was unable to find any information directly concerned with the Yoruba dominating other tribes in Africa. A. B. Ellis, in his book *The Yoruba-Speaking Peoples of the Slave Coast of West Africa* does allude to such a phenomenon, however, in the "conclusions" of his study. While referring to the three books he has written (*The Tshi-Speaking Peoples of the Gold Coast of West Africa; The Ewe-Speaking Peoples of the Slave Coast of West Africa*, and the one mentioned here), he states the following on page 275:

Vodun gods of the Fon and the orixá gods of the Yoruba were similar enough to fuse, and so were united under *Nagô* dominance. These factors, coupled with the experience of facing common problems in exile, spurred the two "nations" into forming the *Gêge-Nagô* complex which exists only in the state of Bahia.

The purpose of dos Santos' study, then, is to point out survivals of the Yoruba complex in Bahia, "whose language and strong cultural elements constitute a form and system which can be said to be autonomous, mingled with, and exerting an influence on the wider 'official culture' in which it is placed." [47] Dos Santos' statement succinctly expresses one of the important aspects of this study. It is therefore important that we review this most recent and unique research project, which has thrown much light on the problem of comparing African and Afro-Bahian cultures and languages.

Concerning the preservation in Brazil of African languages in general and Yoruba in particular, dos Santos informs us that it was the continued practice of the Negro's religion in his forced exile which helped maintain his sense of community, preserved his tradition, kept his racial unity and fortified his psychological integrity.

In Bahia, the Yoruba language was handed down orally from generation to generation and was preserved in the places which had the highest ratio of Africans to Portuguese and where there was very

---

"... three groups of tribes have now been considered, the Tshi, the Ewe, and the Yoruba, who represent three stages of progress, the Tshi being in the lowest stage and the Yoruba in the highest. As these tribal groups undoubtedly had a common origin, it is reasonable to suppose that the Yoruba tribes were once in the social and mental condition in which the Tshi tribes are now, and that, in fact, in these groups we find the same race in different stages of culture. Assuming then, as we legitimately may, that the religious beliefs of the Ewes are modifications of earlier belief (sic) resembling those now held by the Tshis, and that those of the Yorubas are similarly modifications of beliefs like those now held by the Ewes, we here have an opportunity of observing how the evolution of religion may proceed."

If this, in fact, was the case in West Africa during the period of slave trading activities, and if, as the author suggests here, these three stages of development among the three tribes were chronologically simultaneous, then it would have been possible for the culturally superior Yoruba to have overshadowed the Ewe and the Tshi.

See also Chapter II of Samuel Johnson, *The History of the Yorubas*, Lagos, 1946. Here, the Rev. Johnson speaks of the Yorubas as they conquered the aboriginal population of the western territories of the land they now inhabit.

[47] *West African*, p. 8.

little contact with outside Portuguese speakers. Since no writing system existed and since knowledge of the liturgies in the cult houses was kept secret for protection, there are no trustworthy first-hand documents of even the best preserved of Brazilian African vernaculars.

Fortunately, however, some of the cult leaders kept vocabularies and songs transcribed in a crude manner. They were circulated among the cult houses and used only for initiates in the religious groups. In these transcriptions, parallel translations were usually omitted in order to keep the texts from being understood by non-initiates. The writings today are used only for learning the ritual language by heart. Participants know the general sense of each song and formula, the moment when it must be executed, as well as the gestures and dance steps accompanying each song, but literal understanding of each word is far from their grasp.

Dos Santos believes that strong rehabilitative measures have sprouted from among the latest generation of initiates, thus regaining a lost ethnolinguistic heritage. He states:

> In the younger generation there is a great interest in the rediscovery of the language. An intense crusade was launched in order to interest the universities in the teaching of Yoruba, with the result that a Nigerian teacher gave a four year course — 1961 to 1965 — which aroused enthusiastic interest, especially among cult members, others of African descent, and some professional people. Yet this course,... did not fulfill the expectations of those who... flocked to it... This does not mean that the course was not important. It served essentially to inform people of the writing systems used to document the language, as these had been largely unknown until then, to re-establish the correct tonality and its appropriate notation, thus facilitating the introduction and reading of dictionaries in the Yoruba language.[48]

The younger generation's "great interest," to which dos Santos refers, is not borne out by the data which I collected in the city of Bahia. As will be indicated in the chapter dealing with my personal interviews among Bahian initiates, the younger generation shows overt tendencies to discard Yoruba, Ewe, or whatever the language of their particular cult may be, in favor of Portuguese. Also, it is apparent

---

[48] *West African*, p. 14.

that the majority of cult members would not have been able to attend the Yoruba classes offered at the university simply because they were too poor to afford them.

In pointing out differences between African Yoruba and that of Bahia, dos Santos writes:

> Our stay in Yoruba country has merely... led us to conclude that the differences between our Nagô and Yoruba are merely those which may exist between fairly similar dialects. The divergences are not the result of the evolution of a living language, but rather the stratification of a ritual language in which the tones have been weakened, but reappear clearly when the texts are sung. [49]

The following statement indicates that Bahian Yoruba is, in effect, similar to the Yoruba that the slaves brought over with them in the 17th, 18th and 19th centuries:

> With great surprise and delight we found that our Brazilian ritual Nagô was understandable to the Yorubá, once they became accustomed to our accents and archaic usage. When we sang or gave greetings in our Bahian ways, we were repeatedly told that ours is ijìnlèe yorùbá, [50] an expression new to us, meaning "deep Yorubá." [51]

Before examining the cult songs, a short explanation of the origins of the words used for the three drums played during the ceremonies

---

[49] *West African*, p. 17.

[50] Marks above the letters here, as in all the forthcoming chants, indicate tone. They follow the system presented in R. C. Abraham's *Dictionary of Modern Yoruba* (London, University of London Press: 1958), which is:

  A. Static tones:

    There are three main static tones, that is to say, level-tones said on a pitch which does not vary. These are high-tone, mid-tone and low-tone with an equal interval between each of them.

    As usual, high-tone is marked ⟨ˊ⟩. Low-tone is marked ⟨ˋ⟩. Mid-tone is characterized by the absence of any marking.

  B. Gliding tones:

    Gliding tones are marked on each syllable with one of the parts constituting the glide, e.g. èyíí 'this' (low-tone and glide from low to high). Also, in Yoruba orthography, a dot placed below a vowel indicates that the vowel is open: ijìnlẹ́e (ijinlɛe). A dot below 's' indicates a flat, voiceless, alveopalatal fricative: ṣáṣárá (šašara). Apostrophes indicate contractions (p. 28).

[51] *West African*, p. 18.

will help demonstrate additional relationships between Afro-Brazilian and African Ewe and Yoruba:

> It is important for us to record the name "Hun" used for drums, as the instrumental group in the Jêje-Nagô cult houses in Brazil is made up of three drums:
>
> —The Run or ìlù is the largest, beaten with a rod in the right hand... The word ìlù is of Yorùbá origin, just as the name Hun comes from the Fon, the aspirated h having been replaced by r.
>
> —The Runpi... Its name also is of Fon derivation and it seems to correspond to the drum recorded by Clemente da Crus, which Pierre Verger records as Hunpevi.[52]
>
> —The Le is the smallest... It is also known as Omele and its name is derived directly from the Yorùbá Omele.[53]

A passage describing the methods of transcription of the chants and magic formulas which the author recorded will broaden our understanding of the material at hand:

> We have adopted the practice of transcribing the songs in their analytic or oral speech and melodic forms. The tones in the sung text do not always correspond exactly with those in writing. This is also common in Africa. These changes of tones are not arbitrary. They are not distortions, but adjustments used for expressive purposes. Professor R. Armstrong refers to this characteristic feature of Yorùbá as its "expressive system." The analytic form of transcription of the ritual hymns helps us not only to re-establish the "normal" tones, but also to reconstitute the contractions so much used in the language.[54]

The first song is one used in Bahia. The musical form is as follows:

> Ala tí pee èrò mí
> Ala tí pee èrò mí o
> Mò jubà Ogún
> Ògún Àkóroò Òwo nile

---

[52] "Notes sur le culte des Orisa et Vodum à Bahia, la baie de tous les saints, au Brésil et à l'ancienne Coté des Esclaves en Afrique" (Dakar, Memoire 51 de l'Institut Français de l'Afrique, Moire: 1957).

[53] *West African*, p. 25.

[54] *West African*, p. 18.

Oral speech form:

> Ẹnìkan: Alá ti pèé èrò mi
> Alá ti pèé èrò mi

Translation:

> We must call him, my people
> We must call him, my people
> I give you respect, Ògún [55]
> Ògún who has the Akóro [56]

Another song used in Bahia, to honor the saint Nàná, is the following:

> Ẹnìkan: Nana olú odò
> Ọmọ níle kòràjò
> Ègbé: Ná ikú ree
> Ọmọ níle kòràjò
> Nàná funfun lẹ́lẹ́ kòràjò
> Ná ikú ree
> Ọmọ níle kòràjò

Spoken form:

> Nàná olú odò
> Ọmọ onílè kòràjò
> Nàná ikú rèé
> Omo iníle kòràjò
> kòràjò kòràjò
> Nàná funfun lẹ́lẹ́ kòràjò
> Ná ikú rèé (Ná = Nàná)
> Ọmọ onile korajo [sic]

Translation:

> Solo: Nana goddess of the spring
> Daughter of the owners of
> earth, will not depart
> (owners of the earth:
> the spirits of the dead,
> the Ará-Òrun

---

[55] Ògún: One of the spirits worshipped in candomblé: the god of war.
[56] Akóro: According to R. C. Abraham, àkòró means "helmet."

Chorus: Nana is death
Daughter of the owners
of earth, will not depart
Will not depart,
Will not depart,
Nana is death
Daughter of the owners
of earth, will not depart. [57]

More valuable information is afforded us concerning Yoruba songs in Bahia as dos Santos continues his comparison of African and Bahian rituals. The songs presented as occurring in Bahia are used in the *terreiro* of *Axé Opo Afonjá* and have variants in other *terreiros* throughout the city of Salvador. It is fortunate, however, that the monograph containing information about this particular *terreiro* was available to me, for my efforts to obtain personal interviews from the initiates of *Axé Ôpô Afonjá* in São Gonçalo do Retiro in the city of Salvador, as well as from dos Santos himself, were for the most part frustrated.

In the forthcoming examples, only the musical forms will be cited, since the spoken versions are the same except for slight variations in tones, which are not important for our purposes in this study.

Continuing the comparative analysis, dos Santos states the following:

> The name Ìbírí, [58] exclusive to the Ọpáa Nàná is only known in West Africa to some Babaláwo, who belong to a small group which secretly preserves the most orthodox tradition of the cult of Nàná and Ọbalúaiyé. We found the same difficulty in localizing the origin of the Ìbírí, that we found in verifying the information concerning the Àsogba, the supreme head of the Ọbalúaiyé cult...
>
> In Bahia, the Ìbírí is known only by that name and the Àsogba is the person who makes, consecrates and entrusts it ritually to the priestesses prepared to be "mounted" [possessed by spirits] by the òrìṣà. [59]

During the festivals, when the initiates appear in trance, carrying the Ìbírí and dancing with it, a song is sung:

---

[57] *West African*, p. 52.
[58] Ìbírí: a religious charm used for magical purposes during the candomblé ceremony.
[59] *West African*, p. 54.

PREVIOUS STUDIES

Enìkan: Ìbírí otò
Ègbè: Sàlaré
Nana Òlu odò
Ìbírí otò
Ṣálaré
Òlówo sẹn-sẹn

Translation:

Ìbírí is precious
Òrìṣà [60] of justice
Nàná goddess of the spring
Ìbírí is precious
Òríṣà of justice
Owner of the cowries (shells). [61]

Another song used in the *Axé Ôpô Afonjá terreiro* is the following:

Odúun Nàná in Bahia:
Enìkan: Ekún lẹ okò Sàlà
Ègbè: Eé ekún lẹ odò Sàlà
Sàlà i Nana
Sàlà

Translation:

We kneel in the spring
Oh! we kneel in the spring,
Òrìṣà of justice
Òrìṣà of justice. Nàná
Òrìṣà of justice [62]

There is a special song employed in Bahia that requires the use of the *xaxará*, which is a cult instrument made of reeds with a handle at one end and loose fibers at the other. Both song and *xaxará* are used to sweep away evil spirits and foreign bodies that may have intruded into the *terreiro*. The words that are sung are these:

Enìkan: Bálẹ Bálẹ
Ègbè: Ṣáṣárá balẹ̀

---

[60] Orixá (Portuguese spelling): personification and deification of the forces of nature; saint or spirit.
[61] *West African*, p. 55.
[62] *West African*, p. 56.

Ẹnìkan: Bálẹ Bálẹ
Ègbè: Ṣáṣárá balẹ fun wa o
Bàlẹ Bàlẹ

Translation:

If the night comes (during the night until tomorrow)
Ṣáṣárá will take over the ground for us
(will help watch for us)
If the night comes
Ṣáṣárá will take over the ground for us
If night comes [63]

Another song accompanying the movements of the *xaxará* is the following:

Ẹnìkan: Oní f'álejò paramó
Ofì sa Ṣáṣárá d'àgbo

Translation:

He commands that everything foreign
should disappear
He puts the Ṣáṣárá in the medicine water
(of leaves)

In the first line of the song the word *álejò* means "foreign things" or "spirits," who are not benevolent, who do not form part of the community.

Because of the connection of Ọbalúaiyé with shells, the following song is sung for him in Bahia:

Ẹnìkan: Òwo nlá bàṅbà
Òjíṣẹ owó nlá bàṅbà
Òwo nlá bàṅbà

Translation:

Money (shells) great, immense
Messenger of wealth
Money, great, immense

---

[63] *West African*, p. 56.

In Bahia, Ọbalúaiyé made manifest in the priestess is also withdrawn from the public ceremony at the appropriate moment [as is done in Alágbòjé, a little town in Ègbá country, Africa] on the back of a priestess of the òrìṣà Nàná. On this occasion the text sung confirms the action:

> Ènìkan: Koríkoó dé
> Abiyamọ kọ́mọ pọ̀n ó dé ìyà
> Koríkó dé, abiyamọ kọ́mọ pọn ó dé

Translation:

> Koríko (Ọbalúaiyé) has arrived
> Abiyamo put your child on your back,
> he has arrived, make way.
> Koriko has arrived, Abiyamo
> put your child on your back.

The name Abiyamọ is given to the woman who has her child of an age to be carried on her back, in the way children are usually carried in West Africa.[64]

These examples will suffice to point out the relatively close connections which exist even today between West African Yoruba and the Afro-Brazilian *Gêge-Nagô* complexes, for each of the songs or chants included in dos Santos' study (some nineteen in all) taken from the Bahian *terreiro* of *Axé Ôpô Afonjá* was related to a similar ceremonial rendition presently being practiced in the areas of Africa visited by the author.

It is hoped that more comparative studies of this sort will be attempted in the future, for they may aid greatly in helping to solve many problems concerning Afro-Brazilian ethnolinguistics. Intensive research is now being carried on by linguists and sociologists at the Universidade Federal da Bahia in connection with African influences in the coastal region of the state of Bahia around the city of Salvador.

---

[64] *West African*, pp. 69, 70, 72.

CHAPTER II

ORIGINS OF THE AFRICAN TRIBES TAKEN TO BAHIA

The slave traffic from Africa to Brazil exhibits a definite pattern which followed rather well-defined trade routes and caused particular tribes of native Africans to be brought to specific geographical areas in the New World. As a result of this, and of other phenomena which we will attempt to study here, we find that the descendants of peoples of the Kwa and Benue-Congo groups of West Africa predominate among the Afro-Brazilian population in the city of Salvador da Bahia. Melville J. Herskovits, after having studied thoroughly the black population of Bahia, Brazil, and after having compared it with West African culture, came to the following conclusion:

> As in all West African cultures and their New World derivatives — Bahian Negro culture stems principally from Western Nigeria and Dahomey, and from the southwestern part of the Congo — religion is a primary point of cultural focus; and in this intricately organized aspect of life music bulks large. One objective of the research was the recording of Bahian Negro songs, and this afforded an opportunity for close contact with certain of the more prominent Afro-Bahian drummers.[1]

As we will see in a later chapter, musical instruments used in present-day cult houses attest to the fact that the Yoruba and Ewe religions predominated in Bahia. Concerning this, Herskovits states that "the most African use of percussion is in those cults termed

---

[1] *The New World Negro* (Bloomington, Indiana University Press: 1966), p. 184.

Gêge, Ketu, and Jeshá. The first of these stems from the West African culture of Dahomey, the latter two from the Nago-speaking Yoruba folk of Nigeria. The second is at present the most important, and, while the other two have smaller followings now than in earlier years, they still function significantly." [2]

It is not an easy task to find historical information indicating why certain tribes were transported to Bahia, since almost all of the documents concerning the slave traffic were destroyed in 1891, three years after Brazil abolished slavery.

Donald Pierson, in his book *Negroes in Brazil* (Carbondale and Edwardsville, Southern Illinois University Press: 1967), has the following to say about West African slaves taken to Bahia:

> ...the exact date when African importation began is unknown, although it is thought that the fleet which Martim Affonso de Souza in 1531 encountered in the bay at Bahia was engaged in the transport of slaves. Sometime later in this same century the slave trade began to gather momentum, Bahia serving for at least two centuries as the principal port of entry. The traffic opened in Guinea and the island of São Thomé, spread shortly to the Congo and Angola, and finally to distant Mozambique. It continued uninterrupted for nearly three hundred years, assuming its largest proportions in the eighteenth and nineteenth centuries... How many Africans were brought in perhaps never will be known, but the number undoubtedly ran into millions.
>
> Angola furnished most of the importations during the late sixteenth and the seventeenth centuries; Guinea, during the eighteenth and early nineteenth. By 1710 Bahian tobacco was being shipped in quantity to "the Mina coast," which for more than a century thereafter absorbed a full third of Bahia's production. A visitor early in the eighteenth century referred to Bahia as "New Guinea"; while the natives of Guinea were said at that time to have called the outer world "Bahia."
>
> In 1780 fifty vessels were engaged in the Brazilian traffic, "eight or ten with Angola and the rest with the Sudanese coast." In 1800 twenty vessels were plying the trade from Bahia alone. According to custom-house records, 29,172 Negroes from "the Mina coast" and the islands of São Thomé and Príncipe entered Bahia during the decade from 1785 to 1795, and in the last five of these years 17,409 Africans

---

[2] *New World Negro*, p. 185.

ORIGINS OF THE AFRICAN TRIBES TAKEN TO BAHIA 63

came in from Angola. From 1797 to 1806 approximately 47,000 "Minas" and 11,000 "Angolas" entered Bahia.... Thousands of Yorubas, Gêges (Ewes), Haussás, Fuláhs (Fulbis, Fulanis), Ashantis, Tapas, Effans, and Mandingas were imported from the ports of Lagos, Forte de El Mina, and São João de Ajudá (Whydah). [3]

This information is very helpful and is in complete accord with other important data which will be considered concerning the origins of the West African tribal members which were taken to Bahia as slaves. (See Figure 1)

Marius F. Valkhoff, in his *Studies in Portuguese and Creole* (Johannesburg, 1966), states that during the time of the settlement of the three islands of St. Thomas, Príncipe, and Annobón, large numbers of slaves were taken from the mainland directly opposite them. The four areas which are most frequently mentioned in the historical documents dealing with the slave trade here are Guinea, Benin, Gabon, and Angola. After the blacks had been taken to the islands, they were shipped to the New World.

Waldemar Valente, in his book *Sincretismo Religioso Afro-Brasileiro,* devotes some attention to the problem of the origins of black slaves taken to Brazil. Quoting from scholars such as Nina Rodrigues and Arthur Ramos, he states that the principal points from which the slaves were taken extend from the Guinea Coast north to the Senegal and south to the Congo. Valente agrees with Arthur Ramos that there were three main black cultures which served as slaves in Brazil, outnumbering by far all the others: 1) the Fante-Ashante, 2) the Fon, and 3) the Yoruba who had come under the influence of the Bantu before arriving in Brazil. The Bantu themselves, in turn, according to Valente, are not well defined as such in Brazil. There are traces of the Angola and Congolese branches of the Bantu which show up in Rio de Janeiro, and in the states of Bahia and Pernambuco. Waldemar Valente, continuing his discussion of the Bantu, states that the number of these peoples in Brazil is considerably more than most authors who study this problem perhaps realize. This is true especially in the case of Bahia, a state which most scholars consider as having very little Bantu influence.

---

[3] (London, Feffer and Simons, Inc.: 1967), pp. 31-35.

FIGURE 1: Sub-Saharan Africa, Indicating the Major Points from which the Portuguese Imported Slaves to Brazil. (Names of languages are in parentheses)

ORIGINS OF THE AFRICAN TRIBES TAKEN TO BAHIA 65

Valente purports that in those parts of Brazil where slavery was most abundantly practiced, the Bantu were as numerous as the Sudanese. However, the author states that he agrees entirely with Nina Rodrigues that the Sudanese were culturally superior to the Bantu. This is why there are more traces today of the former than of the latter. Valente writes: "... Por isto se destacaram os sudaneses em meio às populações negras do Brazil. Dentro os seus grupos, exerceram função cultural prominente o nagô e o gêge." [4] (... For this reason (cultural) the Sudanese stood out from among the other black peoples in Brazil. Within these groups, the Yoruba and the Ewe were culturally prominent.)

In addition to this, it may be noted that the Bantu, who came mostly from the Congo and Angola, did not bring with them to Bahia such a strong religious fervor as the Sudanese did and were, therefore, even more easily absorbed by the Yoruba, Ijẹsa and Ewe. Bantu traces may still be found, though, in the vocabulary of present-day Bahians, among certain *candomblé* members, and one *capoeira* [5] band, called *Capoeira de Angola*.

Throughout the book, Valente clings to the assumption that the Sudanese, especially the Yoruba and the Ewe, dominated the Bantu: "O culto banto deixou-se progressivamente absorver pela superioridade religiosa, a princípio da simbiose gêge-nagô, e depois quase exclusivamente nagô, em virtude da predominância crescente dos elementos iorubanos." [6] (The Bantu cult became absorbed progressively by the

---

[4] (São Paulo: 1955), p. 35. For additional information concerning the Bantu influences in Brazil, see pages 94 through 103 of this book. Also, more recently, Professor Jeremy Chagas of the Department of Linguistics, University of Southern California, has been investigating Bantu influences in Brazil, and delivered a paper at the 1977 Symposium on Hispanic and Luso-Brazilian Linguistics, which was held at the University of Hawaii at Manoa on July 21, 22, and 23. Her report was titled "Proto-Bantu and Brazilian Portuguese," and it afforded many new and interesting discoveries as concerns the etymologies of some common words used in Brazil.

As to the belief that the Sudanese were culturally superior to other "nations" taken to Bahia, it may be that the final Yoruba dominance in Bahia was a natural result of the much greater numbers of them brought to Bahia in the later periods of the slave trade. The highly ceremonial nature of Yoruba religious practices was probably also a factor.

[5] *Capoeira* is a dance representing a fight between two Afro-Brazilian slaves or between a slave and his master. Songs accompanying the dance used to be sung in Yoruba, but are now all in Portuguese.

[6] *Sincretismo*, p. 95.

religious superiority of the Yoruba-Ewe symbiosis. This symbiosis, in turn, became almost exclusively Yoruba because of the growing predominance of this people.)

This may have been true in Bahia, which concerns us most in this study, but is perhaps too comprehensive a statement to embrace all of Brazil, as the author proposes here. In any case, evidence of the origins of blacks taken to Bahia as slaves will be studied in Chapter IV through attempts to discover the etymologies of certain words used in Bahia today.

Nina Rodrigues, in his study *Os Africanos no Brasil*, emphasizes the numerical preponderance of the Sudanese.[7] Speaking specifically of the slave situation in Bahia, he informs us that the Yoruba and Ewe are by far the most numerous. The best evidence of this is the overwhelming majority of *candomblés* in this part of Brazil which adhere to the religious practices of these two "nations."[8]

Other black peoples which Nina Rodrigues includes in this book as having contributed to the slave trade activities in Brazil as a whole are, in the northern areas, the Hausa, Tapa, Nife (or Nupe), Bornu, Adamawa, Grunci,[9] Fula, Mandinga (or Mande), and toward the south, the peoples of Angola, namely the Ausaze, Pimba, Schinga, and Temba. The Portuguese were also active along the Congo coasts and, according to the author, carried slaves from ports located here to Brazil. Many of these blacks, however, were not natives of the Congo, but were brought by Congolese slave traders from points in the north to the shores of the Congo.

Nina Rodrigues quotes from Spiz and Martius' *Reise in Brasilien* (Zweiter Theil, p. 664) and agrees with them in that there were also slave activities between the eastern shores of Africa, mainly Mozambique, and Brazil. Most of these blacks did not originate from the coastal areas, but rather, as in the case of the Congo, were captured from the central parts of Africa and forced to the sea ports in Mozambique.

---

[7] (See pages 54-59, 62, 63, 69, 71, 77-80, 119, and 136 of Rodrigues.)

[8] (See pages 174-180 of Rodrigues.)

[9] (A people whom the author describes as living north of the Ashanti and next to the Hausa. He explains that the Grunci traded goods with the Hausa. They form a "nation" which was not frequented by anyone and therefore actually contributed very little to the slave trade.)

Pierre Verger [10] divides the Afro-Bahian slave traffic into four periods: 1) The Guinea cycle, during the second half of the 16th century; 2) The Angola and Congo cycle, in the 17th century; 3) The Mina cycle, during the first half of the 18th century; and 4) The Benin Bay cycle, between 1770 and 1850. Most of the Yoruba and Ewe peoples arrived in Bahia during the fourth cycle. According to Verger, their late arrival, coupled with the fact that members of these two tribes were brought to Bahia in very large numbers, accounted for the large influence these Africans had on present-day Bahian customs and language.

Slaves shipped to Bahia from the Bay of Benin, Nigeria, between the early part of the 1800's and 1851 numbered more than all of the slaves brought over from the 16th to the beginning of the 19th century. For commercial reasons having to do with the production of tobacco in Bahia, most of this city's Negroes came from the Benin Bay area. Africans from this region were described as excellent workers, strong and healthy, as well as handsome and skilled at raising tobacco. Slaves obtained from this part of Africa were, therefore, highly valued and greatly sought after because of their extraordinary physical capabilities and assets.

The situation in Bahia contrasts somewhat sharply with slave negotiations in other parts of Brazil, which favored Angola and the Congo for their main sources of black manpower.

Various documents indicating these currents of slave marketing still exist, such as one mentioned by Pierre Verger in referring to a letter sent by the governor, the Conde da Ponte, to Lisbon, in 1807: "Esta colônia (Bahia), pela produção do fumo que lhe é própria, tem o privilégio exclusivo do comércio na Costa da Mina, com, por conseguinte, a importação, no ano passado, de 8.037 escravos Gêges, Ussás, Nagôs, etc., nações as mais guerreiras da Costa da Africa, e, em conseqüência os riscos de subversão são maiores..." [11] (This colony (Bahia), because of its tobacco production, has the exclusive privilege of commerce along the Mina Coast, with, because of it, importation figures for last year, of 8,037 Ewe, Hausa and Nago

---

[10] *O Fumo da Bahia e o Tráfico dos Escravos do Gôlfo de Benim* (Salvador, Fundação Gonçalo Moniz, Publicação do Centro de Estudos Afro-Orientais, Universidade Federal da Bahia: 1966).

[11] *O Fumo*, p. 33.

slaves, etc., these being the most war-like of the African coast, thus increasing the possibilities for subversion...)

Pierre Verger's observations concerning the black slave markets are, in themselves, important documents. In his book *Flux et Reflux de la Traite des Nègres entre le Golfe de Bénin et Bahia de Todos os Santos du XVIIe au XIX Siècle,* Verger demonstrates clearly that during most of the slave trade years (the 17th, 18th, and 19th centuries) there were very active negotiations being carried on between Bahia and the Mina Coast. This area in western Africa is described as lying above the Equator between the Volta and the Lagos rivers. At the same time, there was a minimum of trade between this particular section of Africa and parts of Brazil other than Bahia. The excellent trade relations between Bahia and the Mina Coast were due mainly to the fact that the people of the Mina Coast were the only ones who would purchase the third-class grade of tobacco which the state of Bahia was producing.

The accounts which Pierre Verger affords in his large volume dealing with the slave trade between the Bay of Benin and Bahia carry the reader through an historical journey patterned chronologically and presenting in detail the facts which combined to produce one of the most well developed and interesting slave holding institutions in the Western Hemisphere. In the introduction of the book, Verger informs us that all of the data he has been able to gather point to the Bantu as having been the first blacks to reach Bahia as slaves. These peoples, he writes, were able to speak Portuguese much better than the Sudanese, who came later, and assimilated more easily to the Brazilian way of life than did the blacks from the Mina Coast.

The sixteenth century was marked by active trading on the part of the Portuguese in Bahia along the west African coast south of the Equator. This continued on through most of the following century until the 1680's. During the latter two decades of the seventeenth century strong trade negotiations began to develop north of the Equator along the Mina Coast. This trading was to continue on a grand scale until the year 1851 in spite of the numerous efforts by Great Britain to halt all slave activities north of the Equator.[12] Pierre

---

[12] (A treaty was signed in 1815 between Great Britain and Portugal and Brazil which allowed the latter two countries to deal in slave trading only south of the Equator. The clandestine activities, which are described and annotated very well by Pierre Verger in *Flux et Reflux de la Traite des*

ORIGINS OF THE AFRICAN TRIBES TAKEN TO BAHIA 69

Verger demonstrates how the ships carrying tobacco from Bahia to the Mina Coast and returning from here with Sudanese slaves increased in number from around 1681, and how those vessels engaged in similar activities between Bahia and points south of the Equator decreased from the same year until they finally stopped completely by 1706. Between the years 1681 and 1710, there were 368 ships reported as having traded tobacco for slaves between Bahia and the Mina Coast. During the same time period, only 17 ships carried on trade between Bahia and Angola.[13] Around 1687 voyages from Bahia to Angola, were sharply curtailed because of a smallpox epidemic in this part of Africa. It is easy to see, therefore, why there should be more traces in Bahia of the Sudanese peoples than of any other African "nations."

Pierre Verger reminds us that Luiz Vianna Filho in his writings about the Brazilian slave trade states that between 1815 and 1831, there were heavy negotiations between Bahia and the Bantu areas of Africa. Vianna Filho based his findings on official numbers which were kept by the British. These numbers, however, were in all probability false and registered in the ships logs for the express purpose of deceiving the English so that they, the Portuguese at Bahia, could double or possibly triple their hidden activities along the coasts of Ghana, Togo, Dahomey and parts of Nigeria.

Pierre Verger studies the illegal use of passports issued by Great Britain to the Brazilians for trading in Molembo. The Bahian ships would pretend to go to Molembo, south of the Equator, but always docked somewhere along the Mina Coast to take on slaves. Some captains even went so far as to log trips to an imaginary Molembo

---

Nègres... (see pages 288-290, and 412-431, for example), brought many thousands of Sudanese into Bahia, however, and consequently the trade between this Brazilian city and the Mina Coast did not stop as the British wished it to. As a matter of fact, it increased, for the Portuguese at Bahia had discovered long before 1815 that the best buyers for their tobacco were in the Bay of Benin area of Africa, and that these same blacks were much more suited for the types of agricultural activities carried on in the Captaincy of Bahia than were the peoples who came from the south-central portions of western Africa. The Portuguese in Bahia had many good reasons, therefore, for continuing their trade along the Mina Coast, and so they did, as Verger so aptly explains in the chapter entitled "Ruses et Subterfuges de la Traite Clandestine des Esclaves, 1810-1851," using every trick they could conceive of to evade the British patrol ships.)

[13] *Flux et Reflux* (Paris: 1968), p. 11.

somewhere north of the Equator as an excuse to present to the authorities if the Brazilians should be asked by them to explain their presence in waters of the Gulf of Guinea.

Between 1815 and 1831, according to Verger, there were 300 passports issued to Bahian captains for use south of the Equator. Sixty-five ships having these passports were caught by the British in the process of carrying slaves from the Mina Coast to Bahia. The other 235 vessels in possession of this kind of passport, says Verger, most probably were also engaged in illegal trading north of the Equator. They were just lucky enough to be able to evade the English surveillance. And evasion was more the rule than the exception, as the author of *Flux et Reflux*... demonstrates for the reader.

Once again, all of these accounts spell out the numerical predominance of the Sudanese in Bahia. This, of course, does not exclude the presence of peoples from other parts of Africa, but in Bahia, at least, all of the available historical evidence points to the fact that the majority of the black slaves who lived and worked in this state during the nineteenth century originated from the area in western Africa around the Bay of Benin. [14]

---

[14] (For additional information concerning these events, see *Flux et Reflux*..., pages 207, 288, 290, 309, and 412 to 491. Also see the following references: Amaral (Braz do): "As tribus importadas: Os grandes mercados de escravos africanos," *RIHGB*, vol. X, Bahia, 1915; Boughe (Abbé Pierre): *La Côte des Esclaves et le Dahomey*, Paris, 1885; Bouchot (Auguste): *História do Portugal e suas colónias*, Bahia, 1885; Boxer (Charles R.): (IV), "Negro Slavery in Brazil," *Race*, vol. V. London, 1964; Clarkson: *Résumé du témoignage donné devant le Comité de la Chambre des Communes, touchant la traite des nègres, présenté devant le Congrès de Vienne*, Genève, 1815; Dalzel (Archibald): *The History of Dahomey*, London, 1793; Forbes (F. E.): (II), *Dahomey and the Dahomans*, London, 1851; Goulart (Mauricio): *Escravidão Africana no Brasil*, São Paulo, 1950; Lima (Vivaldo da Costa): *Censo dos Terreiros de Candomblé da Bahia, à paraître*; Lopes (Edmundo Correia): (II), *A Escravatura*, Lisboa, 1944; Newbury (C. S.): *The Western Slave Coast and its Rulers*, Oxford, 1961; Olinto (Antonio): *Brasileiros na Africa*, Rio de Janeiro, 1964; Prado (J. F. d'Almeida): (I), "Bahia e as suas relaçoēs com o Daomé," *RIHGB*, vol. XLIV, Rio de Janeiro, 1949; Ribeiro (René): *Reacçoēs do Negro ao Christianismo na América Portuguesa*, Rio de Janeiro, 1958; Rodrigues (José Honorio): *Africa e Brasil, Outro Horizonte*, Rio de Janeiro, 1961; Simonsen (Roberto C.): *História Económica do Brasil (1500-1820)*, São Paulo, 1937; Snelgrave (William): *A New Account of Some Parts of Guinea and the Slave-Trade*, London, 1734; Taunay (Affonso de E.): *Subsidios para a História do Tráfico Africano no Brasil Colonial*, Rio de Janeiro, 1941; Tavares (Luis Henrique): *História da Bahia*, Rio de Janeiro, 1959: Verger (Pierre): (III), "Note on some

In a letter sent from Brazil in 1815 by Luiz Joaquim dos Santos Marrocos to his family in Lisbon, concerning an uprising of African slaves in Bahia, the common source for Bahian slave importation is mentioned: "Êste perigo não existe no Rio de Janeiro onde chegam negros de tôdas as nações, e por isso inimigos uma das outras, enquanto, na Bahia, há sobretudo, negros da Costa da Mina e muito poucas outras regiões, que são todos companheiros e amigos e que em caso de revolta, formam um blôco unânime e matam os que não são de seu país."[15] (This danger (of revolt) does not exist in Rio de Janeiro, where the Negroes become enemies of one another because they come from different "nations." In Bahia, Negroes from the Mina Coast abound and representatives from other regions are few in number. Here in Bahia, all the slaves are friendly with one another and, if threatened in any way by outside forces, form a unanimous block and kill anyone who does not come from their country.)

An interesting report written in 1848 by Francis de Castelnau, French Consul in Bahia, names the various African peoples held as slaves in this area:

> Os Nagô, que formam provàvelmente nove décimos dos escravos da Bahia e se reconhecem por tres profundos sulcos transversais tatuados em cada lado da face. Quase todos embarcaram em Onim (Lagos) ou Porto Nôvo. Os Hauçá, na sua maioria, empregados na Bahia como negros de "palinquins"; quase todos vem via Onim. Os Gêge ou daomeanos que formam uma nação poderosa e tem numerosos representantes na Bahia; outrora embarcavam em Uida, mas hoje vem a maior parte dêles por Pôrto Nôvo.[16]

(The Nago, which probably form nine-tenths of the slave population in Bahia, can be recognized by three deep transverse lines tattooed on each side of their face. Almost all of them were shipped from Onim (Lagos) or from Pôrto Nôvo. The Hausa, who serve in Bahia for the most part as palankeens, all come from Onim. The Ewe or Dahomeans, which form a very powerful "nation" and are quite numerous in Bahia, used to come from Uida, but today are shipped mainly from Pôrto Nôvo.)

---

documents in which Lagos is referred to by the name 'Onim' and which mention relations between Onim and Brazil," *JHSN*, Ibadan, 1959.

[15] Manuel de Oliveira Lima, *João VI no Brasil*, III (Rio de Janeiro, Livraria José Olympio Editôra: 1945), p. 1008.

[16] *O Fumo*, p. 34.

Confirming what has previously been observed, Francis de Castelnau states that Negroes from Angola, the Congo and Mozambique are somewhat rare in Bahia but particularly abundant in other parts of Brazil, such as Rio de Janeiro.

This historical information can be verified by noting the origins of present-day concentrations of West African religious practices throughout Brazil. Pedro McGregor, in *The Moon and Two Mountains*, draws the same conclusions as I concerning the spread of West African tribes in Brazil, as seen through the development of religious rites. McGregor states the following:

> The religious practices of the Negroes ... developed in two different directions in different regions — one in Rio de Janeiro, São Paulo and Minas, mainly the first-named, where the Negroes of Bantu origin from Angola were less influenced by Yoruba culture and consecuently syncretism with Catholicism and spiritism was more marked; the other in Bahia, with extensions to the North and North-east, where Yoruba influence predominated and Catholic appearances as well as Catholic liturgical obligations were added, but where the influence of spiritism was until recently negligible or non-existent. [17]

McGregor believes that one of the reasons for Yoruba preponderance in the state of Bahia stems from the demographic concentration of Negroes and mulattoes here. It is his opinion that this concentration, plus the advantage of having a city (Salvador) which was not suffering the modernizing influence of industrialization, were coupled together to foment the maintenance of a fairly pure [18] cult among the Yoruba. This relatively pure cult, in turn, in my estimation, would have aided in increasing the possibilities of Yoruba influence over any other tribes brought to Bahia from West Africa. It must be remembered, at the same time, that the Yoruba-Ewe complex in Bahia was very resistent to accepting outside influence and remained culturally independent for the entire time span that these Sudanese peoples spent as slaves. They were the rebellious ones. These things, then, would help to explain the present-day cultural and linguistic monopoly of the Yoruba over the other tribes taken to this area.

---

[17] (London, Souvenir Press: 1966), p. 69.

[18] "pure" meaning not influenced by Catholicism, Indian religious rites or other African orders of worship.

ORIGINS OF THE AFRICAN TRIBES TAKEN TO BAHIA

By studying the religions of the slaves that were brought from West Africa to the city of Salvador, it may be possible to determine why the Yoruba culture prevailed over the others. Fernando Ortiz, in his book titled *Los negros brujos (Hampa afro-cubana: apuntes para un estudio de etnología criminal)* (Madrid, Editorial-América: 1917), believes that the Yoruba were able to overshadow members of other tribes taken to Cuba as slaves largely because these Sudanese peoples had what he terms a more advanced theology and a widely expanded language in West Africa. On the island of Cuba, the Yoruba were successful in implanting their culture and language so firmly that even though the Bantu were more numerous in certain areas, the Yoruba dominated them in almost every aspect of their life styles. [19]

Melville J. Herskovits, in *The Myth of the Negro Past*, substantiates the idea that the Yoruba of western Nigeria were taken to Brazil and Cuba in reasonably large numbers. Even though Professor Herskovits states the fact that historical records concerning slave traffic are not available for Brazil, he does conclude that the data which has been gathered from other sources indicate that the *Nagô* slaves were favored by the Spanish and the Portuguese. It is only logical to assume, then, that Yoruban customs outweigh other African survivals in Bahia and Cuba. Evidences of linguistic and cultural Africanisms in other parts of the slave trade areas in Latin America are not as abundant as in these two places, although it cannot be denied that such traces in other sections do indeed exist. Among other lesser fragments of African ethnic qualities, the Mandingo, Senegalese and Hausa seem to have left some vestiges, especially in Brazil. Some Congo influences may also be found in Latin America, for according to Herskovits, a few names of tribal deities and other linguistic survivals show up here. Among these, the word "congo" itself, as may be evidenced very frequently, for example, on the northern coast of Colombia, where, especially during carnival, one may attire himself as a *congo* and dance in the street. [20]

---

[19] For further references to the origins of blacks taken from the same regions of Africa and brought to Bahia and Cuba, see Nina Rodrigues, *Os Africanos no Brasil*, pages 59 and 60, and also Pierre Verger, *Flux et Reflux*..., page 288.

[20] For additional information on the general impact of West Africans in Latin America, see Sir Harry H. Johnston, *The Negro in the New World* (London: 1910). Also see Peter C. Hogg, *The African Slave Trade and its*

Since Yoruba theogony dominates the Negro religious practices in Bahia, it would be wise to devote some attention to the Yoruba culture in Africa in order to understand the origin and some of the ethnolinguistic traits of these African people who were brought to the New World as slaves.

The Yoruba of West Africa form the third largest ethnic group in one of the country's most populous areas. There are presently slightly more than nine million in the farmland of south-western Nigeria, and a good number in Dahomey and Togo. Their language belongs to the Kwa group of the Niger-Congo family (see Joseph H. Greenberg's classification, Figure 2) which predominates in West Africa. The Yoruba are primarily a farming people. This attribute made these west Africans even more favorable in the eyes of the Portuguese since the Lusitanian explorers were very much interested in gathering large numbers of slaves to till the soil on the Bahian sugar plantations.

The Yoruba also have many ancient towns, so that they appear to be one of the most urbanized of all the people of tropical Africa. It is in the extreme northern portion of the Yoruba's homeland that we find the large city of Oyọ. Ile Ifẹ, the traditional cradle of the race and the spiritual center, is in the forest region toward the southern end of Yoruba territory. There was a great migration southwards during the first part of the nineteenth century, when Oyọ was taken over by the Hausa-Fulani. This move would have facilitated the bartering process among the Portuguese slave traders, since they would no longer have to go very far inland in order to gather fresh supplies of black humans to ship to Brazilian ports.

The African territory mentioned here has undoubtedly been the home of the Yoruba for many centuries. As early as the 15th century, the Portuguese register having found a well developed political organization in this area. And, an examination of the lists of kings and other oral data suggests that this system may have been in existence for several hundred years even before the Portuguese arrived.

According to historians (see Robert S. Smith, *Kingdoms of the Yoruba*; J. A. Ademakinwa, *Ifẹ, Cradle of the Yoruba*; Sir A. Burns, *A History of Nigeria*), the Yoruba have never constituted a single

---

Suppression (A classified and annotated bibliography of books, pamphlets and periodical articles) (Portland) Frank Cass and Company Limited: 1973).

ORIGINS OF THE AFRICAN TRIBES TAKEN TO BAHIA

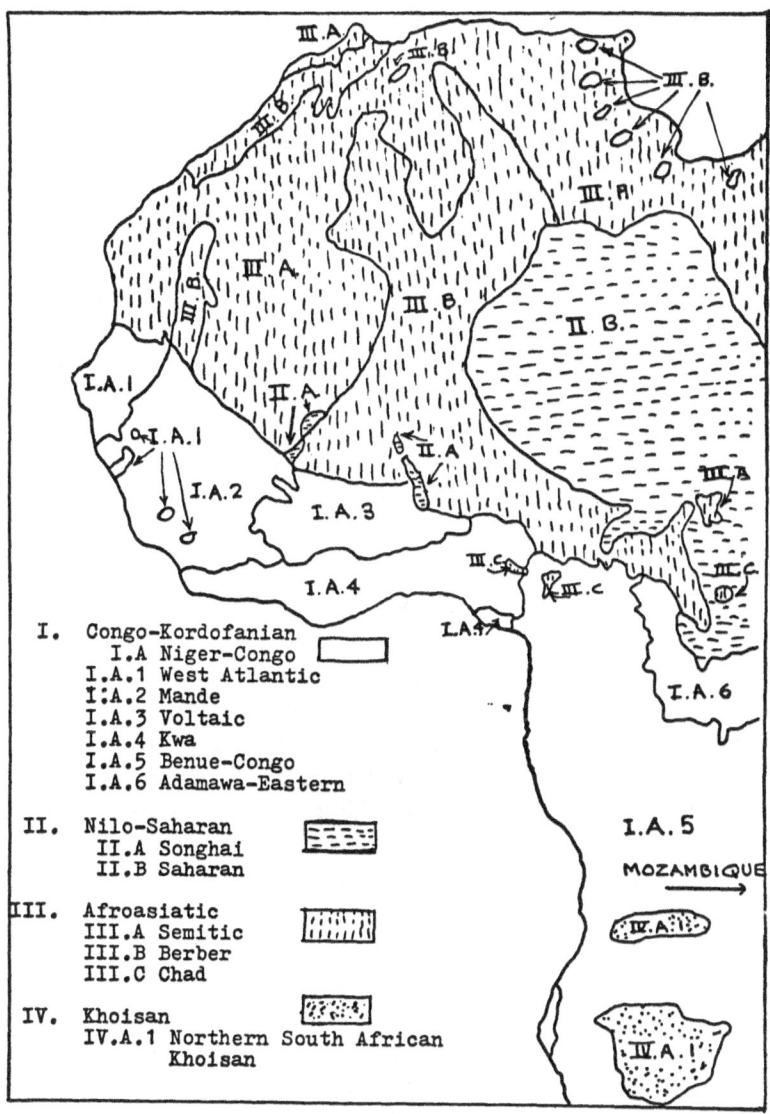

FIGURE 2: Classification of West African Languages (from Joseph H. Greenberg, *The Languages of Africa*, Mouton and Co., the Hague, the Netherlands, 1963)

political entity. Even their name was used only in the northern part of their land, the Ọyọ, the other branches having different nomenclatures according to the various kingdoms. Their language, in spite of the many dialects which help compose it, provides important evidence of a common origin. It is interesting to note that the term sometimes employed to refer to this language, *anago*, has been known to be used by neighboring tribes, especially the Dahomeans. Another name, *Olukumi*, meaning "my friend," is also used by neighbors of the Yoruba to allude to them. *Anago* has been kept in Brazil and Cuba as a term which is used in free variation with *Yorubá*. It shows up as *anagó* in Cuba and as *nagô* in Brazil. *Olukumi* appears in Cuba as *lucumí*, and also refers to these Negro people of West African origin.

A study of certain cycles of myths and legends describing the creation of the world point toward a common origin of the Yoruba people. The names of the gods whom the Yoruba regard as their founding ancestors appear in these tales. One common version of the story of the beginning of the world is that which tells how Ọlọrun, the owner of the sky, let Oduduwa descend to the primordial ocean and form the land masses by tossing some earth into the water. There is a political counterpart to this tale which says that Oduduwa was a son of Lamurudu, King of Mecca, who traveled west until he came to Ifẹ and settled there. From Ifẹ his children became the founders of the kingdoms in all of Yoruba territory. These stories of the creation may be found in all the Yoruba kingdoms, which all trace their descent to Ifẹ. Ọlọrun seems to be the only figure from these legends that took root in Bahia, and that, as a very minor spirit. [21]

The Ijẹṣa, who represent a substantial number of those who still practice *candomblé* in Bahia, stem from the Yoruba. Because of its historical and present-day importance in Salvador, this kingdom merits our attention in this study. The Ijẹṣa kingship derives from Ifẹ whose ruler was Ọwa. The Reverend S. Johnson, in his *The History of the Yorubas*, suggests that the name Ijẹṣa stems from a

---

[21] For additional information concerning the Yoruba in Africa, see A. B. Ellis, *The Yoruba-Speaking Peoples of the Slave Coast of West Africa* (Chicago: 1964). Also see the Rev. Samuel Johnson, *The History of the Yorubas* (From the Earliest Times to the Beginning of the British Protectorate) (Lagos: 1956).

contraction of *ije oriṣa,* meaning "the food of the gods," and refers to a portion of the people who lived in the area east of Ife before the arrival of the founder of the present kingship, and who were considered by their neighbors to be good sacrificial victims. Ajaka, the founder of the Ijeṣa kingdom, is supposed to be a son of Oduduwa by the sister of one of his wives.

One important fact which must not be overlooked when considering Yoruba dominance over other West African tribes brought to Brazil is that of the inseparability in Yoruba life of religious practices and social, economic and political life. Almost everything that happens in life has its cause in the spirits which dominate the course of nature. This is no doubt why neither Christianity nor Islamism have been able to overshadow these Yoruba beliefs. Their dictates so emphatically insist upon the interaction of the powers of the spirits or gods with the very essence of life itself that to counteract this religion would mean the destruction of the true meaning of existence. It is easy to see, then, why the Yoruba remained strong in Bahia in those areas of life centering around religious beliefs.

In addition to the Yoruba and their "first cousins," the Ijeṣa, the Ewe, from Togo and Dahomey, also left an indelible mark on Bahian society. This West African "nation" has much in common with the Yoruba, especially in their religious beliefs. Many of the Ewe gods are the same as those found in Yorubaland with the exception that in Togo they have Ewe names. This is probably why one can find many *candomblé* houses celebrating a complex of Yoruba-Ewe rites under the same roof. It was undoubtedly the strong similarity between the Yoruba and the Ewe religiously centered life sytles which helped keep the Ewe alive.

Melville J. Herskovits, in *The New World Negro*[22] tells of his interview with a West African fellow named Felix, of Dahomey, who told very old tales of Africans being taken from Dahomey to the New World as slaves. Professor Herskovits writes the following about this experience in West Africa:

> Later, as we came to know Felix and he to trust us, we heard from him why he had been so moved that day, and why he was so eager to hear about the Negroes on our side of the Atlantic. Like most Africans, Felix had been trained

---

[22] *New World Negro,* p. 84.

in the traditions of his family. He knew that long ago his ancestors had been decimated by slave raids. He could tell us the story of the wanderings of his family to escape from these raids — how, for example, his people had fled from the Ashanti after a war in which many of his ancestral relations had been lost in battle, either killed or carried off into captivity. He could recount how later, when his family had established a new home, they had had to go farther to the East, and as their enemies found them, farther still, until it had not mattered where they went, for the Aguda, as he called the Portuguese, had continued to clamor for more and more slaves.

During Herskovits' visit to West Africa, the distinguished Africanist was able to gather very important references to the slaving days from the natives themselves. Some of this information is useful in this study, for it concerns activities related to Brazil. Herskovits writes:

> In Dahomey today, there are designations for the countries to which the slaves had gone. They are called from the land of the Nago, the Yoruba of Nigeria to whom the Dahomeans for so many years sent their anual tribute of men and women, and from the countries of the white man. *Yovotome,* white-man's land, had been the name for the countries of the English, but today it is the designation for France. *Ame'ica* is America, *Agudatome,* the land of the Portuguese, or *Blezi,* is the name for Brazil, while *Kpanyo* is Dahomean for Spain, and *Kankanu* the lands of the Dutch. [23]

According to Herskovits, there is a story told by the natives, which deals with one specific case in which a Dahomean woman was sent to Brazil and there established her religion. It is my opinion, based on information such as Herskovits provides here and from data gathered in Brazil, that this story can be generalized to include many similar cases of West Africans who were sold into slavery, taken to Brazil, and there established religious rites. The example given to Professor Herskovits by a native Dahomean, speaks of the enslavement of the mother of Gezo. He writes:

---

[23] *New World Negro,* p. 86.

Gezo was a small boy when his father died, and the kingship went to an older brother, the Adanzan... The father, before his death, had, however, predicted that Gezo would become king. Adanzan was enraged when he learned of this and proceeded to sell Gezo's mother and sixty-three of her supporters into slavery. They were taken by the Portuguese and were sent to Brazil. There, the story goes, they found many Dahomeans. Gezo's mother and eleven others were sent to America, and because she was sad and no longer young she was sold many times. She spent twenty-four years in all in America, and founded the cult of her Dahomean god there.[24]

Melville J. Herskovits, in his study *The New World Negro*, also found that the Yoruba-Ewe complex as found in Bahia, maintained a stronger religious affinity with their West African past than did the other tribes taken to this general area. He states the following concerning this phenomenon:

The many cult-groups found in Bahia, and elsewhere in Brazilian centers with an appreciable population of African descent, differ in the degree of their adherence to African religious custom. The most rigorous — "orthodox," in the African sense — are the Gêge, of Dahomean derivation. Most numerous today among those who hold closest to African procedures are the Ketu, who take their designation from the town of the same name lying on the Yoruba-Dahomean border in West Africa. They are essentially Yoruba in derivation and linguistic expression. Another smaller group, the 'Jesha cult, is to be traced to the Yoruba political group of the same name (Ijesha). It may be regarded as a local variation of generalized Yoruba religious culture that was continued in Bahia. The Nupe, called Tapa, the name even today given them in Africa by the Yoruba, and remnants of the Hausa and their northern and westerly neighbors are incorporated largely into the Ketu group. The Congo-Angola sect, as its name indicates, comes from the more southerly portion of western Africa; its linguistic usages have been traced to Kimbundu, but intensive research, in Brazil, Angola and the western Congo will be necessary before precise provenience can be determined.[25]

---

[24] *New World Negro*, p. 89. For additional information concerning the Dahomeans, see A. B. Ellis, *The Ewe-Speaking Peoples of the Slave Coast of West Africa* (London: 1890).
[25] (Bloomington, Indiana University Press: 1966), pp. 288, 219.

Professor Herskovits' observation is in complete agreement with other Afro-Brazilian historians who maintain that present-day Yoruba-Ewe dominance in Bahia is due mainly to this religiously-oriented life style which, because of its firmly rooted nature, overshadowed the other less rigorously "orthodox" west Africans.

It is interesting to note that even though Roger Bastide, in *Les Amériques Noires,* does not refute any of the foregoing hypotheses of Yoruba dominance over other African tribes brought to Bahia, he seems to insist more heavily upon pure numerical preponderance for the reason behind a cultural supremacy. Professor Bastide writes, while studying the problem of African sources in the Americas:

> ... les négres son davantage originaires de l'ancienne Côte d'Or pour les régions anglo-saxonnes, davantage du Congo et d'Angola pour les pays hispaniques, et pour un même pays, d'une époque à l'autre; ainsi, à Bahia (Brésil) le trafic c'est fait au 16e siècle avec la Côte de Guinée (au sens large du terme), au 17e siècle avec l'Angola, au 18e siècle avec la Côte de Mina, enfin, au cours du 19e siècle, où le trafic devient clandestin, la distribution est plus irrégulière (de 1803 à 1810, 20 navires de la Côte de Mina avec 47.114 Soudains et 31 d'Angola, avec 11.494 Bantous).[26] Or, il est évident que les traits culturels apportés aux 17e et 18e siècles se sont perdus et que les civilisations afro-américaines actuelles se rattachent à la fin de la traite negrière; c'est pourquoi la civilisation justement de la Côte de Mina domine à Bahia sur la civilisation bantoue.[27]

> (... the Negroes sent to Anglo-Saxon areas came mostly from the old Gold Coast, and those shipped to Latin America had their points of origin in the Congo and Angola; thus, in Bahia (Brazil) the traffic was carried out in the 16th century with the Guinea Coast (in the broad sense of this general area), in the 17th century with Angola, in the 18th century with the Mina Coast (see Figure 1) and finally, during the 19th century, when the traffic became clandestine, the distribution becomes more irregular (from 1803 to 1810, 20 ships are registered as having come from the Mina Coast with 47,114 Sudanese, and 31 from Angola, with 11,494 Bantu). It is evident that the cultural traits brought to Bahia

---

[26] The author draws information from Luis Vianna Filho's *O Negro na Bahia,* Rio de Janeiro, 1946.
[27] (Paris, Payot: 1967), pp. 13, 14.

ORIGINS OF THE AFRICAN TRIBES TAKEN TO BAHIA 81

in the 17th and 18th centuries were lost and that the present-day Afro-American civilization reflects the final stages of slave trading; this is why the slaves brought from the Mina Coast in West Africa were able to absorb the Bantu into their civilization in Bahia.)

Of all the slaves brought from the Mina Coast, Roger Bastide reports that the majority were either Ashanti, Yoruba or Ewe.

Even though several authors mention the arrival of considerable numbers of Hausa people to Bahia, Francis de Castelnau informs us that there were very few women among them. This is probably the main reason why few traces of them exist today in the city of Bahia. After the 13 of May, 1888, when Princess Isabel de Bragança signed the *Lei Áurea*, putting a definite end to slavery in Brazil, the majority, if not all, of the Hausa, were absorbed by the Yoruba and Ewe people.

Since historical annals and traces of vocabulary (see Chapter IV) point to the presence of a considerable number of Bantus involved in slave trade activities between Africa and Bahia, a brief word about these peoples is deemed relevant here.

The Bantu "nations" occupy most of the Congo Basin. There are numerous tribes in this region, of whom the Bakongo of the Lower Congo area, the Bangala and the Lunda are among some of the most important. The main languages are Kikongo, Chiluba, Lingala, and Swahili. Of these, it appears that Kikongo was the one taken to Bahia. Also, traces of Shona and Chewa (Southeastern Bantu) are evident in Salvador.

In Angola, we also find the Bantu linguistic group made up of six main ethnic groups, among which the Bambundu and the Bakongo appear in the data concerning African elements in Bahia. The Kimbundu is the second largest ethnic group in Angola. It is at present the one most influenced by European mores and many of the Kimbundu people speak fluent Portuguese. The Kikongo, who live in northern Angola, are relatively closely linked to the peoples of the lower Congo.

The obituaries, containing reports of slave deaths, supply accurate information concerning the numbers of Sudanese and Bantu Negroes during the Brazilian Colonial Period. Eighteenth century reports taken from several files of obituary records show figures designating the geographical areas in Africa from which Bahian slaves came. The list in Table 4, taken from the obituaries of the Santa Casa de Misericórdia do Salvador, covers the years between 1741 and 1799.

TABLE 4

NUMBERS OF SUDANESE AND BANTU SLAVES IN BAHIA BETWEEN THE YEARS 1741 AND 1799

Sudanese		Bantus	
Gêge	1.399	Angolas	7.992
Nagô	385	Benguelas	2.451
Minas	6.244	Cabindas	1
Do Gentio da Costa	388	Congos	30
Do Gentio de Guiné	11	Muxicongo	2
Aussá	6	Gabão	18
Arda	1	Moçambiques	270
Calabar	7	São Tomé	51
Cabo Verde	10	Mbunda	1
Fulanin	1		
Tapa	6		
Ilha do Príncipe	6		

From this chart, a ratio of 4:5 can be established, with the Bantu group claiming the larger number.

As this table indicates, there were more slaves of Bantu than Sudanese origin whose deaths were recorded during these years of the eighteenth century. If these figures are indicative of the actual number of Bantu over Sudanese in Bahia at this time, it would be in order to say that the former should have been able to establish fraternal ties close enough to have prevented any kind of great ethnic dispersion. This type of adhesiveness during the eighteenth century would have counterbalanced the Yoruba-Ewe cultural dominance and probably explains why traces of the Bantu peoples are found in Bahia today in spite of the apparent Sudanese numerical and cultural supremacy during the nineteenth century.

According to sales contracts obtained from the Municipal Archives of Salvador, the years between 1838 and 1860 showed 3,060 Sudanese, 460 Bantu and 4,774 slaves of African descent born in Bahia.

The relative disappearance of the Bantu people in Bahia during the following century can be explained in part by what Carlos B. Ott [28] designates as an inferiority complex among them, which became heightened especially when they found themselves among Sudanese. The effects of this complex may be seen in the fact that the great majority of Bantu *candomblé* houses in Bahia became or fused with either the Yoruba or Ewe houses, thereby adopting many of the Sudanese linguistic and cultural habits.

Turning our attention for a moment to the Portuguese in the interior parts of Africa, we note that E. Franklin Frazier [29] stresses the fact of inland slave trade activities as he writes the following:

> The system of barter which characterized the initial contacts of Europeans and natives in the tropical areas of the world where white settlement was impossible did not always lead to the enslavement of the native on his native soil. In West Africa, which was the source of slaves for the colonizing European powers in the Western World, natives were bartered by native rulers, merchants, and conquerors for the products of European industry. In the Gold Coast, for example, the monopoly of supplying slaves was jealously guarded by the Africans, and the king of Dahomey refused to permit European traders to enter his kingdom. Africans on the coast acted as middlemen and sent their agents inland to purchase slaves. Likewise in Nigeria, the Africans supplied slaves to satisfy the ever-increasing demands of Europeans for labor on overseas plantations. [30]

Nina Rodrigues, in his *Os Africanos no Brasil* (Rio de Janeiro, 1945), p. 194, writing on the subject of slave trading in Africa's interior, states the following:

> A coroa de Portugal acha-se em relação de Protetora ou Aliada para com muitos príncipes do interior da Africa Central; o tráfico de escravos é feito não sòmente na costa como

---

[28] *Formação e Evolução da Cidade do Salvador: O Folklore Baiano* (Salvador, Tipografia Mann Editôra Ltda.: 1955).

[29] *Race and Culture Contacts in the Modern World* (Boston, Beacon Press: 1968), p. 104.

[30] For additional general information on the provenience of slaves throughout the Americas, see Melville J. Herskovits' *The Myth of the Negro Past*, pp. 34 to 41. Also see Melville J. Herskovits, *The New World Negro*, pp. 90 to 94.

também no mais profundo interior, por grande número de
Portuguêses, por mestiços de origem portuguêsa e por negros
nascidos em colônias portuguêsas.

(The crown of Portugal is a type of Protector Ally in its
relationship to many princes of the interior part of Central
Africa; the slave traffic is carried on not only on the coast,
but also in the deepest interior regions, by a large number
of Portuguese, by mestizos of Portuguese origin, and by
blacks born in Portuguese colonies.)

These inland activities would explain the presence in Bahia of the Nupe and the Hausa, who are north of the coasts of Dahomey and Nigeria, the traces of Shona and Chewa, which come from Rhodesia and Malawi, respectively, and the few words of Mang'anja, from the interior regions of Mozambique.

It is not very probable that either Bushmen or Hottentots were brought to Bahia, since no linguistic evidence of these people has yet been found here and since they were highly undesirable specimens for the public market because of a premature wrinkling of the skin, which caused the aesthetic-conscious Portuguese to reject them immediately. A few cases of the sale of Pigmies have been recorded, but these Negroes were not in demand and consequently left no traces behind.

We may conclude, then, that two groups of West Africans had a stronger impact than other "nations" on the Portuguese-Americans in Bahia, both culturally and linguistically. The northern-most group belongs linguistically to the Kwa sub-classification, and the other one, farther to the South, to the Benue-Congo. Both of these groups belong to the Niger-Congo family [31] (See Figure 2). The geographical areas which witnessed more slave activities than others were the regions around Togo, Dahomey, Nigeria, the Congo, and Angola. The Minas who appear in large numbers in the records of the 18th century belong to the Kwa group. These Kwa were referred to as Minas because they were shipped to Bahia from the African port of São Jorge d'El Mina, in Ghana.

Because of the long history of slave traffic and the large numbers of slaves imported, the presence of the black in Bahia was and con-

---

[31] *The Languages of Africa*, p. 8.

tinues to be an important factor, culturally, racially and linguistically. As a matter of fact, the black influence in Bahia has been so prominent that the city became famous because of it. Thales de Azevedo [32] states that the 1775 census showed the city to have 12,720 whites, 4,207 free mulattoes, 3,630 free Negroes, plus 14,696 mulatto and black slaves. Of the total of 35,253 people 36 % were white and 64 % black and mestizo of various kinds, such as mulattoes, *mamelucos*,[33] *cafusos*,[34] *caboclos*[35] and others.

Pierre Verger, in *Flux et Reflux*..., refers to a letter sent by the British consul in Bahia to his superiors concerning the excessively large numbers of blacks in the city and the acute possibility of having a major uprising among them against the white population. The letter, dated May 26, 1827, contains the following: "L'opinion générale, bien ou mal fondée, est que les officiers noirs ont pris part au complot ou en sont les instruments. La quantité de Noirs et de mulâtres armés dans cette ville de Bahia excède à présent de beaucoup le nombre de ceux de toute autre nature. C'est un des résultats de l'expulsion des Portugais. La population blanche est mise ainsi dans une position très dangereuse."[36] (The general opinion, whether or not it is well founded, is that the black officers have taken part in the plot or are the instigators of the same. The quantity of armed blacks and mulattoes in the town of Bahia at the present time greatly exceeds all other kinds of people. It is one of the results of the expulsion of the Portuguese. Therefore, the white population is put into a very dangerous position.)

It is clear that the racial, cultural and linguistic contribution of the Negroes was more lasting than that of the Indians. The latter decreased rapidly because of death from hunger, epidemics and fierce resistance to capture. In 1533, the Jesuits had more than 40,000 Indians in their villages. Thirty years later, there were only 3,400. Today the racial proportions in Bahia are the following: 28 % white, 23 % Negroes, 48 % mestizos, 1 % others, including 0.02 % "yellow."

---

[32] "Índios, Brancos e Prêtos no Brasil Colonial," in *América Indígena*, Vol. XIII, No. 2, April, 1953.
[33] *Mamelucos* — a mixture of Indian and white.
[34] *Cafusos* — a mixture of Negro and Indian.
[35] *Caboclos* — a mixture of white and Indian. Also, a mulatto with kinky hair; a backwoodsman (perhaps the most common meaning).
[36] (Page 309 of Berger.)

CHAPTER III

ETHNOLINGUISTIC DATA GATHERED IN THE
CANDOMBLÉS OF THE CITY OF SALVADOR

The investigation of the cult houses, or *terreiros de candomblé*, cannot be overlooked when studying African influences in Bahia. These cults hold important keys which may unlock doors leading into Bahia's slave-holding multiracial past, for they are the only vestiges alive today which continue to use parts of the ancestral native languages and so provide us with indications concerning the origins of some of the "Africanisms" found in contemporary Bahian Portuguese.

The conservation of African languages within the Afro-Bahian religious circles can be compared to the continued use of Latin in the services of the Roman Catholic Church. Just as Latin remained the official language in which services were conducted in the Church of Rome throughout Europe and the language which spread to the New World in both Spanish and Portuguese territories, so Yoruba or Ewe or Bantu, were brought to the Americas, where they took root and have been used for ceremonial purposes to the present day in spite of the overwhelming influence exerted by Portuguese as the official language of Brazil. And, just as the Roman Catholic Church has, in recent times, begun to employ the language of the host country as the medium of communication to be used in officiating the holy services (for a deeper comprehension by the masses can be achieved through the use of a mutually intelligible tongue), so it is with the cult houses. A growing lack of understanding on the part of the initiates has led to a gradual decrease in the use of Yoruba, or whatever may have been the language of the ancestral tribe, with Portuguese rapidly replacing it.

An easily identifiable comparison of West African languages and culture penetrating Bahia can be made likewise with what has happened in Cuba. When one observes the many studies done by Cuba's own Fernando Ortiz, for example, it is immediately apparent that many of the words used to designate spirits or saints in the Afro-Cuban religious circles are directly comparable to those used in Bahia and both can be traced to a common origin in West Africa.

Although this study does not purport to compare West African vestiges in Bahia, Brazil to those of Cuba, it will be worthwhile to cite some examples of ethnolinguistic similarities found in both of these places, primarily with the expectation that, by so doing, scholars in the field of comparative linguistics will be motivated to carry out extensive research in this area.

Perhaps one of the best focal points for comparison is the worship of African deities in Cuba, known as *santería*. The spirits involved in these religious practices are known as *orisha, babalorisha* and *iyalorisha*. All three are also found in Bahian *candomblé*.

William R. Bascom, who has done a considerable amount of research in Cuban *santería*, writes the following concerning the origins of these Afro-Cuban religious rites:

> The African elements of *santería* are predominantly Yoruba, or Lucumi, as the Yoruba of Nigeria are called in Cuba. In the town of Jovellanos, Matanzas province, where most of the material on which this paper is based was gathered, the importance of Yoruba religion in *santería* is clearly apparent. The Yoruba influence is also recognizable throughout Cuba, despite regional variations, in the names of the Yoruba deities, in similarities to Yoruba ritual, in the Yoruba cities named by Cuban Negroes as homes of their ancestors, and in individuals who can still speak the Yoruba language.[1]

The very extensive studies carried out by Fernando Ortiz in Afro-Cuban matters also point to common origins of the West African slaves taken to Bahia and to Cuba. Two striking examples of musical instruments used both in Cuban religious ceremonies and Bahian *candomblé* are the *maraca* and the *agógo* (*agôgô* in Bahia).[2]

---

[1] "The Focus of Cuban Santería," in *Southwestern Journal of Anthropology* (Volume 6, Number 1, Spring, 1950), p. 64.

[2] See vocabulary in Chapter IV for definitions of these instruments.

Professor Ortiz mentions the fact that the Africans taken to Cuba came from different racial stocks, but that certain of these were more prominent in Afro-Cuban music than others. Concerning this, he writes:

> Al estudiar la música afrocubana habrá, pues, que distinguir al menos, porque la presencia de algunas variedades originarias ha de permitir hacerlo, la música cubana de ascendencia *dajomé, bantú* o *conga*, preferentemente en los bailes más generalizados; tenemos música *carabalí* en los ritos de los ñáñigos; algo de música *arará* o *dahome* y, por fin, esa música africana que en Cuba parece ser la más conservada y varia, la de las liturgias religiosas de los negros *yoruba*, que constituye uno de los más caudalosos veneros de la música negra en la Gran Antilla. Aparte de otras músicas marginales menos importantes, como la de los negros *gangá*, la de los *takuá*, la de los *iyesá*,[3] etc.[4]

> (When studying Afro-Cuban music, one must distinguish, since the presence of some original varieties permit one to do so, Cuban music deriving from *Dahomey, Bantu* or *Congo*, preferably in the more generalized dances; we have *carabalí* music in the rites of the *ñáñigos*; some *arará* or *Dahomey* music, and lastly, that African music which in Cuba appears to be the best preserved and of most variety, that of the religious liturgies of the Yoruba, which constitutes one of the largest sources of Negro music in the Antilles.

---

[3] *iyesá* is *ijexá* in Bahia. This is a good example of some of the phonetic changes which certain West African words underwent in Cuba. The Yoruba for this sub-tribal name, as we have seen, is Ijẹṣa; in phonetic script [ijɛšá]. The Bahian form of this word is phonetically the same as its African original with one small shift of primary stress: [ijɛ'ša]. This is true since, as we shall see in Chapter IV, many of the phones that exist in the Kwa group are also found in Portuguese, making borrowings at the lexical level much more easily adaptable at the phonetic level for the borrowing language, in this case, Portuguese. There are greater differences, however, between the phonetic systems of Yoruba and Spanish, the latter having no direct counterparts for many of the Yoruba phones. Spanish, therefore, when borrowing lexical items, substitutes the nearest phonetic equivalents to the Yoruba sounds which it does not possess. In the borrowing process, then, of the example cited here, three phonetic changes are readily discernable in the passage from Yoruba to Spanish: [j] > [y]; [ɛ] > [e]; [š] > [s]. Shift of primary stress to the final syllable of the word (instead of each syllable receiving equal stress, as in the original Yoruba) also occurs in Spanish as in Portuguese.

[4] *La africanía de la música folklórica de Cuba* (Habana: Ministerio de Educación, 1950), pp. 106, 107.

There are also other minor sources of music, such as that of the *gangá*, the *takuá* and the *iyesá*, etc.)

Additional examples of identical vocabulary items found in Afro-Cuban religious circles as well as in the Afro-Bahian ones are various. Fernando Ortiz, in his book titled *Bailes y el teatro de los negros en el folklore de Cuba*, records several names which I also found in Bahia. In the liturgies connected with *Oru* in Cuba, we find *Echú* or *Eléggua*, who is the god which "opens and closes the road." [5] In certain songs dedicated to the Afro-Cuban *Babalú Ayé*, we find the names of two gods also used in Bahian *candomblé: Ogun*, who is the warrior, and *Ochosi* (*Oxóssi* in Bahia), who is the god of the hunt. Two very popular spirits in *candomblé* worship in Bahia are *Xangô*, the god of thunder and lightning, and *Yemanjá*, the sea nymph. Both of these West African saints play an important part in Afro-Cuban religious ceremonies. In Cuba, their names have been influenced by Spanish pronunciation to a greater degree than they were by Portuguese pronunciation in Brazil, and they are called *Changó* and *Yemayá*, respectively. [6]

---

[5] (Habana: Ministerio de Educación, 1951), p. 202. *Exu*, in Bahia, is also known as the god who watches over the road. He has another name, which is *Elebara* (Elegbara) or Elegba. This is the same as *Eléggua*, that we find in Cuba. See number (3) of Appendix IV. Also see A. B. Ellis, *The Yoruba-Speaking Peoples...*, pp. 64, 65, 66, *The Ewe-Speaking Peoples...*, and Samuel Johnson, *The History of the Yorubas*, among many others.

[6] Note the changes from Yoruba to Portuguese and from Yoruba to Spanish:

Yoruba Iyemoja > Portuguese Yemanjá
[yemɔja]   [yemã'ja]
Yoruba Ṣàngó > Portuguese Xangô
[ʃaŋgo]   [ʃaŋ'go]
Yoruba Iyemoja   Spanish Yemayá
                        [yema'ya]
Yoruba Ṣàngó   Spanish Changó
                        [čaŋ'go]

Since the Caribbean type of Spanish does not have the sounds [š] (generally, although [š] does exist in a sub-dialect) and [j], and Portuguese and Yoruba do, there was a smaller amount of phonetic change which occurred in the transition from Yoruba to Portuguese than from Yoruba to Spanish in these two examples.

For additional comparisons, see Fernando Ortiz, *Bailes y el teatro de los negros en el folklore de Cuba*.

It is also true that comparisons can be made with other areas of Latin America. For example, Melville J. Herskovits, in his *Life in a Haitian Village* (New York, Octagon Books, Inc.: 1964), p. 143, states the following con-

In Bahia, a complete substitution of the African tongue by the Portuguese language has not yet come about. However, present trends, as well as past events, such as the complete disappearance of the use of Yoruba in *capoeira,* indicate that Yoruba and Ewe, as well as other African dialects in Bahia, are slowly disappearing, and that within a relatively short period of time even the *terreiros de candomblé* will be conducting their rituals entirely in Portuguese.

One can readily understand the urgency of extracting as much African dialect material from the cult houses as possible. If proper investigative tasks are not undertaken now, the few remaining traces of an archaic form of language will soon be irretrievably gone, and so will the chances of ever using such information to determine how much of an impact these African tongues actually had on Brazilian Portuguese. Even as the situation stands at the present time, too much has already been lost, so that a complete analysis at all linguistic levels can never be attained.

The conservative nature of the African tongues as used in the religious ceremonies has been investigated in some depth by Professor Yêda Pessoa de Castro of the Universidade Federal da Bahia. In an article entitled "Às Línguas Africanas na Bahia," (African Tongues in Bahia) written in commemoration of the day on which slavery was abolished in Brazil (May 13, 1888), she comments on the singularity of the residual characteristics of African languages in Bahia:

> No resto, as línguas africanas se reduziram à linguagem ritual dos cultos religiosos afro-brasileiros, limitadas assim a um grupo pequeno e bastante conservador, a chamada "língua da gente-de-santo" que, apesar de vir resistindo a interferência do prestígio crescente do português, têm no entanto, com o tempo, dêle recebido uma boa influência morfológica e vocabular, notadamente nos candomblés de origem congo-

---

cerning Afro-Haitian religious practices: "The most striking element in the Vodun cult is the manner in which the gods possess their devotees." According to the author's description, this "manner" is exactly like the way it is done in Bahia. Even the decorations used on Haitian altars in these ceremonies are very similar to the ornaments used to adorn Afro-Bahian *candomblé* altars. Names of gods used in Haiti, such as *Ogun, Shango, Legba* and *Loko,* as well as such words as *zombi,* a type of walking corpse, have direct counterparts in Bahian *candomblé,* and denote a common West African origin. Research carried out by Herskovits concerning the origins of the slaves taken to Haiti confirms these lexical similarities (see pages 17, 18, 19 and 23 of *Life in a Haitian Village*).

angola, os candomblés-de-cabôclo [7] que se acham não só espalhados em sua maioria pelo interior, como isolados de África há pelo menos dois séculos... [8]

(So, the African languages were reduced to the ritual language used in the Afro-Brazilian religious cults, and was thus limited to a relatively small conservative group. This ritual language, called the "language-of-the people-of-saint," which, in spite of the fact that it has tried to resist any interference from the prestige language, namely Portuguese, has, nevertheless, been influenced by this language, both morphologically and lexically, especially in the *candomblés* of Congo-Angola origin, the *cabôclo candomblés*.)

It is important to note, then, the influence which Portuguese has had on the Afro-Brazilian *candomblé* ceremonial language. This influence may not be direct, [9] as Professor Pessoa de Castro suggests, but rather of the type which has caused the gradual disappearance of the dialects brought over from Africa and the substitution of Portuguese in their place. Yet at the same time there has been enough resistance against the invading Portuguese, especially among the Yoruba and Ewe in Bahia, that many of the ritualistic chants in these *candomblés* have been preserved down through the centuries and are still taught to new members who receive the proper initiation. Concerning this matter, Yêda Pessoa de Castro states:

Já nos candomblés de origem iorubá, mais recentes, concentrados em sua quase totalidade na cidade do Salvador, essa resistência por isso mesmo tem sido maior, e a língua vem-se conservando bàsicamente sem alterações, pois há bem um século — contando-se a partir da cessação do tráfico — acha-se resguardada como língua sagrada e ritual de qualquer tipo de interferência lingüística estranha ao meio inclusive

---

[7] *Candomblés* designated as *cabôclo* in Bahia, are those which are a mixture of African and indigenous rituals. Many of the spirits worshipped have Indian names as well as African and Christian counterparts.

[8] In *A Tarde*, sábado, 11 de maio de 1968, Secção "Suplemento," p. 2.

[9] The only instance of direct linguistic influence of Portuguese on an African dialect was registered during an interview with a *mãe de santo* who told me that one of the household words of African origin still used in her home was *mi'lɔŋga*, meaning "plate." Another was *milɔŋ'giña*, meaning "cup." It is obvious that the second one is *mi'lɔŋga* with a Portuguese suffix for the diminutive (*-inho, -inha*). The Kimbundu word *ma'lɔŋga* means "plates, dishes."

de novas ondas lingüísticas da África que viessem renovar ou modificar a sua estrutura arcaizante. [10]

(But, in the Yoruba *candomblés*, which are more recent and concentrated almost entirely in the city of Salvador, this resistance [to the Portuguese language] has been greater. The language has been preserved basically without alterations. It has been kept for more than a century as a sacred, ritual language, completely isolated from Portuguese influence and from any contact with other African languages that may have modified its archaic structure.)

This being the case, one can see that the retention of African forms in Bahia was indeed a strange phenomenon, if not even renovating elements of similar West African dialects taken to Bahia at a later time had any radical effects on changing the language which had already been established there. The fact remains, then, that, according to most Brazilian linguists, the Yoruba and Ewe presently used in the cult houses in Bahia are archaic as well as modified by independent evolutionary processes brought about by separation from Africa. A comparison of Bahian *candomblé* speech with modern Yoruba readily confirms this, as was pointed out in the comparative study made by Deoscóredes M. dos Santos and Juana Elbein. [11]

The "language" of the *candomblé* will be studied in this chapter, for it permits us a glimpse of Yoruba and Ewe almost as they were spoken in the years of colonial Brazil. As Yêda Pessoa de Castro aptly states:

> Nessa "língua," as maiores resistências têm partido das "cantigas-de-santo" — ou cânticos rituais de invocação aos deuses — graças ao seu aspecto não-profano, que faz tôdas elas conhecidas dentro do grupo por um grupo menor ainda, o dos iniciados nos mistérios da seita. Apesar de com o tempo, e por serem aprendidos de oitiva, terem sofrido profundas transformações, conservam inalterado o seu simbolismo significativo, pois para quem canta não interessa saber o que canta, mas para que santo canta.

---

[10] "As Línguas," p. 2.
[11] For additional data on Yoruba, see David L. Olmsted's "The Phonemes of Yoruba," in *Word*, Volume 7, Number 3, Part 3, pp. 245-249.

O fato é que dessa "gente" tem partido o maior número de "brasileirismos" da Língua Portuguêsa chamados de "africanismos," que bem poderiam ser "afro-baianismos." [12]

(In this "language," the archaic or pure forms can be seen in the ritual songs which are used to call the spirits. All of the songs are of a religious nature and are learned by the small group of initiates who take part in the mysterious ceremonies. It is because of their religious nature that they have not changed radically over the years. In fact, it is true that in spite of the long time involved, and in spite of their being learned by oral tradition, they still retain their original symbolism, even though they have changed linguistically. Their original meanings have been lost, for the most part, but this is because in the religious ceremony, the initiates are only interested in knowing what saint they are calling on, and do not really care what the individual words mean.

The fact is that these "people" have contributed a very large number of "Brazilianisms" to the Portuguese language; these also being called "Africanisms," which could well be termed "Afro-Bahianisms.")

The matter of conserving the emphasis on the emotional connotations (*simbolismo significativo*) instead of the denotative meanings of the songs and utterances used during the *candomblé* ceremonies is also, in part, responsible for the disappearance of the African dialects in Brazil, and it has contributed, for the most part, to the inability of the initiates to render literal translations into Portuguese of what they learn to mimic from the *mãe* or *pai de santo*. As a result, the true meanings of many of the archaic words and expressions have been lost. The difficulty of translation is manifest, as we shall see, in the material gathered in personal interviews with *mães de santo*.

As was mentioned in Chapter I, the religion of the Yoruba had set the pattern for all of the neighboring religions, both in Africa and in Brazil. Because of their high social status in Africa [13] and the

---

[12] "As Línguas," p. 2. As will be discussed later, I found that relatively few "Afro-Bahianisms" have come from the *candomblé*. The statement quoted here is probably an exaggeration on the part of the author.

[13] A. B. Ellis, *The Yoruba-Speaking Peoples...*, William Bascom, *The Yoruba of Southwestern Nigeria,* and Samuel Johnson, *The History of the Yorubas,* allude to this high social status, which seems to have been related to a political dominance. A. B. Ellis, for example, states the following: "Of the early history of the Yoruba-speaking peoples nothing is known, except

esteem they were able to attain as slaves in Brazil, the Yoruba in Bahia constituted a type of élite and had no difficulty in imposing their religion on the entire body of Bahian slaves, the great majority of whom had very similar religions in the first place. Edison Carneiro, an authority on *candomblé* in Bahia, states the following concerning Yoruba dominance: "A liturgia nagô serve de padrão e modêlo para as festas de todos os candomblés, com pequenas alterações que não modificam essencialmente a sua fisionomia."[14] ("The *Nagô* [Yoruba] liturgy serves as model for all of the *candomblé* ceremonies, albeit with few minor alterations which do not really modify the basic structure.")

This statement can assuredly be applied to at least 90 % of the total number of cult houses in the city of Bahia. It is possible for me to say this because I was able to observe many Yoruba names of saints and spirits in forty of the forty-four known *terreiros de candomblé* in the city of Bahia, which I visited on several occasions. This being the case, the importance of the Yoruba as a "nation" overshadowing the other tribes in Bahia and influencing to a considerable degree their religion and cultures must be considered when studying the problem of linguistic influence. The socio-cultural dominance of the Yoruba played an important part in determining which African

---

what can be gleaned from Dalzel's *History of Dahomey*, 1793, from which it would appear that, at the beginning of the eighteenth century, all the different tribes were united, and were ruled by a king who resided at Old Oyo, sometimes called Katunga. The kingdom of Yoruba also seems to have been more powerful than the other two great African kingdoms, Dahomi and Ashanti." (p. 6)

Later, in the same book by Ellis, we read: "There is a considerable difference between the Yoruba-speaking Peoples and the Ewe-speaking Peoples. We still find the characteristics which were dominant among the latter, namely, indolence, improvidence, and duplicity, but they are no longer so pronounced,... because life and property are more secure. The Yoruba has more independence of character than the Tshi, Gãs, or Ewes, and servility is rare. He even has the sentiments of nationality and patriotism, and though these are regarded with disfavor by the Colonial Government, they are none the less tokens of superiority. He is a keener trader, is more sociable, and is in all respects socially higher than the tribes of the other three cognate groups...." (p. 32) The author continues to speak about the superior qualities of the Yoruba, and concludes by saying that "at the present day, they are certainly the leading people in West Africa." (p. 32) See also J. F. Ade Ajayi and Robert Smith, *Yoruba Warfare in the Nineteenth Century* (Cambridge: 1964).

[14] *Candomblés da Bahia* (Rio de Janeiro, Brasiliera do Ouro: 1967), p. 101.

language would prevail in the rituals of spirit worship and "black magic" in Bahia.

The preeminence of the Yoruba in Bahia accounts for the presence of some Yoruba vocabulary items in the speech of today's Bahian. However, Yoruba has not monopolized the entire ethnolinguistic terrain. Other "nations" brought to Bahia also established cult houses which, despite the strong Yoruba influence, managed to remain somewhat autonomous, even if it were in name only. Roger Bastide, a French sociologist, was, in fact, impressed by the differences among the cult houses in Bahia. He observes the following:

> À Bahia où les maisons sont innombrables, et elles ne sont pas toutes inscrites à la police, les diverses "nations" se sont conservées bien separées: quetou (j'en ai relevé seize), igeshá (8 ou 9), gêge (probablement trois) dont la principale est appelée Bogoun qui est une déturpation du mot Vodou ou Vodoun, angola (une dizaine, mais dont beaucoup se désagrègent ou se laissent pénétrer par les influences indiennes), congo (deux ou trois) et les candomblés de caboclés, qui constitue la forme bahianise du catimbló; quelques-unes sont enfin mixtes. On n'a malheureusement pas procédé à une étude comparative exhaustive de ces "nations," les africanistes se contentant de descriptions très generales et valables pour toutes les formes de culte. En réalité, les différences sont très grandes, dans les instruments de musique, dans la langue qui varie, Yorubá, fon ou bantoue, dans les cantiques, dans le rythme des tambours, dans les noms des divinités dans le ritual, dans les conceptions de l'au-delà.[15]

> (In Bahia where there are many houses [of *candomblé*], not all of which are registered with the police, the diverse "nations" have been conserved separately: Ketu (I found sixteen of them). Ijesha (8 or 9), Ewe (probably three), of which the main one is called Bogoun, which is a corruption of the word Voodoo or Vodoun, Angola (a dozen, but many of which are breaking up or becoming heavily influenced by the Indian religious practices), Congo (two or three), and the *candomblé* of *cabôclo*, which constitute the Bahian form of *catimbó* [a type of African religious practice]; some are mixed, though. As yet, however, an exhaustive comparative study of these "nations" has not yet been done.

---

[15] *Les Réligions Africaines au Brésil* (Paris, Presses Universitaires de France: 1960), p. 269.

The scholars of African materials are content to give very general descriptions which may be used to describe any of the cult forms. In reality, the differences are very noticeable, when studying the musical instruments, the language, be it Yoruba, Fon or Bantu, the chants, the rythms of the drums, the names of the divinities used in the ritual, or the ideas of the world beyond.)

Perhaps if Bastide had examined the houses he visited more closely, he would have found greater similarities among cults of different names, many of which are based on Yoruba traditions.

Before examining the data collected in various *terreiros* around Salvador da Bahia, a few words about the *candomblé* itself will provide a background for the ethnolinguistic problem being studied.

The term *candomblé* is derived from the name of a dance, *Kandombe*, that was common among the slaves of the early coffee plantations. The dance, in turn, received its name from the drums used to beat out the musical rhythms for it.

The organized cult could not have survived during the era of slavery in the rural areas. In order to maintain such activities, the Negro needed money and liberty, which were attainable only in the large urban centers. The urban blacks in the first half of the 18th century, although not yet free, were able to earn some money and to establish the *Irmandade do Rosário* and that of *São Benedito*, a first step in the foundation of their own religious groups. By the second half of the same century, after they had gained some independence from their white masters, the Afro-Brazilian slaves began to organize into religious groups based upon those which they had brought with them from western Africa. The newly-established cults survived precariously, constantly subject to the whims of political suppression. Even before the slaves finally received their freedom, however, many cult houses had been firmly grounded and were functioning just as they had been in Africa, such as the *candomblé do Engenho Velho* in Bahia, which by 1830 already had a large active membership. [16]

Surveying the present locations of the cult houses, one perceives that practically all of them function within the urban and suburban

---

[16] For additional information concerning the origins and religious framework of the *candomblé* in Bahia, see Pedro McGregor, *The Moon and Two Mountains* (London, Souvenir Press: 1966), pp. 67-85.

areas, with only a few in extremely rural sections. The larger percentage is to be found in the capital cities of each state since they are the largest and serve as important economic centers. In the state of Bahia, approximately forty-four cult houses are to be found in the capital city of Salvador, while only fifteen or so can be encountered in the sugar cane, tobacco and cocoa zones.

Bahian *candomblé* incorporates and blends the various religions of the Guinea Coast with traces of indigenous practices and some features of Catholicism. Altars decked with religious trinkets always have representations of both African spirits and Catholic saints. The initiated participants, however, become possessed only with African spirits, such as *Ogún* (god of iron), *Oxósse* (god of the hunt) and *Xangô* (god of storms). Possession may also be realized with dead ancestors, whose spirits are called *egúns*. The word *egún* is related to the Yoruba *ègungún,* meaning "skeleton." [17] By becoming possessed with these spirits, the mortal cult members can achieve communication and communion with the other world. This spiritual interchange is not merely a symbolic one, nor is it a swift, quickly vanishing mental experience, as with spiritism. In Bahian *candomblé* the world of the spirits and that of flesh and blood become one. The gods of Africa and the dead ancestors become an integral part of those who participate in the ceremony, and they hear the grievances of the cult members, give advice and blessings and bestow remedies for illnesses and consolation for misfortunes. Here, in the *terreiro*, the spiritual world juxtaposes itself on the physical one, and a perfect interrelationship can be established between the two.

The Catholicism permeating the *candomblé* began to filter in as a subterfuge to escape police action against ceremonies, which many times were considered by the authorities to be of a wild and savage nature. As time went on, however, many of the Catholic elements were permanently incorporated into the African rituals, and as a result all of the African spirits have corresponding Catholic names and numerous Catholic gestures are used during the ceremony, such as making the sign of the cross on the floor after entering the *terreiro*.

---

[17] *Candomblés,* p. 183. Confirmed in R. C. Abraham, p. 149, where we find: "eegun = egigun = egungun (1) bone." See p. 107, A. B. Ellis, *The Yoruba-Speaking Peoples*... for a more detailed explanation.

Today most of the *candomblés* do not devote themselves exclusively to the beliefs of one particular "nation," even though they do carry only one name, such as *Nagô, Gêge* or *Ijexá*. They have become so interrelated that many of them hold regular sessions for various cults during different times of the year. Carneiro observed this phenomenon several years ago and commented on possible reasons for it:

> ... Seja porque o chefe atual tem nação diferente da do seu antecessor, e naturalmente se dedica às duas, seja pela grande camaradagem (que entretanto não deixa de supor certa irritação) existente entre as pessoas mais conhecidas de todos os candomblés, o que faz com que se homenageiem tais pessoas, tocando e dançando a maneira das suas respectivas nações. Já não é raro tocar-se para qualquer "nação" em qualquer candomblé. Assim, no Engenho Velho e no Gantois, duas casas onde a tradição keto exerce uma verdadeira tirania, pude ver cantar e dançar para encantados cabôclos. É verdade, que, nos candomblés nagôs, isto raramente acontece, mas é uma diferença a que não podem fugir nem mesmo êsses candomblés.
> A fusão com o espiritismo — ainda mais recente — produziu as "sessões de cabôclo," tendo atingido, em primeiro lugar, os candomblés de cabôclo, mais abertos a influências estranhas do que os demais.
> Os homens do candomblé quase nunca se contentam com ver apenas as festas da sua casa. Freqüentam outras. Há mesmo quem não perca estas festas, sem levar em conta a distância nem o mau tempo. Êstes merecem o nome de "sete roncós" (sete atabaques) ou o apelido nagô de "akirijébó," composto de dois vocábulos yorubás, "Kiri," "procurar," e "ébó," "sacrifício religioso," que significaria, segundo Martiniano do Bomfim, "fiscal de feitiço," mas que, na linguagem corrente, significa apenas freqüentador de candomblés. Êste hábito andejo muito concorre para o sincretismo interior das seitas africanas.[18]

(Whether it be because the present chief is of a tribe which is different from that of his ancestor, and therefore he would dedicate himself to both [tribes], or whether it is because of the great friendship (which, by the way, probably admitted a certain amount of friction) that existed among the more important people connected with *candomblé*, homage is paid to various "nations" within the same *terreiro*. It is not a rarity to celebrate any given "nation" in any *can-*

---

[18] *Candomblés*, pp. 61-62.

domblé. Thus, at Engenho Velho and Gantois, two "houses" in which the Ketu tradition predominates, I saw a ceremony put on for the *caboclos*. It is true that this rarely happens in the Nago *candomblés*, but it is something that does occur here [in the Nago *candomblés*].

The fusion with spiritism — a very recent phenomenon — produced the "*caboclo* sessions," this having happened first among the *caboclo candomblés*, since they were more open to foreign influences than the other "nations."

The *candomblé* members are almost never content to celebrate only their own "nation" in their *terreiro*. They visit other "houses." Many of them will go even if it means buffeting adverse weather or traveling great distances. These people are called *sete roncós (sete atabaques)* or "seven drums," or in Yoruba, *akirijébó*, which is a compound word made up of the two Nago words *Kiri*, "to look for," and *ébó*, "religious sacrifice," which means, according to Martiniano do Bomfim, "controller of magic," but which, in present-day language, simply means "one who frequents *candomblés*." This habit of visitation has a lot to do with the interior sincretism of the Afro-Bahian sects.)

While in Bahia, I visited many cult houses in which certain times of each year were set apart for distinct "nations," so that in the course of twelve months perhaps two, three, or even four different "national" ceremonies could be held in the same house by the members of that house, with visiting initiates representing the "nations" whose beliefs are celebrated at any given time. A case in point is the *Gêge terreiro* of a *mãe* we will refer to as V.M.A.[19] Here regular *Gêge* ceremonies are held in the months of February and April. In June and July, *Nagô* festivities blossom into full ritualism, and there are many guests from different *Nagô* houses who actively participate in all of these activities. September is the month of *Ijêxá* ceremonies at this *Gêge* house, and so changes are made to accommodate certain peculiarities found in this "nation."

This congenial interchange among *terreiros* may be responsible in part for the spread of Yoruba influence throughout the city of Bahia. At the same time, it may be the chief catalyst working to scramble African words of the various "nations" so that many etymologies have become obscured and not even the *mães* or *pais de*

---

[19] The names of all confidential informants have been placed in a file and are available to qualified investigators upon request.

santo are absolutely sure to which "nation" certain words belong. As was mentioned earlier, the question of etymologies in the Afro-Brazilian vocabulary is a difficult one to answer. Nevertheless, in spite of this confusion, Bahian *mães* and *pais de santo* can usually identify the "national" source of most of the songs and utterances used in *candomblé*. And, many of the chants used commonly in the majority of the *terreiros* are consistently identified as being *Nagô* — evidence which corroborates the strong Yoruba influence in Bahia.

As was stated earlier, I was able to visit some forty different *terreiros* in the city of Salvador da Bahia. It was impossible to arrange personal interviews with the leaders of all forty houses; I was able to feet with only five. The information obtained in these interviews may be considered representative of the other thirty-five, however, since about 75 % of the songs and utterances recorded in these five *terreiros* were also taped in the houses where no prolonged contact [20] with any of the members was achieved.

There were many problems involved in obtaining personal interviews. Possibly the outstanding one was the fear that many of the cult leaders and regular members have of disclosing any of their secret songs and phrases, the meanings of which are believed to be known only to initiates of the *candomblé*. They are afraid that the outsider who learns their secrets will use them either to destroy the spirits or do harm to the members of the *candomblé*. This obstacle has been one of the most difficult to overcome, and investigators today are constantly struggling to find some means of penetrating the cult houses.

Bastide experienced the same frustration and noted that the problem was a large one which seemed to admit of no exception. He writes: "Tous les ethnographes qui se sont penchés sur la vie des candomblés ont été frappés par l'importance qu'y joue 'le secret,' comme arme de défense contre les Blancs. Les prêtres n'aiment pas expliquer à de simples curieux les raisons profondes des rites, même publics, de peur qu'on ne s'en serve contre eux, ou que l'on se moque de leurs superstitions." [21] ("All of the ethnographers who have studied

---

[20] The only information that I was able to record at the thirty-five houses where personal interviews could not be obtained was in regard to which "nation" each house represented and for which "nation" each one happened to be in session on the night of my visit.

[21] *Les Réligions*, p. 335.

the *candomblés* have been startled by the importance that 'the secret' has, as a type of defense against the white people. The Negroes do not like to explain to ordinary onlookers the profound reasons behind the rites, even if they are public, for fear that they [the secrets] will be used against them or to make fun of their superstitions.")

My efforts in obtaining cooperation from cult members were highly successful in four *terreiros* and partially so in two others. I can attribute this favorable reception to the fact that I am American and not Brazilian. It seems that the initiates trust Americans more than they do their own kind, especially if they are aware that the American will soon return to his home country and believe that he will not give any of the "secrets" to the Brazilians. Of course, generous amounts of money given liberally to informants also aided in the task of collecting desired information. But in spite of these two assets which I possessed, many potential informants would not submit to being interviewed.

My first successful interview took place with the *mãe de santo* of an "Ewe" [22] *terreiro*. This *terreiro*, according to *mãe* V.M.A., is the only "Ewe" one presently functioning in the city of Bahia. It is approximately three hundred years old.

All of the chants that were given to me have been handed down orally from generation to generation. Even though *mãe* V.M.A. was not able to translate all the songs word for word into Portuguese, she could translate a few of the words and in some instances tell whether they were of *Gêge* or *Nagô* origin.

All the transcriptions presented here are in phonetic script as described in Tables 1 and 2. Word division follows the indications given to me by each informant. The words of the songs are in Bahian "Ewe," except for those which the *mãe* pointed out as being Yoruba. All of the "Ewe" songs here and in Appendix II were checked against the Ewe dictionaries and grammars listed in the bibliography. Many times, words which have the same phonetic values as those in the "Ewe" chants were found in the works consulted, but similarities in meaning were far from discernible. Also, it is practically impossible

---

[22] The word "Ewe" in quotation marks refers to that Ewe which was brought to Bahia from Africa in the 16th, 17th, 18th and 19th centuries, became separate from African Ewe and suffered certain modifications as it remained basically archaic in form. Further references to this kind of Ewe will be indicated by placing quotation marks around the word "Ewe."

to establish definite connections between the "Ewe" songs gathered in Bahia and the Ewe found in Africa when the Bahian *mães* were unable to provide any translation into Portuguese. I have, therefore, not attempted to wager any guesses concerning the songs, as to possible equivalents in Ewe, since such conjecture as it relates to the "Ewe" data, would be of a highly speculative nature. The Ewe words presented here and in Appendix II follow the orthographical system as described in Diedrich Westermann's *Wörterbuch der Ewe-Sprache* (Berlin: 1954).

The first chant, used for opening the ceremony, is called *aju'a mõia*:

(1a) kwɛrɛ'bɛ tã idɛlu

"Vem para a sala."

(Come into the room.)

The following is a song in honor of the saint *jõ'su*, who in *Nagô* is *Abaluaé* (or, in modern Yoruba: ọbaolúwayé, meaning "to appeal to the king of the gods"):

(2a) 'azo a'nu bonu'kaka boja 'gɛre šobo'alɛ

(No translation)

For *Vodúm*,[23] who corresponds to *Orixá* in *Nagô* (in modern Yoruba: òrìṣà, meaning "god"), the following song is used:

(3a) vo'dũ maio'kwɛ šaša'ra zõ lo'i

"O deus está espantando môscas com o xaxará."

(The god is chasing away flies with the swatter.)

The Yoruba word *šaša'ra* (*ṣaṣara*, an adjective meaning "coming apart," in modern Yoruba; also, *Ṣaṣara-ọwọ̀*, a worn-out broom, the tip of a broom) is used in conjunction with the other words that according to the *mãe* are Ewe. *Mãe* V.M.A. was quick to point out, however, that the word was Yoruba and that the "Ewe" word for the

---

[23] *Vodúm*, besides being the name of a specific god, is the generic term for "spirit" or "god" among the Ewe. It is spelled *vodũ* in Ewe.

same object is *ig'biri* (Cf. Ewe *gbidi*, "To rub off, wear out"). The use of the Yoruba word in this context illustrates the language mixture previously discussed.

A chant for the saint *azō'su* is:

(4a) mosɛ'to do'bwe hūjɛbwɛna manag'bɔ
moseto do'gwe

"Cala a bôca!"[24]

(Shut your mouth!)

When asked whether or not either she or any of the members of the *candomblé dos Gêge* could speak fluent "Ewe," the *mãe's* reply was negative. She said that her parents were able to speak it but that she had forgotten many of the words and expressions they had taught her. In fact, she remembered very few utterances. She gave me the following two:

(5a) na za zô "Está doente." (He or she is sick.)

(6a) bɔnu'toi "Cala a bôca!" (Shut your mouth!)

Cf. Ewe dialect Gɛ̃, *bɔ nu*, "shut one's mouth," *bɔ* meaning "shut," and *nu*, mouth.

These were the only two utterances not having to do with *candomblé*. Her inability to speak "Ewe" reveals how much of the "Ewe" language has been lost.

The songs in Bahian "Ewe" presented here and in Appendix II (26 in all) represent about one-third of the total number which are presently being used in the *terreiro*. Of all the ceremonial songs in "Ewe" and Portuguese, well over half are now sung in Portuguese. *Mãe* V.M.A. explained that the younger members of the *candomblé* preferred to sing in Portuguese because it was easier than "Ewe" and they could understand everything they were singing. It is amazing that some seventy-five chants still exist in "Ewe" and are still used,

---

[24] Many of the translations are puzzling, but they are given here exactly as I received them from the *mãe*. For additional "Ewe" songs, see Appendix II. Working from the grammars and dictionaries of the Ewe language available to me, I was unable to identify positively any of the words in these songs as Ewe.

even by the younger generation. Perhaps if it were not for the continued persistence of the *mães de santo* in using "Ewe," and also the belief that the African language possesses strange, occult powers which Portuguese does not, the use of "Ewe" would have disappeared long ago. [25]

The same may be said of *Nagô*. In all of the "Yoruba" [26] *terreiros* which I visited, there were more songs sung in Portuguese than in "Yoruba," and several interviews with Yoruba *mães de santo* confirmed my observations. Nevertheless, the proportion of "Yoruba" songs to Portuguese (roughly about 45 % are sung in "Yoruba") seems somewhat higher than the "Ewe" to Portuguese proportion.

One of my most successful interviews among the *terreiros de Nagô* was with the *mãe de santo* of a *terreiro de Iansã*. [27] The house was founded in 1910 and has had a steady growth since its beginning. The *Nagô mãe* here, whom we will call *mãe* C., informed me that she learned Yoruba from her mother, who was born in Africa and brought to Bahia as a slave when she was a young girl in her middle teens. The mother spoke fluent Yoruba, but *mãe* C. learned only enough to speak in broken phrases and to acquire the songs she needed to know as a permanent member of *candomblé*. *Mãe* C. was 79 years old at the time of the interview and had only a few teeth, a condition which may have hampered her articulation of some sounds. However, she was very cooperative and supplied me with twenty-four songs in "Yoruba" as well as words and expressions not related to *candomblé*.

The translations are presented here as they were given to me by the *mãe de santo*. As expected, they are not all literal, but they purport to convey the general idea of the songs. Again, as with the

---

[25] For comparisons with African Ewe cults, see Melville J. Herskovits and Frances S. Herskovits, "An Outline of Dahomean Religious Belief," in *Memoirs of the American Anthropological Association* (Menasha, Wisconsin, George Banta Publishing Company: 1933), Number 41; Melville J. and Frances S. Herskovits, *Dahomean Narrative*, Evanston, Northwestern University Press: 1958); Melville J. Herskovits, *Dahomey, an Ancient West African Kingdom, Volume II* (Evanston, Northwestern University Press: 1967).

[26] "Yoruba," in quotation marks, refers to the Bahian "Yoruba" as contrasted to the African language. This kind of "Yoruba," just as the "Ewe," is somewhat archaic and mixed with Portuguese.

[27] *Iansã*, a Yoruba spirit, is the wife of *Xangô*, another spirit, and controls thunderstorms. Cf. Yoruba *ìyá*, "mother," and *sán*, "to thunder."

"Ewe" material, attempts to find equivalent expressions in African Yoruba are recorded only when similarities in meaning were discernible. This also includes instances in which analogous utterances in Yoruba appear to fit the context of the *candomblé* ceremonies.

The first song opens the ceremony:

(1b) eua či'rei o'gũ o er'u jo
 jo e'rũ i'ε i'ε

"A gente vai abrir a casa do candomblé, pois a casa está em festa."

(The cult members are going to open the house because the house is going to celebrate a festivity.)

According to my native informant in Yoruba,[28] this song has a contemporary counterpart, which is the following:

ewá ṣiré ògún erú jo diẹ diẹ

"Come all of you slaves and participate in the festival of Ogun, dancing gently."

---

[28] The modern Yoruba cited here and in the rest of this study, was obtained partially through the aid of a native informant. Edward Esan, a graduate student at the University of California, Riverside, from Ibadan, Nigeria, was kind enough to assist me in recognizing many of the words, expressions and songs that I collected in Bahia as "Yoruba" words. Therefore, wherever Mr. Esan was able to recognize elements in the data gathered in Bahia, I present the possible version thereof in modern Yoruba. This comparison with contemporary Yoruba is very helpful in identifying the data as Yoruba and in comparing this older West African language taken to Brazil in the 18th and 19th centuries with its modern counterpart. Of course, we cannot say that those items not recognized by the informant are not Yoruba, for they may be vestiges of an archaic Yoruba which is no longer used in the 20th century. The modern Yoruba appears here and in Appendix III written according to the standard Yoruba orthographical system, as explained in R. C. Abraham's *Dictionary of Modern Yoruba*. This dictionary, the *Dictionary of the Yoruba Language* (London: 1956) published by the Church Missionary Society, the late Bishop Samuel Crowther's 1852 edition of the *Grammar and Vocabulary of the Yoruba Language* (Hanover Square, London), and Crowther's *Dictionary of the Yoruba Language* (Part II) (Lagos, 1931), were also consulted for this study.

Many of the utterances which were not recognized by Mr. Esan have been tentatively identified here through the use of the above-mentioned works. At times, certain words may have more than one meaning and it is very difficult to determine which meaning, if any, would be more appropriate for identification of the chant in question. Again, it must be stressed that these identifications are only tentative.

ETHNOLINGUISTIC DATA

Here, individual words were recognized. They are:

ewá come all of you
ṣiré participate
erú slaves
jo dance
die die gently
ògún the god Ogun

The next song prepares the house to receive the spirits:

(2b)   ai o'gū mɛi'jɛi'rɛ i akoro
              o'gū me'jɛ

"Ogúm é que despacha a casa."

(The god Ogun will preside over the house.)

This may be the archaic version of the modern Yoruba:

aya ògún mejē ṣiré

"Seven wives of Ogun [are coming] to play."?

The individual words here are:

aya wives
mejē seven
ṣiré play

The part of the utterance [i akoro] was not recognized by the informant. According to the dictionaries *akoro* in Yoruba means "helmet."

The following song also serves to open the *terreiro*:

(3b)   abayko'so so i'lɛ o'gū
              kor'gū lo dori'jɛ

"Outra cantiga para abrir o candomblé."

(Another song to open the ceremony.)

My Nigerian informant recognized some of this song, and said that it might be a version of the modern Yoruba:

óbákòsó kòsinlé ógún k'òrìṣà lọ́

"The king is not at home, but has gone away."

108   A BAHIAN HERITAGE

The individual words of the modern Yoruba are:

> óbákòsó — the king is not at home (implying that the king has been captured by non-living gods and has gone off in shame.) This is a polite way of saying that the king has been defeated in battle and humiliated.
>
> It may be noted that there is also the sentence *ọba kò so*, "the king did not hang." This is the triumphant climax of the Shango legend. Briefly, Shango was betrayed and humiliated by leaders among his people. In his shame, he went off into the forest and hanged himself. But when the people who were loyal to him went to look for him, there was a bolt of lightning and a clap of thunder. Out of the thunder, Shango spoke to his people, and ever since they have been loyal to him as the god of thunder and lightning. In spite of the rope and the body, *ọba kò so*, "the king did not hang," but lives on.

kòsinlé   not at home

k'òrìṣà   anything that one worships

lọ́   go

ógún   the god Ogun

The element [kor'gũ] might be a combination of *korin*, "to sing," and *Ogun*.

When the saints begin to appear, the first one to seek recognition in the *Terreiro de Iansã* is usually *Xangô*: [29]

> (4b)   ñi fa o ñi fa ijo o
> ñi fa akara'o
> ɛu vo a'ma ala'ɛ o ñi
> ɛka ori'ša kɛrɛ'wa o de

> "Xangô está pedindo a Deus para coroar êle."

> (*Xangô* wants God to crown him.)

---

[29] *Xangô*, according to Edison Carneiro, *Candomblés*, p. 17, is the "representação das tempestades e dos raios, do trovão e das descargas elétricas, é um orixá fálico. As lendas correntes da Bahia o dão como rei de Óyó e às vêzes, do todo o povo nagô." (the representation of storms and lightning bolts, of thunder and electrical discharges; he is a phallic spirit. Contemporary legends in Bahia describe him as king of Oyo and sometimes as king of all *nagô* nations.)
See Samuel Johnson, op. cit., pp. 34 and 149.

The Yoruba word àkàrà, "cake," was recognized by the native informant. The expression onífa in Yoruba means "worshipper of the god Ifa" (the great consulting oracle in Yoruba country). Ijó is "dance." O in Yoruba can be a personal pronoun in the objective position, an auxiliary verb denoting the future, or an adverb of assent. [ala'ε] could be Yoruba aláde, meaning "one entitled to wear a crown or coronet." The phrase [εu vo a'ma] sounds like Portuguese eu vou amar (I am going to love). (It must be remembered that Portuguese has replaced much of the African languages taken to Bahia.) I was unable to find any Yoruba utterances similar to this.

Xangô becomes hungry and the following song is chanted:

(5b)   ma'la ma'la modo'bi
         εlε modo'bi

"A cantiga de amalá [30] de Xangô. Xangô está comendo o amalá."

(The song of the amalá of Xangô. Xangô is eating the amalá.)

Two words were recognized by my Nigerian informant; Şàngó, the god of thunder and lightning, and àmàlà, meaning "yam flour."

Portuguese shows its influence as Xangô asks for money. Mãe C. explained that the "Yoruba" version of this song has been forgotten. The only word in "Yoruba" is o'o (owo in modern Yoruba), meaning "money":

(6b)   Quem, quem quem dame o'o

"Dame dinheiro quem tem." [31]

(Whoever has money, give it to me.)

This song, as well as many others like it, which have some words in Yoruba and some in Portuguese, provides an example of the transition, which has taken place in the cult houses, from the African languages to Portuguese. The transformation process from one lan-

---

[30] Amalá, a typical Bahian dish, made with flour, water and caruru. (See vocabulary list, Chapter IV, No. 3.)

[31] For additional "Yoruba" songs see Appendix III.

guage to the other begins with the substitution of one or two Portuguese words for African ones, whether they be "Yoruba," "Ewe" or some other; and with time, more and more Portuguese replaces the African tongues until the entire song or phrase is in Portuguese. The following song is a good example of a late transition stage, for here all of the words except one are in Portuguese:

E eu fui para o mato	(I went into the brush
tirar o meu imbé [32]	to get my *imbé*
Nossa Senhora das neves	Our Lady of the snow
dɛso'ña pegou meu pé	dɛso'ña caught my foot
Encontrei com Santa Bárbara	I met Saint Barbara
dɛso'ña pegou meu pé.	dɛso'ña caught my foot.)

The word *imbé* did not appear in any of the texts consulted. (*im(b)é* in Tupi means "to be." However, in the song the word is used as a noun.) [dɛso'ña] may be divided into Yoruba *dẹ*, "to set a trap" and *sòna*, "to hold at bay."

Mixing phrases of "Yoruba" and Portuguese is also somewhat common in *candomblé* ceremonies and again shows transition from one tongue to the other:

Na beira do mar azul	(On the shores of the blue sea
encontrei uma seréia	I found a mermaid
ɛ ko'ã kosa 'ɲiña ɲi ko'ã	
olhe o bote da cobra	look at the snake jump
koča 'ɲiña ɲi ko'ã	

The translation for the lines in "Yoruba" were given to me as follows: "Quer dizer êsse cavalo [33] vai lhe explicar o que veio dizer." (It means that the spirit will explain what he came to say.)

---

[32] *Imbé*, according to the *Nôvo Dicionário Brasileiro Melhoramentos*, 2a edição, II, D-I (São Paulo, Edições Melhoramentos: 1964), p. 807, is a "planta da família das Aráceas (Philodendron imbe), cujas raízes, em forma de cipó são largamente usadas na feitura de cestas, covos e outras peças da indústria da pesca no litoral, graças à sua resistência à água salgada." (A plant of the Aracea family (Philodendron imbe), the roots of which, in the form of vines, are commonly used to make baskets, fish nets and other items used in the fishing industry along the coast, due to their endurance in salt water.)

[33] *Cavalo*, used in this sense, means "spirit" or "saint." The word is very common among *candomblés de caboclo*. The use of the word for "horse" in this context could come from the idea of being "mounted" when possessed by a spirit. In Portuguese, the initiates say, *O orixá monta nela*, "the spirit

The songs presented here, as well as the words and expressions which *mãe* C.'s mother taught her,[34] are indicative of 19th century "Yoruba" as it was spoken in Salvador da Bahia.[35]

The data listed in Appendix III, numbers 54 through 64, were obtained from a *pai de santo* who refused to state his name. The material which he gave me may be an example of the *língua geral* once spoken in this area, since it was consistently described by all of the *mães de santo* who heard it as being "a mixture of many languages."[36]

An interview in the same area furnished more data of a similar nature. The *mãe de santo* supplying the information here will be referred to as *mãe* Z. When asked whether or not she or any of the members of the house could speak the African languages in which they sang, her reply was negative. Their only *língua*,[37] as they refer to it, consisted of what they learned for purposes of participating in the *candomblé* ceremonies. Part of the ritual languages used in this house has been handed down orally and part has been learned from a book which Deoscóredes M. dos Santos wrote, *Yorubá Tal Qual Se Fala*, which was purchased at the Mercado Modêlo[38] in Salvador. Dos Santos' book contains a number of words and expressions which are used in his cult house and which have been transcribed according to the system of Portuguese orthography with some slight variations. The book is now out of print, however, and copies are difficult to obtain.[39]

A final interview, which was frustrated in part, was one I had with Deoscóredes M. dos Santos and his wife, Juana Elbein. I was

---

mounts her." On the other hand, it might be the result of a confusion between two Yoruba words, one *ẹsin*, "horse," and the other *èsin*, "religion, creed."

[34] See Appendix III.

[35] For comparison with African Yoruba, see William R. Bascom, "The Sociological Role of the Yoruba Cult-Group," in *American Anthropologist* (American Anthropological Association, Volume 46, No. 1, Part 2: 1944); Eva Krapf-Askari, *Yoruba Towns and Cities* (Oxford, Clarendon Press: 1969); William R. Bascom, *Ifa Divination* (Bloomington, Indiana University Press: 1969).

[36] See Appendix III.

[37] The *palenqueros* of the Atlantic coast of Colombia also refer to a creolized form of Spanish which they still speak as *lengua*.

[38] The Mercado Modêlo was completely destroyed by fire in November, 1969.

[39] See Appendix IV for examples.

able to obtain very little Bahian "Yoruba" from him. He repeated "The Lord's Prayer" and the "Ave Maria" in African Yoruba; he had learned these in classes which he attended at the Centro de Estudos Afro-Orientais in Bahia.

Dos Santos was kind enough to comment on the African influences in Bahia. He said that the *Nagô* spoken in Bahia is definitely an archaic language preserved only in the *candomblé* circles. He recalled that his grandmother spoke fluent Yoruba. This bit of information, together with what *mãe* C. said about her mother's being able to speak "Yoruba," enable us to draw the tentative conclusion that the disappearance of "Yoruba" in Bahia is a fairly recent phenomenon. Dos Santos stated that "Yoruba" as a spoken household language began to disappear about forty years ago. He agreed with Juana Elbein that the members of the various *terreiros,* who must learn "Yoruba" in order to acquire membership, learn only what is required within their religion and speak Portuguese at all other times. As far as the initiates are concerned, "Yoruba" is a foreign language.

Speaking of the *língua geral,* dos Santos stated that, in his view, it never existed. He called the *língua geral* a myth and dismissed the matter.

In his cult house, *Axé Ôpô Afonjá,* as in the majority of Bahian cult houses, the "Yoruba" used during the ceremonies is learned by the *orixás* through oral tradition. A teacher designated by the *mãe de santo,* or the *mãe de santo* herself, has the responsibility of teaching the students the language. After a period of practicing "Yoruba" among themselves, they are able to utter some sentences and carry on very basic conversations in the language. Dos Santos informed me that in his home the members of the family speak some "Yoruba" at times but that they do not worry about speaking it; when they do, he acknowledged that they usually mix it with a great deal of Portuguese. If what dos Santos said is true, and I assume it is, then his family and *terreiro* are rare cases in Bahia; for none of the other cult houses investigated could boast of such "fluency" in any African language.

Dos Santos said that "Yoruba," among the older members of the cult, is considered to be a very special language and that they take pride in being able to say a few things in it. He did not mention the reluctance on the part of the younger initiates to learn the African tongues — a reluctance which I recorded first-hand in interviews with some young initiates.

Juana Elbein mentioned an interesting point about *cabôclo* cult houses. She said that the language often called *Nagô* is not pure Yoruba as used in *Axé Ôpô Afonjá*, but a mixture of several African languages, Portuguese and Tupi-Guarani. We encountered an example of what seems to be this kind of "language" in the utterances which were recorded from the *pai de santo*. The problem of separating the African languages among themselves and from the Tupi-Guarani is far from being solved. At present, an expert in Brazilian Indian languages, Dr. Friedrich Edelweiss, is studying the problem of etymologies, but as yet only very few answers have been found.[40]

As far as conclusive statements about the materials gathered in personal interviews and general observations of the Afro-linguistic situation in Bahia are concerned, only a small portion of the data can be objectively studied because of their highly ambiguous nature. In the first place, there is not enough of it to be able to arrive at definite answers at any linguistic level except the lexical one, and here only in part; and in the second place, practically no direct translations are available for the few archaic forms that still remain. Most of the conclusions reached with the available data, therefore, must be of a tentative nature.

---

[40] See Frederico G. Edelweiss, *Estudos Tupis e Tupi-Guaranis* (Confrontos e Revisões) (Rio de Janeiro: 1969).

Chapter IV

LEXICAL AFRICANISMS IN BAHIAN PORTUGUESE

The penetration of African languages into Bahian Portuguese is immediately evident at the lexical level. Some words found in Bahia can be tentatively identified as having their origin in one or more of the many West African dialects. As we saw in Chapter I, there are some studies which have attempted to postulate definite connections between African languages and Brazilian Portuguese at all linguistic levels. There are also more contemporary theories suggested by certain Brazilian linguists which point to possible morphological and syntactic influences of West African languages on Brazilian Portuguese. It is my contention, however, that proof of African influences at linguistic levels other than the lexical one has not yet been found. By way of introductory remarks to this chapter, I hope to be able to demonstrate that such influences may not, in fact, exist at all.

A worthwhile study of linguistic evidence at any level other than the lexical one would have to include data from the Benue-Congo and Chad groups as well as other languages and dialects of Kwa in addition to Yoruba, Ewe, and Ijesha. Historical evidence of the Brazilian slave trade carried on at certain geographical points in Africa, as we saw in Chapter II, substantiates this. Also, the tentative identification of words found in Bahia as stemming from languages which are classified under these groupings would indicate that African influences present in Bahian Portuguese at any linguistic level should come from the same languages which were responsible for augmenting the vocabulary.

In order to be absolutely accurate, a comparative investigation of this sort should be based on these various West African languages as they were spoken in the sixteenth, seventeenth, eighteenth, and nineteenth centuries, during the slave trade period. Such a task would, of course, be impossible, since there are no written records of these dialects for the early centuries of Brazilian colonization. Therefore, one has to rely on contemporary linguistic information concerning the African languages in question.

When Bahian Portuguese is compared to European Portuguese on all linguistic levels, it becomes apparent that there are no phonemic (as opposed to phonetic) or morphological differences between the two, so it may be concluded that the African languages have had no influence on Bahian Portuguese either phonemically or morphologically.

There are certain phonetic differences between European and Bahian Portuguese which at first glance might suggest the possibility of African influence. One is the phenomenon of the palatalization of [t] and [d] before [i] in Bahian Portuguese. This occurs with speakers of all social levels. Although these affricate sounds which result (i.e. [č] and [ǰ]) from the palatalization are found in many of the languages of West Africa,[1] it is impossible to obtain positive proof that these sounds influenced the Portuguese language in Bahia. It is more likely that the palatalized sounds found here have come about by the simple fact that the palatal character of the vowel [i] came to be anticipated by a palatal release of the alveolar plosives [t] and [d]. This palatal release perhaps began as a semi-consonant sound [y] and later became a full palatal [š] or [j], forming [tš] and [dj] (herein written [č] and [ǰ]).

Another factor to be considered here is that this phenomenon of palatalization does not occur in some parts of Brazil where the percentage of blacks is very large. A case in point is the area encompassing the states of Sergipe, Alagoas, and Pernambuco. In addition to this, the lack of any palatalization in the Portuguese Creole spoken in either Guinea or in the interior of Surinam,[2] strengthens the argument in favor of a natural, logical phonetic change in one dialect

---

[1] See, for example, Peter Ladefoged, *A Phonetic Study of West African Languages* (Cambridge: 1968); Frederick W. Migeod, *The Languages of West Africa* (London: 1971); Robert G. Armstrong, *The Study of West African Languages* (Ibadan: 1964); Diedrich Westermann, *Practical Phonetics for Students of African Languages* (London: 1949).

[2] See Marius F. Valkhoff, *Studies in Portuguese and Creole* (Johannesburg: 1966), p. 91.

of Portuguese over the possibility of this shift having been caused directly by sounds which were present in the West African languages.

Another phonetic difference between European and Bahian Portuguese which piques one's curiosity as to the possibility of West African influence is a change that occurs with word-initial and intervocalic [r̄] > [x]. A similar phenomenon may be observed in the shift from breath-group final [r] > [x] > silence. Again, this is found at all social levels. Although the voiceless velar fricative does occur in some West African languages (see Peter Ladefoged, op. cit.), and even though one of these is Ewe (see Diedrich Westermann, *A Study of the Ewe Language*, Oxford: 1954, p. 14), where it is found word-initially and intervocalically, there is no reason to believe that the [r̄] > [x] change had any connection with the [x] sound either in Ewe or in any of the other West African languages where it occurs. Why should a [x] in some West African languages cause a [r̄] or a [r], and not some other sounds in Portuguese, to become velar, voiceless, and fricative? Also, [x] does not appear in breath-group final position nor word-final position in any West African language. And, when one considers the geographical areas in which this sound shift has taken place, the theory of African influence does not seem viable. For example, the change occurs in areas where there are large percentages of blacks, such as Bahia, Rio de Janeiro, and Pernambuco, but it may also be found in places where there are relatively few blacks, such as the state of Rio Grande do Sul and Santa Catarina. Comparing this with Spanish-speaking America, we see that the same shift from [r̄] > [x] word-initially and inter-vocalically has happened at all levels of society in Puerto Rico, where the black population claims a relatively high percentage. Yet in areas which contain larger percentages of blacks than can be found in Puerto Rico, such as the Atlantic and Pacific coastal areas of Colombia, the Dominican Republic, and Cuba, the [r̄] > [x] change has not taken place. Here, too, we find no breath-group final or word-final [r] becoming [x]. Breath-group final [r] does disappear into silence, however, in all of these Spanish-speaking areas, especially among the lower social levels. This phonetic change may not be attributed to African influence, though, since we see that it is also found in certain parts of Spain, such as the Madrid area, where the black population is very minimal.

With this kind of evidence, the most obvious reasons for such sound changes as have been discussed here must be those which would account for simple dialect variation. There are, of course, other differences in the phonetic realization of phonemic patterns between European and Bahian Portuguese, as there are between the various dialects of the language spoken in Portugal and Brazil. None of these differences, however, purport to be due to African influence.

There are, in the syntax of spoken Bahian Portuguese, two peculiarities which almost never manifest themselves in European Portuguese. Both of these phenomena can be found in all levels of society: the repetition of *não* and the placing of subject pronouns in objective positions after the finite verb. As to the first of these, negative formations in the West African languages do not suggest the development of this kind of a double negative construction in Portuguese (see F. W. Migeod, op. cit., volume I, pp. 218-227). The use of *não* in this fashion, usually appearing before and after the verb, which is so prevalent in Bahia and in other parts of Brazil (even where the black population is practically nil) is probably due to the fact that the early Portuguese slave traders and colonists in Brazil overemphasized negation (as they no doubt overemphasized almost everything they said) in order to make themselves understood when attempting to communicate with their black slaves. This, of course, is "standard procedure" whenever the formation of a Pidgin "language" is involved, as was certainly the case with the Portuguese and the Africans. Marius F. Volkhoff, op. cit., informs us that there is strong evidence to believe in the existence of a double negation of this type in the African variety of the Portuguese lingua franca. He says that Hugo Schuschardt came across the same thing in secondary Creole on the Loanga Coast in Africa. It also exists in Afrikaans.

The same reasons given here for the usage of the double negative *não ... não* may be posited for the peculiar placement of subject pronouns after the finite verb, where they become the object pronouns. That is, for purposes of simplification, the Portuguese probably repeated the subject pronouns and emphasized them while talking to the black slaves. This seems logical, especially since the subject pronouns in Portuguese are much easier to perceive in an utterance than are the direct object forms. [3]

---

[3] The direct object pronouns in Portuguese, especially the third person singular and plural, which perhaps have a higher frequency of usage than the other persons, are made up of a single vowel, i.e., *o*, *a*, or a single vowel plus "s," i.e., *os*, *as*, and are many times difficult to hear in an utterance. The

By way of final remarks concerning theories of direct influences of African languages on Bahian Portuguese at linguistic levels other than lexical, it may be said that the problem is one of dealing with a Creole or what Valkhoff, op. cit., terms a form of Low Portuguese. This is the same as the Portuguese lingua franca which originated on some of the western coastal areas of Africa during the second half of the 15th century. Since the same linguistic phenomena in Brazilian Portuguese discussed here may also be found in other parts of the world, such as India and Ceylon, where there were no Africans, and where the Portuguese sailors where active,[4] and since these same linguistic traits do not manifest themselves in some areas of relatively high black concentrations either in Spanish- or Portuguese-speaking America, it behooves one to conclude that the languages spoken by slaves taken from Africa to Bahia did not, in fact, have any direct influence on the Portuguese spoken here in the New World as far as phonetics, phonology, morphology, and syntax are concerned. In other words, there occurred a natural pidginization of the Portuguese language that later developed into a Creole which was nothing more than a "low" or different form of this European language.

Since the vocabulary of a language is the most transient feature of its structure and lexical borrowings among languages are more frequent than at any other linguistic level, it is not surprising to find that a fair number of West African words have been permanently introduced into Bahian Portuguese. It is equally understandable that the pronunciation of the vocabulary items which have been borrowed into Portuguese adhers to the phonetic structures of this language as it is spoken in Bahia, rather than retaining the original sounds of each African language from which they come (which, of course, would not be in accordance with basic linguistic principles).

Before presenting the list of words which I have tentatively identified as having a sub-Saharan origin, a brief statement concerning the methods used in gathering the vocabulary would be useful at this time. It was my intent to compile a list of words of supposed African origin which could be checked against grammars and dictionaries of

---

third person singular and plural subject pronouns contain more phonemes, i.e., *êle, ela; êles, elas*, and are more easily perceived, especially by a foreign ear.

[4] See M. F. Valkhoff, op. cit.

African languages [5] and with native informants, whenever possible. Sixty-five copies of the list were attached to questionnaires which solicited the following information about each person completing the form: name, age, race/color, sex, place of birth, number of years having lived in Bahia, profession, birth place of parents, education, number of trips and destinations of same, yearly income, and size and location of their homes. The questionnaires were circulated among Bahians of all social levels and racial backgrounds for the purpose of determining the existence and frequency of usage of each word at the different social levels. By doing this, I hoped to be able to discover how much lexical penetration of African origin can be found in each social class of the Bahian population.

In order to compile the list of words of supposed African origin for the preparation of questionnaires to be circulated among the Bahians, I gathered vocabulary items from five sources, i.e., Edison Carneiro's *Candomblés da Bahia*; three books by Deoscóredes M. dos Santos, *Contos de Nagô*, *Axé Ôpô Afonjá*, and *Contos Negros da Bahia*; and Renato Mendonça's *A Influência Africana no Português do Brasil*. These books were chosen because they purport to contain a very large percentage of the African words that were brought to Bahia. That is to say, these books represent efforts by authors interested in the black African influences present in Bahia and therefore are excellent source materials for initiating the investigation of vocabulary usages of black origin among the Bahians.

Of some 1,740 lexical items of supposed non-Portuguese (presumably African) origin gathered from these authors, 428 were chosen for inclusion in the questionnaire. The other 1,312 words were eliminated because they could not be found in either the *Grande Dicionário Etimológico-Prosódico da Língua Portuguêsa* [6] or the *Dicionário Etimológico da Língua Portuguêsa* (1st edition, 1952, by José Pedro Machado), as having some etymological connection with the languages of sub-Saharan Africa. Many of the words chosen for the questionnaire were found registered in the etymological dictionaries as simply "of African origin," or "supposedly African," without any guess as

---

[5] The bibliography contains a complete list of the references which were consulted for this study.

[6] See *Grande Dicionário Etimológico-Prosódico da Língua Portuguêsa* by Francisco da Silveira Bueno (catedrático de Filologia Portuguêsa da Universidade de São Paulo), São Paulo, Edição Saraiva: 1963.

to specific languages or dialects. Both José Pedro Machado and Francisco da Silveira Bueno rely rather heavily on Renato Mendonça's *A Influência Africana no Português do Brasil* for etymological information. As part of my research efforts, I have consulted as many grammars and dictionaries as possible, and conferred with native informants to check the 428 words against Machado's and da Silveira's words, in order to achieve a more accurate study.[7] (Words that could not be identified by any of these sources were not included on the list which appears in this chapter.) In doing this, I have been able to identify, on a tentative basis, the languages of sub-Saharan Africa which have left some of their lexicon enbedded in the Portuguese language of Bahia.

The sixty-five questionnaires were circulated among Bahians of all socio-economic levels. Approximately one-third of these was distributed to members of the upper classes, one-third to those of the middle classes, and the remaining one-third to people of the lower levels of society. Six of the questionnaires were read to illiterate Bahians, all of whom were members of the lower classes. The instructions on the questionnaires were such that each informant was required to indicate whether or not he or she could give one or more definitions for each word recognized. Any items which were identifiable as part of the Bahian dialect, yet for which no exact definitions could be given, had a question mark placed by them. Those words not recognized were not marked by the informant. This procedure was followed so that the vocabulary items could be categorized. The words for which definitions were given by a majority (over 50%) of all the informants were placed in an "active vocabulary list,"[8] and

---

[7] In addition to dictionaries and grammars of sub-Saharan African languages, which are listed in the bibliography, I also checked my list of words against the following studies of the Tupi language: Antonio Ruiz de Montoya, *Gramática y Diccionarios (Arte, Vocabulario y Tesoro) de la lengua tupí o guaraní* (Paris: 1876); Federico G. Edelweiss, *Estudos Tupis e Tupi-Guaranis (Confrontos e Revisões)* (Rio de Janeiro: 1969); Plínio Ayrosa, *Têrmos Tupis no Português do Brasil* (São Paulo: 1937); Octaviano Mello, *Dicionário Tupi (Nheengatu) Português e Vice-Versa* (São Paulo: 1967); Pe. A. Lemos Barbosa, *Pequeno Vocabulário Tupi-Português* (Rio de Janeiro: 1967); Anselmo J. Peralta y Tomás Osuna, *Diccionario Guaraní-Español y Español-Guaraní* (Buenos Aires: 1950). I also consulted other studies dealing with the Tupi-Guarani, which are listed in the bibliography.

[8] Words from the "active list" are indicated in the numbered list which follows with an asterisk.

those which received only a question mark by a majority were classified as "passive."

In addition to the questions concerning name, age, place of birth, etc., it was also required of each informant to state whether or not he or she had some kind of affiliation with any of the cult houses, and if so, to what extent. This was done for the purpose of discovering correlations between certain groups of Brazilians and cognizance of the words on the list. The results of this methodology are stated in the final chapter of this study (Chapter V), since it is here that I attempt to investigate the problem of identifying links between socio-economic and racial categories of the Bahian people and the usage of African-related terminology.

From the list of 428 words, 217 were identified by Bahian informants as being either a part of their active or passive vocabulary. Only 10 of these words were found in the songs and utterances gathered in the *candomblés*. They appear below as the first words of the list. This small number would indicate that the vocabulary found in present-day Bahian cult chants and expressions is not indicative of the relatively large number of African words that were introduced into Bahian Portuguese. In effect, all of the sub-Saharan vocabulary borrowed into Bahian Portuguese from cult songs pertains only to *candomblé* and is used in no other context. This means that a considerable amount of the Afro-Bahian vocabulary did not enter Portuguese through the cult houses but rather by direct contact between the black slave and his or her white master.

The following collection of 217 vocabulary items gathered from the sources herein mentioned and checked against the grammars, dictionaries, and native informants so indicated, appears in alphabetical order within each separate category in which the words are listed. Each word is spelled according to the orthography used in Brazil and is immediately followed by the meaning(s) which the word has in Bahia. (Portuguese words occurring in some expressions are placed in parentheses.) The tentative African equivalents with their respective meaning(s) are then included in phonetic script (tone markings have been omitted since tone is not important to this study.) This phonetic script is used to provide a uniformity of appearance in order to facilitate interpretation. The heterogeneousness of the spelling systems used in the various grammars and dictionaries of sub-Saharan African languages and dialects has made the use of these phonetic symbols obligatory in this chapter. At times, more than one tentative source for the Bahian words has been recorded. This procedure was deemed appropriate since some of the words on the list were found to be similar both phonetically and semantically to utterances in several of the sub-Saharan African languages. In many cases, this is due to the fact that the languages are genetically related. Of course, it would be impossible, in such instances, to know which language from among the several possibilities was the one that did, in fact, contribute to Brazilian Portuguese. Occasionally, the semantic and/or phonetic fit between a Bahian word and its corresponding African entry may not seem relevant. In such cases, I have included the African lexical item(s) so as not to undervalue the possibility of some seemingly irregular semantic and/or phonetic changes having occurred either during or after the borrowing process. These entries have a question mark in parentheses (?) after them, denoting their highly tentative nature.

First, the words which appear in the chants gathered in *candomblés* and form part of either the active or passive vocabulary of the contemporary Bahian, are the following:

(1) *AGÔ*,[9] the word used to ask for any type of permission, such as that required to enter the *terreiro* or to address one of the dignitaries of the house.
Yoruba: *ya go*, abbreviated to *ago*, "give way," "let pass."
Fante-Ashante: *ɐgo'*, "a salutation in or before entering a house by day or by night, announcing that a visitor is coming."
Twi: *agɔ'*, "Let me pass."

(2) *AGOLELÊ*,[10] an apparently meaningless expression used in many samba bands. (For *AGO*, see word number 1.)
Kimbundu: *lele*, "light in weight." *lelela*, "to be easy"; "to lull to sleep."
Ewe: *lele*, "to cry."
Kikongo: *lele*, "weariness."
Hausa: *lela*, "a dance performed by young men."

---

[9] See Appendix III, number 8.
[10] See Appendix III, number 18.

Fulani: *lela,* "to sing" (especially a battle song); *leli,* "song."
Fon: *lele,* "to revolve."
Mende: *lɛlɛ,* "slowly."

(3) AMALÁ,[11] a special dish prepared for *Ogum* and *Xangô*, made of flour, water, okra, shrimp, and *dendê* oil.
Yoruba: *amala,* "a pasty food made of yam flour."

(4) DAHOMEY,[12] the country which was once a French West African colony and is now the independent country of Dahomey. It is the home of the Ewe.
Ewe: *dahomey,* "the country of Dahomey."

(5) GÃ,[13] a musical instrument made of metal, similar to the *agôgô* (#41), but having only one bell-shaped piece.
Efik: *ŋkɔŋ,* "an instrument made of iron of one funnel, beat in play."
Fon: *gã,* "metal."

(6) OGUM, *[14] the god of iron who is represented by various tools such as the ax, scythe, hoe, shovel and pick. His Catholic counterpart is St. Anthony, who in Bahia is the captain of the national army. He is also considered to be the keeper and controller of the high-ways. He does not have a wife and lives alone in the jungle eating goat meat, chickens, oil from the *dendê* palm and corn.
Yoruba: *ogũ,* "god of war and of iron."

(7) OQUICÓ,[15] also spelled OKIKO, is a word for chicken.
Yoruba: *akuk,* "cock."

(8) ORIXÁ,[16] the personification and divinization of the forces of nature; spirit or saint.
Yoruba: *oriša,* "anything one worships."

---

[11] See Chapter III, number 5b.
[12] See Appendix II, number 18.
[13] See Appendix II, number 9.
[14] See Chapter III, number 1b. Also see Appendix III, numbers 69-72. For detailed information concerning the Yoruba gods, see the Rev. Samuel Johnson, *The History of the Yorubas* (Lagos: 1956).
[15] See Appendix III, number 9.
[16] See Chapter III, number 4b.

LEXICAL AFRICANISMS IN BAHIAN PORTUGUESE 125

(9) *VODUM*,[17] spirit or saint. It is essentially the same as the Yoruba *orixá*. Edison Carneiro comments that the "voduns jêjes... são menos conhecidos pelos seus verdadeiros nomes, menos do que os orixás nagôs em virtude da popularidade dos deuses de Yorubá."[18] (the Ewe *voduns* or spirits... are not as well known by their real names, less [well known] than the Yoruba spirits because of the popularity of the Yoruba gods.)
Ewe: *vodu*, "deity."
Fon: *vodũ*, "a good or evil spirit."

(10) *XAXARÁ*,[19] a sheaf of fine pieces of straw decorated with very small sea shells. It belongs to the spirit *Omolu* (#37).
Yoruba: *šašara*, "falling apart."
Yoruba: *šašara ɔwɔ*, "a worn-out broom; the tip of a broom."

The other 201 words from the questionnaires were divided into meaning and grammatical categories. The definitions given for the active vocabulary items are those received on the questionnaires. The passive words were identified by four Bahian informants[20] who have a special interest in Afro-Brazilian culture and, therefore, were able to supply the accurate meanings which the words have in Bahia today. All of the lexical explanations taken from the questionnaires have been translated into English. Portuguese words have been placed in parentheses.

The first category contains the names of gods, spirits and dignitaries in Bahian *candomblé*.

(11) *ABIÃ*, a girl who has arrived at the stage in the induction process before final initiation as a *filha de santo*. She is a member of a group which is not officially a part of the *candomblé* and is usually under the direction of the *mãe-pequena* or of an

---

[17] See Chapter III, number 3a.
[18] *Candomblés*, p. 86.
[19] See Chapter III, number 3a.
[20] The informants were Thales de Azevêdo, age 63 at the time of the interview, medical doctor and Professor of Sociology at the University of Bahia; Elyana Barbosa, age 27, university student and part-time secretary at the Centro de Estudos Afro-Orientais; Yêda Pessoa de Castro and her husband, Guilherme Sousa de Castro, ages not available, both Professors of Linguistics at the Centro de Estudos Afro-Orientais.

older *filha de santo*. The initiation procedures are elaborate and in some cases may extend over several months. The candidate for the position of *abiã* must first save enough money to be able to pay for certain initiation expenses. She then must abstain from sexual intercourse and observe various dietary taboos. Following these initial steps there is a series of purification rites which must be performed and a learning period during which the girl memorizes many chants and shouts in either *Nagô, Gêge* or *Ijexá* (depending on which "nation" her *candomblé* represents) and in Portuguese. After a long period of preparatory ceremonies, the student is finally ready to become *feita* ("made") and is received as a bonafide member of the fetish cult house.

Efik: *abia,* "a practitioner or one who professes something." It is used in many compound words, such as *abiamfa* or *abiãfa,* "a practitioner of Mfa, a kind of incantation."

Fante-Ashante: *abia,* "in the way of helping."
Yoruba: *abi,* "that which possesses."

(12) ABÓ, the name of the sacred ram spirit in "Yoruba" *candomblés*.

Yoruba: *agbo,* "ram."

(13) ACUCÓ, the name of the sacred chicken spirit in "Yoruba" *candomblés*.

Yoruba: *akukɔ,* "cock."

(14) ALUFÁ, *pai de santo,* the masculine counterpart of the *mãe de santo*. The Bahian "Yoruba" BABALORIXÁ, which is evidently known only among initiates since it was not identified on the questionnaires as even part of the passive vocabulary, is a synonym.

Yoruba: *alufa,* "priest, clergyman."
Yoruba: *babaloriša,* "idolatrous priest."

(15) BABÁ IFÁ, the fortune-teller spirit. He is called upon by the *mãe* or *pai de santo* to reveal the future for any non-initiate who may wish to pay the price of such services.

Yoruba: *baba ifa,* "a man capable of talking to a god." The word *baba* is "father," and *ifa* is "any kind of god."

(16) *CUMBA*, a "Yoruba" witch doctor. This term is not frequently used in Bahian *candomblé* circles but is more often employed in *macumba* in Rio de Janeiro.

Kikongo: '*kumba* (superscript ' indicates stress), "to make a noise, a roar; to be amazed." The word *macumba*, meaning "black magic, or a ceremony of singing and dancing for purposes of creating black magic," may be a combination of the Kikongo prefix *ma*, the common Bantu plural (inanimate) prefix, plus '*kumba*, "to make a noise."

Kimbundu: '*kumba*, "to make a groaning noise."

Vai: *kumba*, "a personal name."

Wolof: *kumba*, "a personal name."

Umbundu: '*kumba*, "to roar."

(17) *ELEDA*, the guardian angel who watches over all of the members of the cult houses.

Yoruba: ɛlɛda, "Creator of the world, the Supreme Being."

(18) *EXU*[21] *ONÃ*, the *Nagô* spirit of the highways. *Onã* was translated into Portuguese as *do caminho* (of the road).

Yoruba: *ešu ɔna*, "spirit of the road."

(19) *IÁ Ô*, an initiate of Bahian *candomblé*.

Yoruba: *iyawo*, "wife." The implication being that the initiate is "married" to the *candomblé*.

---

[21] See Appendix IV, number 1. Edison Carneiro, in his *Candomblés da Bahia*, p. 83, describes the spirit *Exu* in the following manner: "... Exu não é um orixá — é um criado dos orixá e um intermediário entre os homens e os orixás. Se desejamos alguma coisa de Xangô, por exemplo, devemos despachar Exu, para que, com a sua influência, a consiga mais fàcilmente para nós. Não importa a qualidade do favor Exu fará o que lhe pedirmos, contando que lhe demos as coisas de que gosta.... Se o esquecemos, não só não obteremos o favor, como também Exu desencadeará contra nós tôdas as fôrças do Mal, que, como intermediário, detém nas suas mãos." (... Exu is not a god — he is a servant of the gods and an intermediary between men and gods. If we wish for something from *Xangô*, for example, we should call on *Exu*, so that, through his influence, he can get it for us more easily. The quality of the favor is not important; *Exu* will do what we ask of him, just so long as we give him what he wants ... If we forget this, not only will we not obtain the favor, but *Exu* will unleash all of the evil forces against us, for he has the power to do so.)

(20) *IYALAXÊ ÔPÔ AFONJÁ,* the *mãe de santo* of the *terreiro de Axé Opô Afonjá,* in the *Gonçalo do Retiro* area of Salvador.
    Yoruba: *iyalaše,* "the wife of the chief priest"; *opo,* "pillar"; *afōja,* "a family name."

(21) *IYALORIXÁ,* the *mãe de santo* of any cult house.
    Yoruba: *iyaloriša,* "mother of something worshipped."

(22) *IYÁ NASÓ,* the "Yoruba" designation for *mãe senhora,* which is a synonym for *mãe de santo.*
    Yoruba: *Iya-Naso,* "one of the Ladies of the Palace in the hierarchical system of government of the Yoruba."
    Yoruba: *iya,* "mother or elderly woman."
    Kimbundu: *nasoma,* "queen."
    Igbo: *nsɔ,* "sacredness."

(23) *MUZENZA, filha de santo* in any Bahian *candomblé.*
    Kikongo: *'ndumba' 'muēnze,* "a young virgin."
    Kikongo: *mu'nzenzi,* "guest." (?)
    Shona (Rhodesia): *mu'dzenza,* "within the generation." (?)

(24) *OBÁ,* an important dignitary of Bahian *candomblé.* My informants did not know what his functions were.
    Yoruba: *ɔba,* "king."

(25) *OBÁ ORUM,* the great spirit, lord of all things.
    Yoruba: *ɔba orũ,* "the Lord of Heaven."

(26) *ODI,* the great wise man.
    Yoruba: *odi,* "deaf man." (?)
    Gũ (Ewe): *odi,* "scroll." (?)
    Twi: *ɔdɛfo* (possible apocope), "a title of respect." (?)
    Bini (So. Nigeria): *odayi* (possible syncope), "a young man functioning as the senior of his ɛgbɛe." (?) [22]

---

[22] See Lorenzo Turner, *Africanisms in the Gullah Dialect* (New York: 1969), p. 143.

(27) OGÃ, a non-initiated patron or supporter of the religious cult chosen by the *orixás* and "confirmed" by means of a public festival. The *ogãs* generally take turns playing the musical instruments for the *candomblé* ceremonies.
Yoruba: ɔga, "boss." (?)

(28) OMI XUM, the waters of the spirit OXUM,* who is the goddess of the springs and brooks. Her Catholic counterpart is the Lady of the Candles, and her day of celebration is the 2nd of February. She is a child goddess; her place in the *terreiro* is always filled with toys.
Yoruba: *omi*, "water"; ɔšũ, "a river goddess."

(29) OSSI IYALAXÉ, the third in rank below the *mãe de santo*.
Yoruba: *osi*, "left-hand woman"; *iyalašɛ*, "wife."

(30) OTUM IYALAXÉ, the second in rank after the *mãe de santo*.
Yoruba: ɔtũ, "right-hand woman in spirit-worship ceremonies"; *iyalašɛ*, "wife."

(31) OXAGIYAN, a synonym for the god *Oxalá*.[23]
Yoruba: *orišajiyã*, "the name of the god *orišala* as he is known in the township of Ejigbo." *orišajiyã* is contracted to *ošajiyã*. The name *oša'la* is a combination of two Yoruba words: *oriša*, "anything worshipped," and *ninlá*, "big." *oriša ninlá* contracts to *ošanla*, and shows up in Bahia as *oša'la*.

(32) OXALUFAN, the name given to *O Senhor do Bomfim* (the Christ of the Bomfim Church) in *candomblé* circles. This is a very famous church in Bahia to which many people go to pray for miracles, for it is believed that through this church thousands of miracles are performed every year. Members of the Bahian cult houses gather annually at the *Igreja do Bomfim* (Church of the Bomfim) to wash the front steps as part of a religious act connected with *candomblé*.

---

[23] *Oxalá* is one of the many spirits worshipped in *Nagô* cult houses. No indication of his being recognized was obtained on the questionnaires.

Yoruba: *Oṣalufan,* "god of the city of Ifan."
Yoruba: *oriša oluofi,* "the name of the god *orišala* in Iwọ̀fin." (?) *oriša oluofi > ošalufi > ošalufã.* (?)

There are many *orixás* in Bahian *candomblés*. In fact, they are so numerous that not even the *mães de santo* can remember them all. Besides Ogum* and Oxum,* which have already been discussed, there are seven other important or popular saints that were identified on the questionnaires:

(33) IANSÃ,* the wife of *Xangô*. She is honored with special ceremonies every 4th of December.[24]
Yoruba: *iyãsã,* "the wife of *šaŋgo*."

(34) NANÃ,* also called *a Senhora Sant'Ana*, is the oldest *mãe-d'água* (water sprite) and mother of all *orixás*. Whenever she dances, it is as if she were carrying a small child in her arms.
Yoruba: *nana,* "a common family name in Ghana." (?)

(35) OMOLU,* the god of smallpox and other related diseases. He may appear as *São Lázaro*, an old man, bent and crooked, or as *Obaluayé*, a strong man. He always carries a *xaxará* (sheaf).
Yoruba: *omolu,* "child of God." *omolu* is an abbreviated form of *omo oluwa*. The name *Obaluayé* comes from a Yoruba verb, *ɔbaoluwaye,* "to appeal to the king of the gods."

(36) OXÓSSI,*[25] the god of the hunt, whose Catholic name is *São Jorge*. He is represented in *candomblé* wearing armor, carrying a sword and fighting a dragon. At times he also carries such gear as a bow and arrow, quiver, rifle and a knapsack. Special ceremonies are held in his honor on the day of Corpus Christi.
Yoruba: *oriša osi,* "one of the national gods of the Yoruba."
In Bahia, *oriša osi > ošosi > ɔ'šɔsi.*

---

[24] See Chapter III, footnote number 27. Also Appendix III, numbers 8, 16, and 17.
[25] See Appendix III, numbers 7 and 72.

(37) *OXUNMARÊ*,* the rainbow, is *São Bartolomeu* in the Catholic Church. His day of celebration is the 24th of August. He was brought up as a child by *Xangô* and has the form of a snake. His clothes consist of white linen, strings of small seashells (*búzios*) and yellow beads. In his hand he carries a trident.
Yoruba: *ošumare*, "rainbow."

(38) *YEMANJÁ*,*²⁶ the young and beautiful *mãe-d'água* who among the Catholic saints is the *Senhora da Conceição*. She wears strings of beads and carries a sword and an *abébé*²⁷ with the figure of a mermaid in the center. In Bahia this goddess is perhaps the best known of all the *orixás*. Her picture can be purchased in almost any stationary or dime store in the city and is found hanging in many public buildings and private homes.
Yoruba: *iyemɔja*, "mermaid."

(39) *XANGÔ*,*²⁸ the god of thunder and lightning. He is also called either *São Jerônimo* or *São Pedro*, depending on the color of his garments. On some occasions he may even turn into a female, who is then identified with *Santa Bárbara*.
Yoruba: *šaŋgo*, "the god of thunder and lightning."

The number of minor *orixás* runs into the thousands, and no one knows the names of them all. One of the better known among Bahian cult circles, *Oxalá*,²⁹ was not recognized by any of the informants

---

²⁶ See Appendix III, numbers 66-68.

²⁷ *Abébé* is a circular metal fan painted white and engraved with the figure of a mermaid representing the goddess *Yemanjá*.
Yoruba: *abɛbɛ*, "fan."

²⁸ See Chapter III, footnote 29 and Appendix III, number 18.

²⁹ Edison Carneiro, in *Candomblés*, page 78, describes *Oxalá* in the following way: "...identificado com o Senhor do Bomfim, e mais raramente com o Divino Espírito Santo, recebe — como entre católicos da Bahia — as homenagens que se deveriam prestar a *Olorum*.... É considerado o pai de todos os orixás e, portanto, avô dos mortais — donde se chamar a sua morada, a igreja do Bomfim, Lançaté do Vovô." (...identified with the Christ of the Bomfim Church, and rarely with the Holy Spirit, he receives — as among the Catholics of Bahia — the homages which should be given to *Olorum*.... He is considered to be the father of all the gods and, therefore, grandfather of mortals — whence the name of his dwelling-place, the Bomfim Church, *Lançaté de Vovô* — grandpa's place.)

who submitted questionnaires. Some of the less important *candomblé* spirits were identified by informants and are listed in Appendix V.

The next category includes articles, shouts, functions and other miscelaneous words connected with *candomblé*.

(40) *AGÔ*,[30] permission.

(41) *AGÔGÔ*, a musical instrument of two metal bell-shaped chambers of unequal size which are struck with a rod of the same material. It produces a hollow metal sound. The *agôgô* is used in *candomblé*, samba and *afoxé*.
   Yoruba: *agogo*, "bell, metal musical instrument."

(42) *ALABÊ*, the person in charge of selecting all the musical instruments and songs to be used on any occasion in the "Ewe" cult houses.
   Yoruba: *alabɛ*, "one who circumcises." (?)
   Arabic:[31] *al'be*, "someone who is wealthy or in a position of authority." (?)

(43) *AMALÁ*,[32] the special dish prepared only in the cult houses for certain spirits.

(44) *ATÔTÔ*, the expression used to salute[33] the spirit *Omolu*.
   Yoruba: *toto*, "praise to thee." This is an expression used in religious contexts.

(45) *AXÉ*, an expression equivalent to Christianity's "Amen."
   Yoruba: *aʃɛ*, "Amen."

(46) *AXÊXÊ*, a term used to describe a cult house which has been temporarily closed because of the death of one of its members.
   Ewe: *ʃēʃē*, "interval."
   Yoruba: *aʃɛ*, "Amen; law, commandment." (?)

---

[30] See word number 1 of this chapter.
[31] Arabic words may have filtered in through Hausa.
[32] See word number 3 of this chapter.
[33] In Bahian *Candomblé* every spirit has his or her own *saudação* or "salute" which is used by the initiates to summon their own saint or to render to any particular *orixá*.

LEXICAL AFRICANISMS IN BAHIAN PORTUGUESE 133

(47) *BÚZIO*, a very small sea shell used in large quantities to make necklaces, bracelets and ornaments for the *terreiro*. *Búzios* of a special shape and color are worn by the *mãe* or *pai de santo* and are supposed to have certain magical powers.

Ewe: *busu*, "misfortune." Perhaps the *búzios* were worn to guard against misfortune. (?)

Ewe: *buzabuza*, "plentiful." (?)

Kikongo: *'bunzu*, "honor, respect, esteem, influence." (?)

(48) *CANJERÊ*, a formal meeting of Negroes whose purpose is to practice some form of black magic or to sing and dance in honor of the spirits.

Bambara: *kaŋgεrε*, "provocation, incitement." (?)

Shona: *kan'jεrε*, "a small bit of wisdom." (?)

(49) *CANZUÁ ~ GANZUÁ*, the cult house.

Ewe: *ganua*, "tin." Houses originally made of tin or metal. (?)

(50) (DAR) *DOBALÉ*, the act of stretching oneself out on the ground face down to give due respect to a spirit. It is practiced by all of the *filhos* and *filhas de santo* during some of the ceremonies.

Yoruba: *dobalε*, "an utterance used to refer to a male who prostrates himself before an elderly person out of respect for that person.

(51) (DAR O) *IKÁ OTUM IKÁ OSI*, a dance maneuver which requires that the initiate, kneeling, sway from right to left with the entire body and touch the ground with the head. Only cult members who have female guardian angels may do this.

Yoruba: *yika ɔtũ yika osi*, "to prostrate oneself toward the ground, then roll to the right, then to the left."

(52) *EBÓ*, an evil spell which the *mãe* or *pai de santo* may cast upon anyone.

Yoruba: *εbɔ*, "a sacrifice made to the devil."

(53) *EIRU*, an ox tail, used as a magic charm.

Yoruba: *iru*, "any tail that wags."

(54) (FAZER O) *OSÉ*, to clean and decorate the *terreiro* in preparation for a ceremony.
   Yoruba: ɔʃɛ, "soap."
   Akan: osɛ kɛtɛ, "spreading a mat." (?)
   Gũ (Ewe): osɛ, "blossom." (?)
   Gũ: osɛ̃, "god of the sky." (?)
   Gũ: sɛ, "to gleam."

(55) (FEIXE DE) *ATORI*, a reunion of several spirits during a ceremony.
   Fulani: *tori*, "a kind of large drum used by Fulani slaves." (?)
   Yoruba: *atori*, "whip; a very tough tree." (?)
   Tiv: *tori*, "chief." (?)

(56) *FILÁ*, a type of hood made of straw which the female initiates wear when representing certain spirits.
   Yoruba: *fila*, "any kind of covering for the head."

(57) *GÃ*,[34] the metal musical instrument.

(58) *GANGA*, the chief of a *Cabinda*[35] cult house.
   Ngangela: *ŋgaŋga*, "a wicked witch doctor."
   Shona: *ŋaŋga*, "witch doctor."
   Igbo: *ŋgaŋga*, "a proud person." (?)
   Mang'anja (interior Mozambique): *gaŋga*, "a brave strong man." (?)

(59) *GONGÁ*, a sanctuary where the more important spirits live.
   Umbundu: *'koŋga*, "to meet, get together." (?)
   Kimbundu: *'ŋgoŋga*, "a bell which is in an enclosed area, such as a sanctuary." (?)

(60) *IXÊ*, the post or pole which is found in the center of all Bahian *terreiros* and which represents the bridge or connecting point between the earth and the sky.

---

[34] See word number 5 of this chapter.
[35] *Cabinda* is a branch of *Umbanda*, the black magic type of spiritualism prevalent in Rio de Janeiro. The word *umbanda* means "medical science" in Kimbundu.

Gũ (Ewe): šẽšẽ, "between." (?)
Kimbundu: 'iši, "earth, ground." (?)
Yoruba: iši, "a tree with edible fruit." (?)

(61) MANDINGA, witchcraft. Also, a tall Negro of West Sudan.
Mandingo: a tribe of Senegal, Guinea, and extreme S. W. Mali, known among neighboring tribes for their skills in witchcraft.
Yoruba: atiŋga, "witchcraft." (?)
Mandinka: man'diŋka, a reference to this language of Gambia. (?)
Kimbundu: mandiŋga čivī, "evil doers; evils."
Kimbundu: ma'ni'ŋga, "blood." (?)

(62) MIRONGA, a doctrine professed in the *macumba* cult.
Shona: mu'roŋgwa, "order or plan." (?)

(63) MULUNGU, an African idol worshipped in *macumba*. The word also refers to a tambourine or small drum having one side covered with leather.
Kikongo: mu'luŋgu, "idol."
Chewa (Malawi): mu'luŋgu, "God."
Mang'anja: mu'luŋgu, "God."

(64) ÔBI, the name given to a nut (*noz-de-cola*) used in the religious ceremonies.
Yoruba: obi, "cola nut."

(65) ÔLUBAJÉ, popcorn which is given to the guests of a *candomblé* ceremony. It is to be eaten during the ceremony.
Yoruba: olu, "god," plus Yoruba: gbaje, "to take and eat."
The Yoruba expression olu gbaje has to do with the belief prevalent among some western Nigerian peoples that if something is dropped on the ground, especially food, one should not pick it up because oluwa ilɛ, the god of the ground, will eat it. Part of this idea is still retained in Bahian *candomblés*, since it is true that at several times during the ceremony, popcorn is thrown on the floor of the *terreiro* and is not picked up.

(66) ORIKI, a greeting used to salute particular saints.
Yoruba: oriki, "the history of a family, family tree." (?)

(67) ÔRÔBÔ, a type of fruit used in black magic ceremonies to strengthen a curse already invoked. It is believed that when the person casting the spell chews the ôrôbô, the spell cast will not fail.
    Yoruba: *orogbo*, "nut." In western Nigeria, the *orogbo* is a symbol for old age. Both it and the *obi*, a symbol for productivity, are used in wedding ceremonies.

(68) OSSÉ, the act of offering food to the *orixás* who protect the *terreiro* and all its members.
    Ewe: *sẽ*, "to bring fruit."
    Igbo: *ose*, "pepper."
    Ewe: *se*, "a deity." (?)

(69) PADÊ, the invocation of the spirit *Exu*.[36] He is called upon by the use of this expression and is entreated to cause the religious ceremony to be a great success.
    Yoruba: *bade*, "to be suitable." (?)
    Yoruba: *ešu*, "spirit."

(70) PEJI, the main altar in all Bahian *terreiros*. It is always decked with images and pictures of the principal spirits as well as with *búzios* (strings of small shells) and religious ornaments of all kinds. During the ceremonies, the initiates gather around this altar and offer gifts to the spirits.
    Yoruba: *pe*, "to assemble," plus Yoruba: *ji*, "to give one a present."

(71) PEJI GÃ, the person in charge of arranging and taking care of the main altar.
    (See #70 for *peji*)
    Ewe: *gã*, "respected, distinguished." (?)
    The supposition here is that the person in charge of the altar is a respected individual.

(72) RUM, RUMPI, LÉ, the three drums used to beat the many rhythms in all *candomblé* ceremonies. The *rum* is the largest or tallest, the *rumpi*, the middle-sized one, and the *lé* is the smallest.[37]

---

[36] See word number 18 of this chapter.

[37] The drums are listed together because they form a unit in *candomblé*. The three are always played together, each being used to produce a different rhythm, yet all in harmony with one another. See Chapter I for tentative origins of the words for these three drums.

(73) *XAXARÁ*,[38] Omolu's sheaf.

(74) *XERÉS*, a gourd in the form of a spindle filled with dry seeds and used as a musical instrument in the religious ceremonies.
Yoruba: šɛkɛrɛ (possible syncope), "a rattle made from a calabash netted with strings of cowries.

During a *candomblé* ceremony one may hear many isolated shouts either during the beating of the drums or when they are silent. These loud exclamations serve to enliven the spirits so that they will respond to the initiates and possess them. Each separate shout corresponds to a different god. According to the *mães* and *pais de santo* whom I interviewed, there are thousands of shouts (called *gritos* or *saudações especiais* in Portuguese). One would expect to find a large number of them, since we know that there are theoretically thousands of spirits. Nine *gritos* of approximately twenty listed on the questionnaires were recognized by informants as having some connection with *candomblé*. They are listed in Appendix III.

The third category, that of foods, shows a higher percentage of active vocabulary than the previous two. Present-day Bahian culinary arts include a wide variety of dishes of African origin which still use many ingredients from plants that were brought from Africa. Darwin Brandão, in his descriptive cookbook of Bahian recipes, *A Cozinha Baiana*,[39] lists sixty-three salt dishes (*comidas de sal*), sixty-two sweet ones (*doces*) and ten drinks and appetizers (*refrigerantes, licores e aperitivos*) stemming from Africa. One of the national dishes of Brazil, which is by far the most common in Bahia, the *feijoada*, uses many ingredients and skills of cookery introduced by Negro slaves.

The following Afro-Brazilian foods were recognized on the questionnaires:

(75) *ACAÇÁS*,* a mass of cooked corn prepared with *vatapá*.[40]
Twi: *akasã*, "corn porridge."
Gẽ (Ewe): *akasã*, "porridge."

---

[38] See word number 10 of this chapter.
[39] (Rio de Janeiro, Tecnoprint Gráfica, S. A., Coleção Brasileira de Ouro: 1967).
[40] A dish of shrimp, fish or chicken with a flour base.

(76) *ACARAJÉ,* * balls of mashed black beans fried in *dendê* oil and often eaten with shrimp and black pepper. It is as popular as Bahian *feijoada* and can be purchased from Afro-Brazilian "mammies" on almost any Bahian streetcorner.
    Yoruba: *akara,* "cake," plus Yoruba: *jɛ,* "eat, ate."
    Igbo: *akara,* "fried cake, commonly made with bean meal."

(77) *ANGU,* * gruel made from ground cassava.
    Kimbundu: *'angu,* "grass, straw." (?)

(78) *BEIJU,* * a dish prepared with manioc.
    Yoruba: *beju,* "food made of cassava."
    Curiously enough, Plínio Ayrosa, in his book *Têrmos Tupis no Português do Brasil,* lists *beiju* as coming from Tupi *mbeiú* or *mbeyú,* meaning "rolled up." Father A. Lemos Barbosa, in his *Pequeno Vocabulário Tupi-Português,* lists *beju,* "bread, cake."

(79) *BÔLO,* * cake.
    KiKongo: *'mbolo,* "cake."

(80) *CACHAÇA,* a strong alcoholic drink made from rum which has been buried in a coconut.
    Mang'anja: *ka'šasu,* "wine; strong beer."
    Cinyanja (Mozambique): *ka'šasu,* "whiskey."

(81) *CACULA,* a tonic drink.
    Kimbundu: *'kakula,* "a tonic drink."

(82) *CURAU,* gruel made of ground or sliced green corn cooked with sugar.
    Kimbundu: *'kuria,* "food." (?)
    Hausa: *kuresa,* "a bunch of corn." (?)
    Vai: *kura,* "green, fresh." (?)
    Ewe: *ku,* "corn." (?)
    Nupe: *kuru,* "cake." (?)

(83) *FUBÁ,* * cornmeal.
    Nupe: *fura,* "a drink made from Indian or Guinea corn." (?)
    Kimbundu: *'fufu,* "cornmeal."
    Fon (Ewe): *fufu,* "food made from maize, fish and palm oil." (?)

Akan: *fufu*, "any starchy food which is mashed up." (?)

(84) *GARAPA*,* a soft drink made from sugar cane juice. The only reference found to this word as being of African origin was in Juan Corominas' *Diccionario crítico etimológico de la lengua castellana*, volume II (Berna: 1970), pp. 814, 815, where we find the following:

"El Sr. Fernando Ortiz (*Glos. de Afronegrismos*, s.v.) documenta satisfactoriamente el hecho de que *garapa* designa una bebida de gusto dulzón y alcohólica, derivada del maíz y de la yuca, en Angola, Benguela y el Congo. Como esto coincide con la temprana aparición en el Brasil, justamente en la forma *garapa*, y con la atribución del vocablo a los esclavos por parte de Tirso, parece probado en este caso el origen africano de la palabra."

(Mr. Fernando Ortiz (*Glos.* of *Afro-Negrisms*, s.v.) satisfactorily documents the fact that *garapa* designates a drink, which is sweet and alcoholic, and made from corn and manioc, as coming from Angola, Benguela and the Congo. Since this coincides with its early appearance in Brazil, in exactly the same form, *garapa*, and [since the 17th century Spanish playwrite] Tirso [de Molina] attributes the word to the slaves, it seems that the word is most likely of African origin.)

José Pedro Machado lists the word *guarapa*, and states that it comes from Tupi. However, the same word, in the masculine gender, with the same meaning that it has in Bahia, i.e., *guarapo*, is very common in Colombia, where there are no Tupi Indians. Since large numbers of West Africans were also shipped to Colombian ports during the slave trade, it would seem more feasible to consider the word as having an African origin rather than an Indian one.

(85) *INHAME*,* any of various yams and aroids.
Yoruba: *iyã*, "pounded yam."
Mende: *ya, 'yambi*, "wild yam."
Twi: *nyam nyam*, "food."
Fulani: *'ñama*, "to eat." (?)

(86) *MARUFO*, a fermented drink extracted from the sweet sap of raintree saman.

Kikongo: *ma'lafu,* "a fermented drink."
Kikongo: *ma'lavu,* "wine made from parts of a felled palm tree."

(87) *MOCOTÓ,** a dish made of cow's knuckles.
Yoruba: bɔkɔtɔ̃, "food made from cow's knuckles."

(88) *QUENGA,* chicken stew.
Bobangi (Congo): 'ŋkeŋgɔ, "a steamer for cooking." (?)

(89) *QUITUTE,** any food which is especially delicious. There is a chain of restaurants in Brazil which has adopted this word for its name.
Twi: *æku'tudie,* "the eating of oranges." (?)

(90) *UMULUCU,* a dish made of black beans, *dendê* oil, a number of condiments and shrimp.
Yoruba: *mulukɛ,* "a dish of black beans cooked with oil, found in the extreme southwestern part of Nigeria."

(91) *XIMXIM,** a popular chicken dish seasoned with salt, garlic, lemon juice, onion, shrimp and roasted peanuts. It is served with *farofa* (ground manioc) and *dendê* oil.
Twi: *æsiŋsiŋ,* "parts, pieces, fragments," (?) referring to the ingredients of the dish?
Twi: *sīnsīn,* "to cut, carve, peel." (?)

(92) *XUXU,** the chayote squash.
Nupe: *šu,* "to make into a ball." (?)
A possible reduplication, this could refer to the shape of the squash.

Turning to Frederick W. H. Migeod's *The Languages of West Africa,* we find the following concerning the verb: "The conjugation of the verb is, on the whole, simple in all the languages of West Africa. ... it may be said generally that it is rare to find in any language that the stem or root of the verb is not clearly discernible, any prefixes or suffixes that may be added for conjugational purposes being simply added without any modification resulting therefrom." [41]

---

[41] (London: 1971), p. 191.

The readily identifiable stems in the verbal systems of West African languages may have been responsible for a greater ease in the borrowing process of verbs into Portuguese. Also, the regularity of these West African verbs may have accounted for the fact that all of the ones tentatively identified here as sub-Saharan are of the -ar conjugation in Portuguese and none is irregular. In any case, it may be said that when Portuguese acquired African verbs, or any morphemes or combinations of morphemes which it might have transformed into verbs either during or after borrowing, it fit them into the productive subclass of regular -ar verbs. This paradigmatic subclass was probably automatically selected because it has the highest frequency of usage of the productive subclasses of verbs in Portuguese.

The verbs identified by Bahian informants and tentatively identified as being of African origin are the following:

(93) *ABOMBAR*, to stop a march or walk because of intense heat.
   Ewe: *abo*, "suffocation." (?)
   Kikongo: *bombo'moka*, "be boiled to pieces." (?)
   Kikongo: *bombo'mona*, "to boil to pieces." (?)

(94) *BANGOLAR*, to float around aimlessly without direction.
   Lingala (Kinshasa, Upper Zaire): *'bongola*, "to turn around and around."
   Fulani: *'bange*, "roundabout." (?)

(95) *BINGAR*, to blow on the horn of an animal.
   Ngangela: *'mbinga*, "the horn of an animal."

(96) *BRIQUITAR*, to hesitate or fluster over something in a very undecided way.
   Yoruba: *bikita*, "to disregard." (?)

(97) *CAFUNGAR*, to sulk with a very long face.
   Shona: *ka'funga*, "to think very deeply with a pensive expression."
   Kimbundu: *ka'fuka*, "to become angry."
   Nupe: *kafũ*, "indolence." (?)

(98) *CAMBAR*, to twist and turn while walking, running or dancing.

Shona: *ka'mbaira*, "to crawl like a baby."
Tiv: *kamber*, "to coil something up." (?)
Kikongo: *'kamba*, "to show." (?) The idea being "to show off." (?)
Hausa: *ka'mbama*, "flattery." (?)

(99) (CATAR) *CAFUNÉ*,* the act of one person embracing the head of another with the fingertips. Also, to pretend to be delousing someone.
Kikongo: *ka'funa*, "to strike, hit." (?)

(100) *CUFAR*, "to kick the bucket," to die.
Kimbundu: *kufua*, "death."
Ewe: *kufia*, "the sentence of death"; (with change of tone) "the king of death."
Swahili: *kufa*, "to die by pestilence."

(101) *CURIAR*, to eat.
Kimbundu: *'kuria*, "food."

(102) *GUNGUNAR*, to grumble or gripe over something.
Shona: *ŋu'ŋuna*, "to grumble."
Shona: *gu'ŋguta*, "to grumble."
Kimbundu: *ŋgu'ŋguna*, "to complain."
Hausa: *gu'ŋguni*, "murmuring."
Mang'anja: *ŋgu'ŋgudza*, "to grumble, gripe."
Cinyanja: *ŋgu'ŋgudza*, "to grumble, gripe."
Chope (Mozambique): *ŋguŋgu'ruka*, "to grumble or murmur in a low voice."

(103) *MANGAR*,* to make fun of or verbally reject someone or something.
Kimbundu: *ma'ŋgala*, "to have fun, joke around."
KiKongo: *maŋga*, "to object to, disapprove."
Shona: *'maŋga*, "to tell lies." (?)

(104) *TUNGAR*, a verb with five different meanings in Bahia, which are: 1) to insist upon or argue stubbornly; 2) to persist in doing something; 3) to beat, knock, thump or bang; 4) to deceive; 5) to evade.
Hausa: *duŋga*, "to persist in or continue doing something."
Hausa: *tuŋga*, "obstinacy."
Kimbundu: *'tuŋga*, "a fool"; "to confuse, perplex."

Fulani: *'tuka,* "to press the point."
Fulani: *'tuŋkur,* "the sound of pounding in a mortar."
Shona: *'tuŋga,* "to knock or butt with the head."

(105) XINGAR,* to abuse, criticize or speak evil of someone.
Kimbundu: *'šiŋga,* "to insult someone."

(106) ZANZAR,* to walk about with no destination.
Shona: *zu'ŋgaira,* "to walk around with no destination."
Ewe: *zãnzɔla,* "one who walks in his sleep."

(107) ZOMBAR,* to mock or make fun of someone.
Ngangela: *sompa,* "to censure; to rebuke, scold."
Kimbundu: *'somba,* "to judge."
Shona: *'ñomba,* "to mock." (?)

(108) ZURRAR,* to make silly or nonsensical remarks.
Shona: *'zu'a,* "to brag." (?)

Twenty words from the questionnaires were identified as adjectives. They are listed here in the masculine singular form. Eight of them are invariable in gender, seven of which end in the letter "a." Invariable Portuguese adjectives with final "a" which derive from Latin roots are not common in the language. Unfortunately, the reason for the high frequency of occurrence of these words which have an African origin remains a mystery.

The Bahian adjectives of supposed African origin recognized by informants are the following:

(109) BAMBO,* having no equilibrium, faltering or staggering.
Kikongo: *ba'mbala,* "to wriggle (as a wounded snake), flounder about."
Chewa: *'bambo,* "an old man." (?)
Kimbundu: *'mbamba,* "nervous (used especially to refer to pregnant women)." (?)
Kimbundu: *'mbambi,* "trembling due to fever." (?)

(110) *BANGUELA,* * lacking one or more front teeth.
Hausa: *Ba'ŋgale,* "to break off." (?)
Renato Mendonça gives an interesting etymology for this word. He writes: "provém do costume dos banguelas [or Benguelas, an African tribe from Benguela] que arrancavam os dentes da frente em criança." [42] (it comes from the Banguela custom of extracting the front teeth from children.)

(111) *BOBOCA,* * stupid, not intelligent.
Vai: *bobo,* "a person who cannot talk."
Hausa: *bo'bawa,* "unintelligible speech." (?)
Ewe: *bɔbɔ,* "to be inferior." (?)
Swahili: *bo'boka,* "to talk indiscreetly, to blabber." (?) This is probably only a chance occurrence, since the Portuguese had no slave trade activities in the eastern areas of Africa where Swahili is spoken.

(112) *BOCÓ,* * incapable of doing anything correctly.
Hausa: *boka,* "quack doctor."
Kimbundu: *mbo'koto,* "rogue." (?)
Ewe: *bokɔ,* "diviner, priest." (?)
Ewe: *bɔkɔ,* "slowly, calmly." (?)
Twi: *bɔkɔ,* "soft, tender." (?)
Kikuyu: *'mboko,* "awkwardness in the use of one's hands." This may be a chance occurrence, since the Portuguese had no slave trade activities in Kikuyu territory.

(113) *BUZUNTÃO,* dirty and sloppy (of a person). The *-ão* is a typical Portuguese suffix.
Hausa: *'buzu,* "slave; a serf of the Azbeu people; an undressed skin-mat; a loincloth."

(114) *CAFUNGA,* sad and silent.
Kikongo: *ka'fuŋga,* "silent."
Shona: *ku'fuŋga,* "to think deeply." (?)

(115) *CAMBAIO,* crippled, unable to walk because of some physical defect.
Kimbundu: *'kamba,* "to lack something." (?)
Ngangela: *ka'mbana,* "to obstruct." (?)
Shona: *ka'mbaira,* "to move slowly." (?)

---

[42] *A Influência,* p. 196.

(116) *CARCUNDA* ⋆ or *CORCUNDA*, ⋆ hunchback.
Kimbundu: kari'kunda, "hunchback."

(117) *CASSANGE*, an adjective having three meanings: 1) describing anything having disparaging characteristics; 2) customary, frequent or commonplace; 3) mistaken.
Hausa: ka'sanče, "to remain, continue."
The Kasanzi, pronounced [ka'sanji], is a tribe in Angola located between the Tala Mungongo depression and the Kuangu River. The adjective may have referred to these people. (?)

(118) *CUMBA*, very strong, tough or bruttish in the sense of being a bully or braggart.
Umbundu: 'kumba, "to roar."
Kimbundu: 'kumba, "to roar; to scandalize; slander."
Kimbundu: 'kumba, "to howl, yelp."
Ngangela: 'ŋkumba, "insolence."

(119) *CUTUBA*, of extreme excellence, extraordinarily perfect or exact.
Ngangela: ŋku'tuva, "an ornament worn by the Vankumbi people." This may possibly have referred to the perfect design of this ornament. (?)

(120) *DENGOSO*, ⋆ prudish, prim, coy. This is used to describe a person with a lot of *dengue* (affection). *-oso* is a typical Portuguese affix.
Ewe: deŋgɔ, "progressive, going ahead." (?)
Kikuyu: nde'ŋgere, "neatly or daintily formed." This may be a chance occurrence. (?)
Twi: dēn, "expensive." (?)

(121) *DUNGA*, of exceptional or incomparable qualities.
Kimbundu: 'nduŋge, "intelligence, expertise."
Fulani: 'duŋga, "to approve."

(122) *EMPALAMADO*, ⋆ anemic. The *-ado* is a typical Portuguese affix.
Kimbundu: pa'lama, "to be condemned, cursed." (?)

(123) *(EN)GANGENTO*, ⋆ extremely boring, wearisome or tedious.
Kimbundu: 'ŋganzi, "pain; anger." (?)

(124) *MANGALAÇO*, rascally, knavish, vagrant. *-aço* is a Portuguese affix.
   Kimbundu: *ma'ŋgala*, "to have a good time, play around."

(125) *MIXE*, insignificant, of very little value.
   Ewe: *miči*, "snot, nasal mucus."
   Gũ (Ewe): *emisi*, "mud; diarrhea."
   Tiv: *'miši*, "sprinkle." (?)

(126) *MOLONGÓ*, frail, sickly, indisposed; soft when something is ordinarily hard.
   KiKongo: *mo'ŋgola* (possible metathesis), "timorous, easily frightened, shy, skittish."

(127) *QUIBA*, an adjective used to refer to animals which are very strong and muscular.
   Hausa: *'ḳiba*, "fat; to grow fat." *'ḳiβa*, "to mark off as exceptional."
   Bobangi: *'kiba*, "to be complete." (?)
   Kimbundu: *'kiba*, "skin." (?)

(128) *XÔXO*,* dried up, shriveled because of loss of juice, water, etc.
   Ewe: *xoxo*, "old."[43] The idea here being that whatever is old is shriveled.

It is generally believed that the African Negro is very musically inclined. The slaves who were shipped to Brazil brought with them a whole array of songs and dances as well as many of the musical instruments that accompanied them. As a result, Brazil is probably the South American country which can boast of having more African influence in its music than any of the others. Brazil's most popular dance, the samba, for example, is a direct offspring of the music played in *candomblé*, *macumba*, *umbanda* and *xangô*. Many of the instruments used in these cult ceremonies were borrowed by the Por-

---

[43] The voiceless velar fricative of the Ewe word could have been interpreted as a palatal fricative by the Portuguese. European Portuguese has no voiceless velar fricative. Changes in the manner of articulation of fricatives have been attested in the process of borrowing from one language to another. A classic example is Spanish, which borrowed Arabic [š] and changed it to [x] in the borrowing process. European Spanish has no [š]. Arabic [ša'rab] (noun) "drink" > Spanish [xa'raβe] "syrup," is one example.

tuguese and are presently employed in a variety of musical beats which have become typically Brazilian.

Nine words on the questionnaire were recognized by Bahian informants as being Afro-Brazilian musical instruments. They are:

(129) *AGÔGÔ,* * the metal, gong-like instrument.[44]

(130) *ATABAQUE,* * a drum.
José Pedro Machado states that this word comes from the Arabic *aT-Tabq*, meaning "plate." (*Dicionário Etimológico*, p. 275) I was unable to find it in any of the sub-Saharan grammars and dictionaries checked. Most Brazilian linguists believe the word to be of sub-Saharan origin, however, and that is the reason I include it here.

(131) *BERIMBAU,* * a pole about one and a half inches thick and about three feet long with a wire very tightly attached to both ends. An empty gourd is affixed to the wire with a heavy string. Two distinct tones are produced by alternately pressing and releasing a coin against the wire and striking it with a slender wooden stick. The empty gourd serves as a resonance chamber. This is the principal instrument used in *capoeira* (a dance originating in the days of slavery), and every *capoeirista* (he who dances *capoeira*) knows how to play it.
In the past few years the *berimbau* has also become an important instrument in samba orchestras. Anyone can purchase a *berimbau* for just a few dollars at any music store or souvenir shop in Bahia, and most tourists do not leave the city without buying one. It is the most popular Afro-Brazilian musical instrument in Bahia.
Igbo: *ŋgbirigba*, "bell, especially a hand bell." (?)

(132) *CAXIXI*, a small, enclosed basket-like cup made of reeds with dry seeds inside. When shaken, the seeds make a sound similar to that of a maraca. It is used mostly in *capoeira* and samba bands. In spite of its use in Bahian musical ensembles, it was not readily identified by informants.
Hausa: *kašiu 'gwaŋki*, "a prostrate gourd." (?)

---

[44] See word number 41 of this chapter.

(133) *CUÍCA*, a barrel-like percussion instrument producing grunting sounds.
   Kimbundu: *kwika*, "to resound, reverberate, to sound."

(134) *ENGOMA*, a type of drum.
   Umbundu: *'ŋgoma*, "drum."
   KiKongo: *'ŋgɔma*, "drum."
   Kimbundu: *'ŋgoma*, "a dance accompanied by drums."
   Cinyanja: *'ŋgoma*, "drum."

(135) *GÃ*,[45] the metal instrument.

(136) *GANZÁ*, a percussion instrument similar to the *reco-reco*.[46]
   KiKongo: *'ŋganza*, "percussion instrument."

(137) *MULUNGU*, a tambourine or very small drum with only one leather cover.
   KiKongo: *mulu'ŋgawa u'tari*, "metal in a circular shape." (?)
   KiKongo: *mu'luŋga*, "bracelet." (?)

(138) *QUÊRÊRÊQUÊXÊ*, another word for reco-reco.
   Kikuyu: *kererekeše*, "maracas."
   KiKongo: *kele'kesa* (possible reduplication of syllable -le-; 1 > r), "to grate."
   Swahili: *kere'keta*, "to scratch."

Carnival in Brazil is famous the world over, and the African influence enhancing this yearly festival is what makes the entire affair so unique. Much of the music played during carnival is of African origin; many of the components which are involved in making up the carnival, besides the musical instruments already mentioned, are from Africa. They form an integral part of the celebration, and without them the Brazilian carnival as it is found today would not exist. Four of these components were identified on questionnaires:

---

[45] See word number 5 of this chapter.
[46] *Reco-reco* is a round, hollow, oblong piece of wood which has ten or fifteen notches carved along one portion of it. It makes a grating sound produced by rubbing a stick over the notches. The same instrument is used in the Caribbean area where it is called a *güiro*. The word *reco-reco* is probably an onomatopoeic one representing the sound that the instrument makes when played.

LEXICAL AFRICANISMS IN BAHIAN PORTUGUESE 149

(139) *AFOXÉ*, a group of men who call themselves the *Filhos de Gandhi* (Sons of Gandhi) and perform only during carnival. They play variations of one basic rhythm on large drums as they parade through the streets. They wear white tunic-like costumes copied after those used by many western African nations.

Yoruba: *afɔšɛ*, "fortuneteller; priest who can predict the future."

(140) *BATUCADA*,* the rhythm or chant of the *BATUQUE*,* which is a very fast beat produced by percussion instruments. It is very similar to the samba and is played mostly during carnival by samba orchestras.

Yoruba: *batakoto*, "a kind of drum."

(141) *CONGADO*, a type of dance stemming from western Africa. *-ado* is a typical Portuguese affix.

Kikongo: *e'koŋgo*, "Congo country."

(142) *CONGO*, a dance of African origin similar to the *congado*.

Kikongo: *e'koŋgo*, "the Congo."

The dances *congo* and *congado* ostensibly come from what became the Republic of the Congo in south-central Africa.

(143) *SAMBA*,* the most popular Brazilian dance of African origin. It has urban and rural varieties. Singing usually accompanies the musical instruments, and the dance steps require a great deal of hip-swinging. The music is composed of a double beat, one faster than and superimposed on the other. The accompaniment, whether it be voices or instruments, is syncopated.

Ngangela: *samba*, "to jump around."
Tshiluba (Congo): *'samba*, "to jump around."
Hausa: *sa'mbale*, "a dance for young people."
Bobangi (Congo): *'somba*, "to dance the divination dance."
Kimbundu: *'samba*, "to be very excited, to be boiling over."
Umbundu: *'samba*, "to applaud." (?)
Yoruba: *samba*, "a small drum." (?)

150   A BAHIAN HERITAGE

Among the words on the questionnaire, four were identified as articles of clothing or items of adornment. They are:

(144) *BURUCUTU*, a necklace made from small metal disks.
   Yoruba: *burukutu*, "sorghum seed."

(145) *MISSANGA*,* a decorative string of beads.
   Shona: *mi'saŋga*, "a string of beads."
   Chewa: *mi'saŋga*, "a string of beads."

(146) *TANGA*,* a loincloth.
   Kimbundu: *'taŋga*, "cloth, clothes."
   Umbundu: *'taŋga*, "to make a net or lace."
   Twi: *ntama*, "clothes, African wrap-around dress." (?)

(147) *XOKOTÓS*, a kind of very specially decorated pair of pants, often used by members of samba bands or dancers.
   Yoruba: *šokoto*, "pants native to Nigeria."

Many of the terms for animals and plants represent geographical shifts of context. This is especially true in the case of naming animals, for when the Africans were brought to Brazil they gave African names to many Brazilian species having characteristics similar to those of animals in their own native land.

Brazilian animals that acquired Negro African names and were identified by Bahian informants are:

(148) *ABÔ*, ram.
   Yoruba: *agbo*, "ram."

(149) *CATENDE*, a lizard.
   Kimbundu: *ka'tende*, "a small lizard."

(150) *CAXINGUELÊ*, any kind of squirrel.
   Kimbundu: *kašin'zeŋgele*, "squirrel."

(151) *KELÉ* (also spelled QUELÉ), a certain kind of climbing bird of Africa and Brazil.
   Kimbundu: *'kēle 'kēle*, "a bird which has a loud call and lives on the river banks."
   Yoruba: *kele*, "a young lizard." (?)

(152) PEPEYÉ, duck.
Yoruba: pɛpɛyɛ, "duck."

(153) ZIMBO, a univalve mollusk, the shell of which was once used for money by the Congolese.
Kikongo: 'nzimbu, "money; beads."

Some names for plants were geographically shifted from one continent to another. In a few cases, however, the plant itself was taken to Brazil, retaining its original name. Informants recognized the following:

(154) BORI, a palm tree.
Swahili: ma'bori, "the fruit of the mkunazi tree." (?) This is probably a chance occurrence.

(155) DENDÊ,* a palm tree which grows abundantly in the Congo and Guinea Coast. It was transported from Africa to Bahia, where it is now very plentiful. Many of the Afro-Bahian dishes listed in the category of food are prepared in the oil extracted from the fruit of this palm. The oil has a thick texture and is dark red in color. It has one of the highest rates of consumption of any of the Afro-Bahian culinary ingredients.
Ngangela: ndende, "palm oil."
Kimbundu: 'ndende, "palm tree."

(156) MACONHA,* a hallucinogenous plant known as Indian hemp. Also used for marijuana.
Kimbundu: ma'kaña, "tobacco."
Tshiluba: ma'kaña, "tobacco."

(157) MULUNGU, the coralbean plant.
Kikongo: mu'luŋgu, "a plant used for medicinal purposes and for witchcraft.

(158) MUTAMBA, the bastard cedar.
Shona: mu'tamba, "a bush-like tree which grows to a height of about twenty feet."

(159) RÔKO (also spelled RÔCO), a very large fig tree.
Yoruba: iroko, "a very large timber tree."

(160) ZANZO, a wild plant called the broomjute sida.
Shona: 'sanzu, "a big branch of a plant."

Four words identified on the questionnaires are names for dwelling places:

>(161) *CUBATA,* a shack where black slaves used to live, very similar to the *senzala.* The *cubata* was considered a very filthy place to live.
>Gɛ̃ (Ewe): *kubaλa,* "to lie in agony."

>(162) *QUILOMBO,* * a hiding place deep in the jungle where runaway slaves used to congregate and establish small communities.
>Kimbundu: *ki'lombo,* "house."

>(163) *SENZALA,* * the plantations' slave quarters where Negroes had to live under very cramped and filthy conditions. [47]
>Kimbundu: *sa'nzala,* "village."

>(164) *TATA,* a small fortified village where several chieftains live with their families and flocks.
>Ewe: *tatɔ,* "chief." (?)

Names of African languages and tribes were checked by Bahian informants:

>(165) *CABINDA,* the language of a group in Angola belonging to the Bantu.
>KiKongo: *ka'binda,* "a Portuguese-ruled enclave north of the mouth of the Congo River. It is the smallest administrative district of the Portuguese territory of Angola."

>(166) *CASSANGE,* the name of an African tribe.
>KiKongo: *ka'sanzi,* "a tribe in Angola living between the Tala Mungongo depression and the Kuangu River, east of Malange." [48]

>(167) *IJEXÁ* * (also spelled *IJESHÁ*), [49] an eastern kingdom of the Yoruba nation.
>Ijesha: *ijɛ'ša,* "the Ijesha people, part of the Yoruba nation."

---

[47] See Gilberto Freire's *Casa Grande e Senzala.*
[48] See L. Turner, op. cit., p. 106.
[49] See Chapters II and III, and Samuel Johnson, op. cit., p. 20.

(168) *NAGÔ*,*[50] the Yoruba.
    Fon (Ewe): *nago*, "the Yoruba language."
    Ewe: *anago*, "Yoruba."

Afro-Brazilian terms with sexual denotions are:

(169) *BINGA*,[51] a man whose wife betrays him by having sexual relationships with someone else. The active word in Bahia for cuckold is *cabrão*.
    Kimbundu: *'mbiŋga*, "an animal horn; the vagina." Both meanings fit the Brazilian significance well. In the Latin tradition (especially Portuguese and Spanish) the horns of an animal are generally placed above the door of a cuckold. The meaning "vagina" is self-explanatory.

(170) *COMBOÇA*, a "lover."
    Tiv: *kombo*, "the various magic articles for producing fertility."

(171) *QUENGA*, a prostitute.
    Bobangi: *'ŋkeŋgɔ*, "a perforated bowl."
    An extension of connotative meaning is possible in this case.
    Kimbundu: *'keŋga*, "to be concave."
    Again, extension of meaning is possible.

Several vocabulary items belong in the category of undesirable persons:

(172) *BAMBAMBÃ*, a braggart or loudmouth.
    Vai: *gbaŋ gbaŋ*, "loudly."
    Tiv: *bãm* (possible reduplication), "a contentious person."

(173) *CAFUÇU*, a worthless person.
    Nupe: *kafunči*, "a lazy person."

(174) *MANGÔLÔ*, an extremely lazy person.
    Kimbundu: *ma'ŋgoña*, "laziness, worthlessness." (?)

---

[50] See Chapters II and III.
[51] *Binga* may also mean a bag of water or a type of animal horn.

(175) *MANZANZA*, a foolish, indolent person.
    Shona: '*nzenza*, "foolish," with Bantu plural prefix *ma-*

Names for individuals who may be considered sneaky in certain aspects:

(176) *CAPIANGO*, an extremely dexterous thief.
    Kikongo: *kapi'aŋgu*, "thief."

(177) *CAXINGUELÊ*,* [52] a meddlesome, intrusive individual.
    Kimbundu: *kašin'zeŋgele*, "squirrel."
    Possible extension of meaning.

People of extraordinary traits:

(178) *BAMBA*, anyone who is admired because of some capacity possessed.
    Kimbundu: '*pamba*, "to be prominent, salient, important."
    Nupe: *bāga*, "belovèd." (?)
    Kikongo: '*bamba*, "middleman in trade; a native broker." (?)
    Mang'anja: '*bambo*, "a title of respect."
    Cinyanja: '*bambo*, "master" (used for addressing someone).

(179) *FIOTA*, a dandy or dude.
    Ewe: *fiɔdua*, "rich."
    Gẽ (Ewe): *fiɔfitɔ*, "thief." (?)

Undesirable or impudent traits, actions, and attitudes:

(180) *CAFANGA*, an outward display of scorn or disdain for something which has been offered to someone.
    Kimbundu: *ka'foka*, "to become angry."

(181) *CANDONGA*, false affections; flattery.
    Kimbundu: *ka'ndoka*, "to be bold."
    Possible extension of meaning.

---

[52] See word number 150 of this chapter.

LEXICAL AFRICANISMS IN BAHIAN PORTUGUESE 155

(182) CHICANA,* behavior indicating that one does not believe what another says. The expression used with this word is *agir por meio de chicana*. (to act doubtingly)
Hausa: *an 'šika 'hanya*, "the way has been missed." This expression could have been reduced to [ši'kana] very easily.
Kikongo: *ši'kama*, "to awake, be aroused." (?)

(183) INGANJA,*⁵³ a reaction causing an uproar over some insignificant thing which had long been forgotten by everyone. The common expression is *fazer inganja*.
Kimbundu: *'ŋganzi*, "pain; anger." (?)

(184) MUNGANGA,* funny or "smart" faces.
Mang'anja: *mu'ŋguña*, "to pout the lips."

(185) QUISILA, a superstitious antipathy which many Afro-Brazilians hold concerning certain foods and actions. Any prejudice or antipathy toward anything in general.
Kimbundu: *ki'sola*, "love." This may be a possible reversal of meaning.

Words denoting physical imperfections or sickness:

(186) CAOLHO,* a one-eyed person.
Hausa: *kal'o*, "gaze, stare."

(187) CARCUNDA,*⁵⁴ hunchback.
Kimbundu: *kari'kunda*, "hunchback."

(188) MONDRONGO,* an extremely fat, heavy person.
Shona: *mo'ndoro*, "huge in size."

As might be expected, names for evil spirits stem from African vocabulary:

(189) CAPÊTA,* a small demon.
Igbo: *ŋkapI*, "mouse" plus *nta*, "small," (?) *ŋkapI nta* > *ka'pIta* > *ka'peta* (?)
Mang'anja: *ka'peta*, "a kind of mouse." (?)

---

⁵³ See word number 123 of this chapter.
⁵⁴ See word number 116 of this chapter.

(190) *ZUMBI,* * a mummified dead body which walks around at night.
Kikongo: *'nsumbi,* "devil." [55]
Tiv: *sumbe,* "an evil-smelling tree-cat." (?)

Places which are dark and dismal also form part of the Afro-Brazilian vocabulary:

(191) *CAFUA,* * any enclosed, dark room.
Kikongo: *'kafua,* "someone who has died and gone to a dark place." The word is part of an enfatic expression, *'kafua 'kwandi.* The word *'kafua* stems from *fua,* "dead."
KiKongo: *ka'fwalala,* "dark, somber." (?)

(192) *CAFUINHA,* * the diminutive of *cafua.* A small room which served as a kind of prison for bad students in the schools of past centuries.

(193) *CAFURNA,* any dark, damp room, similar to that of a dungeon.
Hausa: *kafau,* "mire, swamp." (?)
It could stem from Kikongo *'kafua.*

Words falling under the category of noise and commotion:

(194) *FUÃ,* noise caused by a fight or brawl.
Kikongo: *'fwa,* "noise."
Gũ (Ewe): *fũ ahwa,* "to undertake in warfare." (?)

(195) *FUZUÉ,* confusion or any disturbance of the peace.
Nupe: *fuši,* "anger, rage." (?)

(196) *MIRONGA,* any kind of fight, usually involving the fists.
Kimbundu: *mi'lɔŋga,* "disputes."

(197) *MUXINGA,* a beating or spanking; a whip.
KiKongo: *mu'singa,* "whip, cord, rope."
Shona: *mu'šiŋgwa,* "one that endures." (?)

---

[55] See Robert A. Hall, Jr., *Pidgin and Creole Languages* (Ithaca: 1969), p. 92.

(198) **SANGANGU**, a great amount of disorder in a large crowd of people, generally involving fist fights, etc.
Ngangela: *saŋgu'muna*, "to provoke disorder."
Kimbundu: *saŋgu'luka*, "to frolic." (?)
Kimbundu: *'saŋga*, "to dance." (?)
Shona: *sa'ŋgano*, "a large gathering of people."
Kikongo: *'saŋga*, "the clamor of warriors; to leap with joy; to mix." (?)
Mang'anja: *saŋga'niza*, "to mix, confuse."

Lexical items for receptacles are entered in another category:

(199) **CAÇUA**,* a basket used to carry merchandise on horseback.
Hausa: *kasuwa*, "a market in which some special article is sold." (?)
Tiv: *kasua*, "a market." The Tiv is a borrowing from the Hausa.

(200) **CAPANGAS**,* a sack or bag, usually made of leather, used on the *sertão* (backlands) for various purposes.
Kikongo: *ka'paŋga*, "the name of a town in the Congo, east of the Lulua River, in the southern province of Katanga." (?)

(201) **GONGA**, a small basket with a top.
Kimbundu: *'koŋga*, "a gourd shaped like a bottle." (?)

Parts of the human body:

(202) **BIMBA**, the penis of a small child; the thigh.
Ngangela: *mbimba*, "cork." (?)
Kimbundu: *'mbinda*, "reed, pole." (?)

(203) **BUNDA**,* the rear end, buttocks.
Kimbundu: *'mbunda*, "buttocks."

Terms for money:

(204) **JIMBO**, money.
Kimbundu: *'nzimbu*, "beads, money."
Kinkongo: *ŋkua 'jimbu*, "rich."

(205) *TUTU*,* money.
   Yoruba: *otutu*, "green beads used as a form of money. The devotees of the god Sọpọna (small pox) receive them as part of payment for having buried someone who died of small pox." [56]

Names of chiefs or people in head positions:

(206) *GUNGA*, chief; the head man; ranch foreman; "big shot."
   Kimbundu: *'ŋguŋgu*, "magnate, rich person."
   Umbundu: *'ŋguŋga*, "an only son." (?)

(207) *SOBA*, the chief of an African tribe; a bossy person.
   Kimbundu: *'soba*, "a native chief."
   Kikongo: *'soba*, "chief."

Terms for members of the family:

(208) *CAÇULA*,* the youngest child of a family, the "baby."
   Ngangela: *kasule*, "an adopted child."

(209) *MABAÇA*,* twin.
   Kikongo: *ma'pasa*, "twin."
   Shona: *ma'pačka*, "twins."

(210) *MUCAMA*,* the favorite slave girl of the master of the big house on Brazilian plantations of the 18th and 19th centuries.
   Fulani: *makama*, "formerly, one of the Emir's chief slaves who acted as almoner."
   KiKongo: *mu'kami*, "pupil, small child, orphan." (?)
   Shona: *mu'koma*, "a way of paying respect to a more important person." The idea being that the slave girl in question was more "important" than the other slaves. (?)
   Kikongo: *ma'kama*, "dowry." (?)

The final category is that of miscelaneous items which do not fit into any of the above groupings:

---

[56] See S. Johnson, op. cit., p. 28.

LEXICAL AFRICANISMS IN BAHIAN PORTUGUESE 159

(211) *BENGALA,** cane, walking stick.
Kimbundu: *mba'ŋgala,* "a stick."

(212) *CABALA,** a swear word.
Bambara: *kabala,* "admirer." (?)
Mende: *kabala,* "roasted cassava and groundnuts beaten together." (?)
Tshiluba: *kabala,* "a native wooden sandal." (?)

(213) *CACHIMBO,** pipe.
Kimbundu: *kašimbu,* "pipe."
Mang'anja: *ka'šimbo,* "pipe."

(214) *CAFIFA,* chance, luck.
Hausa: *kafi, kafe,* "a charm used to establish the prosperity of a house, town, etc."

(215) *CAMBONDO,* a very close friend.
Kimbundu: *'kamba,* "a friend." (?)

(216) *CAXINJE ᔕ CAXIXE,* swindling.
Hausa: *kaši,* "a violent beating; a killing." (?)

(217) *ENGOIO,* the act of becoming sad or downhearted.
Kikongo: *'ŋgawa,* "sad, sorrowful."

(218) *FULO,** a Negro who is light in color.
This no doubt refers to the Fulanese people, who are generally light in color.

(219) *IXES,* manual labor.
Yoruba: *išɛ,* "work."

(220) *MATACA,* soil in which Kaffir corn has been planted.
Lingala: *ma'taka,* "soil."
Shona: *ma'daka,* "muddy soil."

(221) *QUITANDA,** a vegetable and fruit store.
Kikongo: *ki'tanda ka mu'lele,* "a package of materials, fabrics." (?)
Kimbundu: *ki'tanda,* "the Portuguese language and customs." (?)

(222) *TITICA,** dung.
Kimbundu: *'titi,* "refuse."

(223) *XARÁ,* namesake.
Yoruba: *ara,* "relative." (?)

It is interesting to note that of the 217 vocabulary entries in this chapter, about 50% of the suggested African origins appear to be relatively well established. This percentage is divided between Yoruba on the one hand, and Kimbundu-Kikongo on the other hand. There are also a few etymologies that seem rather clearly to be either Ewe, Hausa, or Akan.

The problem of intonation in Brazilian Portuguese is a very delicate one which needs much careful study. Melville J. Herskovits, in *The Myth of the Negro Past*, discusses the fate of the tonal elements of West African speech in the New World. He writes that

> ... it is a most difficult problem requiring a long-term and highly technical analysis of Negro speech in various parts of the New World. That the peculiarly "musical" quality of Negro English as spoken in the United States and the same trait found in the speech of white Southerners represent a non-functioning survival of this characteristic of African languages is entirely possible, especially since this same "musical" quality is prominent in Negro-English and Negro-French everywhere. [57]

The "musical" quality which Professor Herskovits noted in Negro-English and Negro-French is also found in Bahian Portuguese. As a matter of fact, one can hear this "musicality" in all areas of Brazil where there are heavy concentrations of blacks and mulattoes, such as the states of Bahia, Guanabara, Rio de Janeiro, Sergipe, Pernambuco, etc. In these areas, the "musicality" is perceived as a very wide range of pitches which rise and fall to a relatively great degree, even within short utterances, especially when compared to the Portuguese spoken in other areas of the country, such as Rio Grande do Sul, or that of Portugal, where the absence of such wide pitch variations is easily noticeable. Whether or not this phenomenon is due to the influence of phonemic tonal elements which were present in the African tongues brought to Brazil remains to be seen. A comparison of Negro-Brazilian Portuguese (that Portuguese spoken by Brazilians in areas where the percentage of blacks is high) to the rest of the Portuguese spoken in Brazil (where the Negro influence has been minimal) and to the language as it is found in Portugal, would certainly seem to

---

[57] (New York: 1941), p. 291.

indicate that the African tonal systems influenced Brazilian intonation patterns in the areas where the black slave trade flourished.

Curiously enough, there is a place on the Atlantic coast of Colombia called Palenque, which was one of the earliest congregations of run-away slaves in the New World. [58] These slaves were brought from approximately the same geographical areas in West African as those which were taken to Brazil. The Spanish of the *palenqueros* who live in Palenque today is notably marked by a similar degree of wide variations in musical pitches as that noted in areas of high black population in Brazil. This linguistic peculiarity helps strengthen the theory that the sub-Saharan tone languages may have influenced the intonation patterns of the Portuguese language in certain sections of Brazil, as they seem to have done in Palenque.

The information on intonation found in Lorenzo Turner's book, *Africanisms in the Gullah Dialect,* also suggests that African tone languages may have been instrumental in causing the intonation in Gullah to appear "strange," as the author states.

No matter what these above observations seem to indicate, the fact of the matter is that no definite conclusions can be drawn from present data concerning the influences of African tonal languages on Indo-European languages since these data are highly subjective in nature. Only careful studies carried out with the aid of the good ear of a linguist acquainted with a variety of African tone languages will be able to yield positive results in helping to solve this most intriguing problem.

---

[58] See Roberto Arrázola, *Palenque, primer pueblo libre de América* (Cartagena, Colombia: 1970).

Chapter V

THE BAHIAN PEOPLE AND THEIR LANGUAGE IN DIFFERENT LEVELS OF SOCIETY

The first phase of ethnic encounters between the Portuguese and the West Africans taken to Brazil as slaves was characterized by contrasts that were not truly social, since these persons with different racial and cultural backgrounds were not members of the same moral order. Even if it is true that they considered each other quite odd, the African slave being on the defensive side and the Portuguese master on the offensive one, they no doubt regarded one another as something less than completely human. The first conflicts which developed, then, between these two distinct peoples in Brazil, were on a biological level. Certain physical changes were imposed on the slaves by the dominating Portuguese and during the period of these changes, there were symbiotic relations established on American soil between the European and the African. Out of such relations there evolved an ecological organization that took the shape of racial divisions of labor, which, in turn, affected the ethno-economic structure of Brazilian society in that the Negro found himself at the poverty end of the economic spectrum and the white European took complete control of the opposite portion of this spectrum. Moreover, in as much as the racial divisions of labor are part of an impersonal process, the labor status of the black race in Brazil was determined by certain socially acquired characteristics. The habits and attitudes of the slaves, which occupied a certain caste position in the society, are the direct result of psychological and social adaptations to their status.[1]

---

[1] See Florestan Fernandes, *A Integração do Negro à Sociedade de Classes* (São Paulo: 1964).

Coming from relatively sophisticated cultures, however, the Negroes were able to maintain certain personal qualities in the face of the European culture. As Melville J. Herskovits so adroitly states in *The Myth of the Negro Past,* concerning the black men:

> Instead of representing isolated cultures, their endowments, however different in detail, possessed least common denominators that permitted a consensus of experience to be drawn on in fashioning new, though still Africanlike, customs. The presence of members of native ruling houses and priests and diviners among the slaves made it possible for the cultural lifeblood to coagulate through reinterpretation instead of ebbing away into the pool of European culture. In some parts of the New World full-blown African civilizations resulted from successful revolts which permitted the establishment of independent or quasi-independent Negro communities. Elsewhere the process of acculturation resulted in varied degrees of reinterpretation of African custom in the light of new situations. [2]

Concerning the process of acculturation as experienced by the Negro in America under the bonds of enslavement, Herskovits brings out some very important and basic facts which must be considered when studying the ethnolinguistic and socio-economic interchange among whites, mulattoes and Negroes in Brazil. He writes the following, while discussing some of the stereotyped misinterpretations of the Negro and his culture as seen in a predominantly white society:

> As has been indicated, the current point of view, which emphasizes the acquiescence of the Negro to slavery, is an integral part of the "mythology" sketched in our opening pages. As such, it reinforces certain attitudes toward the Negro and is thus of practical as well as scientific importance, the latter deriving principally from the fact that this phase of the Negro past aids in understanding the rate and the nature of the acculturative process prior to the abolition of slavery. Slaves who acquiesced in their status would be more prone to accept the culture of their masters than those who rebelled; hence, if the slaves were restless, as recent studies have indicated, and if this restlessness caused revolt to be endemic in the New World, then the reluctance to accept slave status might also have encouraged the slaves to retain

---

[2] (New York: 1941), p. 297.

what they could of African custom to a greater extent than would otherwise have been the case.[3]

The last statement of this quotation may help to explain one of the basic reasons for the retention and spread in Bahian society of the *candomblé* and other of the West African elements identified here. It must be remembered, when attempting to decipher why so much of the African influence found in white society has come from the religious angle of Negro culture, that, as Herskovits states, "underlying the life of the American Negro is a deep religious bent that is but the manifestation here of the similar drive that, everywhere in Negro societies, makes the supernatural a major focus of interest."[4]

Another very important principle, functional in Negro cultures, which surely contributed toward the preservation and penetration of African elements into American society, is discussed by Professor Herskovits:

> A factor of importance, consistently unrecognized in evaluating the acculturative process operative among the Negroes, has been found to be the African traditional attitude toward what is new, what is foreign. Aboriginally manifested most strongly in the field of religion, where both conquered and conquerors often took over the gods of their opponents, it has operated to endow the African with a psychological resilience in facing new situations that has proved of good stead in his New World experience. To term an old deity by a new name is but one manifestation of a device which, in the field of social organization, has made for disregard of European sanctions underlying family structure while accepting European terminology relating to the family; for the adaptation of African patterns of mutual self-help in matters pertaining to death to outward Euro-American conventions of lodges and funerals; for the reworking of song and dance in accordance with the demands of the new setting. In instance after instance that has been cited from the literature bearing on the highly acculturated Negroes of the United States, it has been demonstrated how a proper assessing of these vestigial forms of African practice has led to the recognition of slightly modified African sanctions supporting forms of a given institution that are almost entirely European. This principle of disregard for outer form while retaining

---

[3] *Myth*, p. 86.
[4] *Myth*, p. 207.

inner values, characteristic of Africans everywhere, is thus revealed as the most important single factor making for an understanding of the acculturative situation. That it reveals intellectual sophistication rather than naïveté negates the proposition in the mythology which holds that the force of superior European custom was so overwhelming that nothing of Africa could stand in the face of it. [5]

These basic truths concerning African influences in a predominantly European-type culture will aid us in our understanding of some of the reasons for the presence of black vestiges in Brazilian language and culture. We may see then, in a general and panoramic way, how and why the African slaves that were brought to Brazil, were able to preserve many of their ethnolinguistic habits, and how some of these habits became an integral part of the Brazilian society, especially in Bahia.

This socio-linguistic situation in the state of Bahia manifests its own peculiarities, slightly different from those in the rest of Brazil. Speech patterns and vocabulary usages vary in accordance with the degree of African penetration into the three main social classes of the city. Since historically the black has spent most of his time at the bottom of the social scale because of the long period of slavery he had to suffer, membership in the high ranks of society has been much more difficult for him to attain than for the white person, who already held a high position upon arriving in Brazil. Those African linguistic characteristics which became an integral part of Bahian Portuguese in particular and of Brazilian Portuguese in general, had to filter upward from the lower to the higher classes. As a linguistic phenomenon this infiltration of languages which were considered culturally and socially inferior to the conquering language, represents somewhat of a victory of the "inferior" language over the dominant one. Ordinarily one might expect the resulting linguistic situation in Bahia to be similar to that of the African or Indian languages vis-à-vis the English language in the United States. African influence on Bahian Portuguese is, however, relatively great in comparison to the African or Indian influence on English in the United States. [6]

---

[5] *Myth*, pp. 297, 298.
[6] Perhaps one could compare African influences in Bahia to those on English in the Gullah dialect found in South Carolina and Georgia. This dialect is studied thoroughly by Lorenzo D. Turner in his book, *Africanisms*

THE BAHIAN PEOPLE AND THEIR LANGUAGE 167

Perhaps the explanation for the admittance of such a comparatively large amount of African vocabulary into Bahian Portuguese can be found in the psychological nature of the Portuguese people and in their attitude toward miscegenation. As Gilberto Freire so graphically points out in his *Casa Grande e Senzala*, the Portuguese colonizer, in contrast to the Spanish, English, French or Dutch, was the one who best succeeded in fraternizing with members of what were considered to be inferior races. The greater social, cultural and psychological plasticity of the Portuguese enabled him to realize an innate inclination toward intimate contacts with the people of other lands.

The mating in Brazil of Portuguese men with African women, which was a general practice during colonial times because of the scarcity of white European women, may have been facilitated by the fact that many of the early colonizers were Mozarabs [7] from the southern part of Portugal, who were dark in color and perhaps, therefore, not so "racially conscious" as the lighter Portuguese. The genealogical constitution of the Portuguese conqueror already contained many African characteristics even before his arrival in Brazil. This Portuguese disposition to welcome intermixture with the African greatly enhanced the possibilities for linguistic interchange.

Portuguese influences on the Africans taken to Brazil were also very strong. The amalgamation which resulted from this Portuguese-African contact was partly due to a friendly type of personal relationship between the two cultures, but more so to the Portuguese acceptance of intimate relations with other races. In Brazil, especially in Bahia, relatively little hostility on the part of the Portuguese toward their black slaves has been noted by historians of colonial times. [8]

In chapter five of Sir Harry H. Johnston's *The Negro in the New World* there is a discussion of the relatively benign treatment that the black slaves received in Brazil. This information is corroborated in Pierre Verger's *Flux et Reflux....* For example, on page 489 of the edition previously cited, we find the following:

---

in the Gullah Dialect (New York: 1969). According to Turner, this dialect has a substantial amount of influence from many of the languages of West Africa.

[7] Mozarab-Luso-Hispanic Christians living under Arab rule on the Iberian Peninsula. Many of these people were darker in skin color than the average Iberian owing to inter-marriage with the conquering Arabs.

[8] See Gilberto Freire, *Casa Grande e Senzala*, and Donald Pierson, *Negroes in Brazil*.

Les documents les plus connus traitant de la situation des Africains esclaves et affranchis dans la société brésilienne sont les récits des voyageurs. Ces "etrangers" de passage, citoyens de pays dans les colonies desquels l'esclavage avait été aboli, professaient en général des idées "philanthropiques" avec d'autant plus d'ardeur que la conversion de leur propre pays à ces principes généreux était de date récente. Leurs écrits sont teintés en général de ce vertueux point de vue.

Parmi les voyageurs qui ont échappé à ces excès, on peut retenir quelques citations de certains d'entre eux.

Thomas Lindley écrivait en 1802: "Au souvenir des derniers événements de Saint-Domingue (Haiti) et en raison des très nombreux eslaves qu'il y a au Brésil, on pourrait penser que la tranquillité publique pourrait être troublée. Mais c'était de loin le contraire, car toutes licences y était tolérées, et les nègres y sont joyeux et contents, n'étant pas surmenés de travail, et disposant de la même nourriture que dans leur pays d'origine."

(The best-known documents dealing with the situation of African slaves and free blacks in Brazilian society are the accounts of travelers. These "strangers" who visit, citizens of countries the colonies of which have abolished slavery, generally profess Philanthropic ideas with much more ardour than [they do when speaking of] the conversion of their own country to these noble principles, which occurred fairly recently. Their writings in general are tainted with this virtuous point of view.

Among the travelers who have not exaggerated the matter, one can find certain quotes [which enlighten us as to the situation].

Thomas Lindley wrote in 1802: "Opon remembering the latest happenings in Santo Domingo (Haiti) and because of the very large numbers of slaves in Brazil, one would think that the public tranquility would be disturbed. But this is not the case at all, since all kinds of permissiveness was tolerated here, and the blacks are very happy since they are not overworked and have the same kinds of food that they had in their native land.")

The following paragraphs of this chapter in Verger's book contain quotes of the same tone as this one. They all point to the fact that the black slaves in Brazil were, on the whole, treated much better than in other parts of Latin America, North America or Europe.

It is interesting to note, at the same time, that Charles R. Boxer in an article titled "Negro Slavery in Brazil" in *Race* (the Journal of

THE BAHIAN PEOPLE AND THEIR LANGUAGE 169

the Institute of Race Relations), London, 1964, calls attention to an anonymous pamphlet, the *Nova e Curiosa Relação*, which he refers to as "one of the few works printed in the eighteenth century which criticise the mistreatment of Negro slaves in Brazil." (p. 38)

There is no doubt about the fact that the black slaves were mistreated in Brazil, but if so few documents as the one discussed by Boxer here can be found, then one could assume that the need to criticise the mistreatment of slaves in Brazil was not of great magnitude because the mistreatment itself was not of such a nature that would warrant heavy amounts of criticism. This corroborates the relatively humane treatment of slaves which was observed by the travelers mentioned in Verger's book.

It is also equally interesting to note that on comparing certain methods of torture of slaves used in different parts of the New World, one immediately becomes aware of the fact that the Portuguese were not as savage-like in their "torture chambers" as were the Spanish, French, British, and especially the Dutch (see Sir Harry H. Johnston, *The Negro in the New World*).

One of the circumstances in Bahia which has greatly favored white-black miscegenation has been the congenial attitude taken by white males of upper-class families toward sexual affairs with their black or mulatto servant girls. This type of intermingling continues today and has broadened into what Brazilian sociologists call *mancebia*, that is, extra-conjugal unions in which there is a certain degree of permanency. Also, many pre-marital informal unions are entered into by young men and women of all colors, and these unions contribute further to the racial mixture of the Brazilian population. In Bahia miscegenation is also facilitated by the desire which many Negro women have to bear children lighter than themselves, since they feel that this will help the child to attain a higher social and economic status within the community.

The most obvious effect of racial mixture has been to reduce physical differences. With this reduction there has come a great affinity among all Brazilians toward a leveling process, which has aided in the cultural, social and linguistic acceptance of each other's ways of life. This breaking down of the color line, then, permitted the prestige language, namely Portuguese, to become peppered with many lexical items from the so-called and so-considered "inferior" languages of the Negro slaves.

A very good way to understand how the process of miscegenation has helped to reduce social, psychological, cultural, and linguistic barriers is to compare race relations in Brazil and in the United States. If this is done, it becomes apparent that the creation of the mulatto in Brazil affords unique possibilities for the realization of cross-cultural phenomena. Carl N. Degler, in his book *Neither Black nor White* has defined the "catalyst" of this cultural "symbiosis" as what he terms "the mulatto escape hatch." Degler states the following concerning this:

> The key that unlocks the puzzle of the differences in race relations in Brazil and the United States is the mulatto escape hatch. Complex and varied as the race relations in the two countries have been and are today, the presence of a separate place for the mulatto in Brazil and its absence in the United States nevertheless define remarkably well the heart of the difference. Let us look for a moment at some of the ways in which the mulatto escape hatch distinguishes race patterns in Brazil and the United States.
>
> The existence of the mulatto, for example, makes most difficult, if not impossible, the kind of segregation patterns that have been so characteristic of the United States. With many shades of skin color, segregating people on the basis of color would incur both enormous expense and great inconvenience. Facilities, for instance, would have to be duplicated several times, beyond reason and financial feasibility. Furthermore, in a society in which distinctions are made among a variety of colors, rather than by race as in the United States, families would be split by the color line. Children of mulattoes, after all, vary noticeably in color. In view of the high value that western society places upon the nuclear family it would be neither practical nor likely that a system of segregation that would disrupt families would be permitted to develop. Moreover, in a society in which the mulatto has a special place, a racist defense of slavery or of Negro inferiority cannot easily develop, for how can one think consistently of a white "race" or a Negro "race" when the lines are blurred by the mulatto? The search for purity of race is thus frustrated before it begins. Similarly, the existence of the mulatto escape hatch helps to explain why relations between the races in Brazil have been less rigid and less prone to hostility than in the United States. The presence of the mulatto not only spreads people of color through the society, but it literally blurs and thereby softens the line between black and white. To seek out the origins of

the mulatto as a socially accepted type in Brazil, then, is to be on the trail of the origins of significant differences in the race relations of Brazil and the United States.

... ...

Put another way, I am contending that when a society develops a place for the mulatto, as occurred in Brazil, then certain other responses to the presence of black men in a white-dominated society, such as those that were worked out in the United States, for example, are foreclosed. The mulatto escape hatch serves as a symbol, actually a condensation of a range of relationships between blacks and whites and of attitudes toward one another. If we focus attention upon that symbol and seek to explain its historical development, then an explanation for the whole range of social attitudes and behavioral patterns for which that symbol stands is also accounted for.

It is in that sense that I call the mulatto escape hatch the key to the difference between race relations in the United States and Brazil. It does not encompass all that we want explained, but it is a crucial part of the answer. [9]

Bahian society exemplifies that kind of social stratification in which racial and ethnic variables do not have so heavy a bearing on the criteria for status as may be noted in other parts of Brazil, especially in the Southern states, and in many sections of Spanish America. It is a multiracial class society; the fact of being a Negro, although still a handicap to marriage into the upper classes, which because of historical factors are predominantly white, is not an absolute barrier against rising socially and may be overcome with the help of such assets as wealth, intelligence or occupational proficiency. The first of these assets carries the most weight in such matters.

Two important studies concerning race relations in Brazil will help demonstrate the apparent wane in racial prejudices evidenced here. The first, titled "Racial Identity in Brazil," by Marvin Harris, while admitting that the alleged absence of "barriers of racial prejudice" is in reality a myth, also concludes that "the larger significance of confusion about racial identity in Bahia is that it clearly precludes systematic discrimination and segregation." [10] According to Harris'

---

[9] (New York: 1971), pp. 224, 225.
[10] In *Luso-Brazilian Review*, Winter, 1964, University of Wisconsin Press, p. 28.

study, racial identity in Brazil involves a very complicated set of calculations. Concerning Bahia, the author states that he is "of the opinion that we shall never be able to state the general cognitive formula by which particular Brazilians assign a racial identity to themselves, or by which particular Brazilians are assigned a racial identity by others." [11] As part of a survey carried out in a small fishing village twenty-five miles north of Salvador, Bahia, Harris elicited forty different racial terms from a set of nine portrait drawings, each varying in degree of hair color, texture, nasal and lip width and skin tone. This confusion of nomenclature was compounded by the fact that the informants describing the drawings were found to be in disagreement when asked to describe the abstract qualities designated by a particular term. From this and other impressions gathered in the state of Bahia, Harris states that "the use of racial terms appears to vary from individual to individual, from place to place, time to time, test to test, observer to observer." [12]

The author concludes that "ambiguity, both of a definitional and referential sort, appears to be built into the meanings of these terms, and is in a sense a more important feature of the system than the attention which is supposed to be paid to actual physical appearance." [13] It is interesting to note, at this point, that Harris draws a parallel between the "semantic confusion surrounding the racial identity of the people of Arembepe" and the "actual behavior" of these people. According to the author's observations, "race is not a vital issue at any point in the life cycle ... Under these circumstances, ambiguity about racial identity is probably an ideological manifestation of the egalitarian patterns which predominate in the fishing industry upon which the life of the community depends." [14]

The second article, by Conrad P. Kottak, poses the same problem as the one by Harris, and its author arrives at very similar conclusions. Kottak also studies racial terminology and classification as seen in Arembepe, Bahia. He states that

> ... the data presented in this paper indicate that neither from observer's nor actor's point of view is race an important

---

[11] "Racial Identity," p. 23.
[12] "Racial Identity," p. 27.
[13] "Racial Identity," p. 27.
[14] "Racial Identity," p. 27.

focus of life in Arembepe. This is suggested by the profound ambiguity which pervades the entire system of racial classification, by the fluidity of racial terminology in exactly that area in which most Arembepeiros would be classified, and by the fact that this fluidity indicates semantic blurring and the inability of terms to designate significant structural groups. [15]

Kottak then extends the Arembepe example to the whole of Brazil, concluding that the situation in this small Bahian village "should indicate that there is a good deal of explicable variation in awareness and expertise throughout Brazil. Brazilian racial nomenclature," he concludes, "which is admittedly as rich in Arembepe as anywhere else in Brazil, simply reflects a more sensible way of treating the tremendous range of phenotypes normally encountered in any human population than the American system which recognizes only two social races." [16]

Even though Kottak admits that the size of the Brazilian racial vocabulary is important, in conjunction with what Charles Wagley in his "On the Concept of Social Race in the Americas," [17] has written, namely that "a social system which includes a large number of social racial categories in its terminology is incompatible with intense racial discrimination," he states that the most important variable to be considered when explaining differences in racial terminology in Brazil "is not the size of the racial vocabulary... but the efficacy of this vocabulary in designating socially significant groups..." [18] "How could segregation possibly exist," he writes, "how could there be directed discrimination, if the members of the unit in question are unable to decide on which groups they are to discriminate against and on what the constituency of these groups is?" [19]

Although this may be the case in Arembepe, the lack of racial prejudice here is certainly not as great in other parts of the state of Bahia, especially in the city of Salvador. As the famed anthropologist

---

[15] "Race Relations in a Bahian Fishing Village," in *Luso-Brazilian Review*, Vol. IV, No. 2, December 1967, p. 49.
[16] "Race Relations," p. 50.
[17] *Actas* from the 33rd International Congress of Americanists, San José, Lehmann I, pp. 403-417.
[18] "Race Relations," p. 50.
[19] "Race Relations," p. 50.

Thales de Azevedo has stated very well in his book, *As Elites de Côr*, racial antagonism does exist in Bahia, among the mulattoes and the blacks as well as among the lighter population, even though it is true that this tension is not as strongly felt in Bahia as in other parts of Brazil.

Yet the fact remains that since a black cannot escape the color he was born with, he immediately tends to be categorized as a member of the low status group, even in Bahia. The reasons behind such class distinctions, which at first sight seem to be directly based on racial attributes (yet upon closer consideration are found not to be) may be made clearer by examination of the unique perspective of status groups into which Bahian society split during colonial days and through most of the 19th century. These corresponded to lines of race and color as well as to position in economic stratifications. [20]

The main criterion for social classification during the slave-holding period was the distinction between free man and slave. Since the former were white and the latter either Indian or black, physical type and ethnic origin became such important factors of class significance that they themselves were indicative of status. The prevailing economic system of colonial Brazil did not allow for any other way of life. As Fernando de Azevedo so succinctly states concerning this situation:

> Since Brazil's first social classification was based upon pigment, this distinction of classes established on an economic basis met in the distinction of races a material and visible sign of differentiation. Lords and slaves, whites and Negroes. The races, white and African, formed an ethnic stratification, the layers of which correspond exactly, as you see, to social stratification, to the two classes with the plantation system of monoculture and the slave system separated and superimposed, raising the lords of the sugar plantations to the category of nobility, and degrading to the lowest level the masses of slaves. [21]

---

[20] For detailed information concerning the historical background of racial prejudices in Bahia, in particular, and in Brazil in general, see Charles Wagley, *Race and Class in Rural Brazil* (Holland, UNESCO: 1952), pp. 143-154, Charles Wagley, *An Introduction to Brazil* (New York, Columbia University Press: 1963), pp. 134-146, and Jorge Prado Teixeira and Rubens da Silva Gordo, "O Negro — O Preconceito — Meios de Sua Extinção," in *O Negro Revoltado* (Rio de Janeiro, Edições GRD: 1968), pp. 75-89.

[21] Fernando de Azevedo, *Brazilian Culture* (New York, New World: 1950), p. 129 (translation; translator not given).

THE BAHIAN PEOPLE AND THEIR LANGUAGE 175

The population was divided by law and custom into two main racial categories that could not legally mix or mate. Nevertheless, the miscegenation which developed came to weaken the strictness of government policies which had no social justification and did not coincide with the attitudes and behavior of the colonists. Even before the civil authorities decided to act in favor of what was happening, the priests began to bless unions between people of different races. By the second half of the 18th century, the Brazilian colonists, convinced that the best move toward political and moral unity was in the legalization of miscegenation, enacted a decree providing that mulattoes be accepted in civil and military posts. [22] The same decree provided for the legal marriage of whites with mulattoes and blacks. In spite of such governmental enactments, however, there still existed separate brotherhoods and professions for white and black. The struggle upward had not yet ended for the man of color.

This struggle, forming a part of the "racial democracy myth" which may be observed in a general way throughout Brazil, is an important facet of the whole "social disorganization," as Florestan Fernandes terms it, prevalent here. Professor Fernandes, in *The Negro in Brazilian Society*, [23] has made a very complete study of the socio-economic rôles of the white, the mulatto and the black, specifically in São Paulo, and generally in all of Brazil. In order to comprehend the plight of the black man in Bahian society, which is what interests us at present, I should like to reiterate some of the points Fernandes makes in his book, since many of the facts he records are also applicable to the Bahian situation.

Speaking of the assets and liabilities of life in the cities which developed in Brazil during the period between 1880 or so and 1930, Fernandes states that "the advantages offered by urban life to the individual and to the community did not appreciably alter the position

---

[22] For additional information concerning the rise of the mulatto in Brazilian society, see Donald Pierson, "Ascensão Social do Mulato," in *Antologia do Negro Brasileiro* (Rio de Janeiro, Tecnoprint Gráfica, S. A.: 1967), pp. 196-200.

[23] Florestan Fernandes, *The Negro in Brazilian Society* (New York and London, Columbia University Press), a translation, by Jacqueline D. Skiles, A. Brunel, and Arthur Rothwell, of *A Integração do Negro à Sociedade de Classes*.

of the Negro and mulatto in the economic and social levels."[24] Continuing, the author writes the following:

> ...throughout the period under consideration, they [the Negro and the mulatto] remained in the same position in which the emergence of the competitive social order and the urban revolution had found them. They were totally excluded by the new socioeconomic mechanism of occupational screening and thus totally unable to adopt the new patterns of living associated with the more promising and remunerative urban occupations. Strictly speaking, they did not simply remain on the fringes of the process of economic growth... they shared in the occupations and opportunities opened by the urban style of life in such a fashion that they perpetuated the inevitable initial maladjustments derived from the breakdown of the old order and soon were in a state of chronic social disorganization.[25]

Under the socio-economic conditions developing at this time, Fernandes informs us of the following:

> ...that two social groups benefited broadly from the economic, social, and political consequences of industrialization: those who retained the role of capitalist, as owners of developing industries, and those who could sell their labor as workers. Although Brazilian elements existed in both groups, participation of the Negro and mulatto was practically nil. With the exception of rare cases of racial mixture in important families, the advent of urban, industrial capitalism was prejudicial to the independent Negro and mulatto entrepreneurs, who were irremediably ousted from every favorable position they had achieved in the past. As for the free labor market, we have also seen how unfavorable it was to those who came out of slavery or from the free labor associated with slavery.[26]

The fact of the matter is, then, that the black and the mulatto were automatically relegated to the lower level of society, not only in São Paulo, but in Bahia and throughout Brazil. In the third chapter of *The Negro in Brazilian Society*, Fernandes explains the paradoxical situation arising in Brazil which created a racial heteronomy in Brazil-

---

[24] *Negro in Brazilian Society*, p. 72.
[25] *Negro in Brazilian Society*, p. 72.
[26] *Negro in Brazilian Society*, p. 73.

ian class society. Attempting to interpret the white man's reasons for certain racial adjustments during the early 1900's in São Paulo, the author mentions two facts which may also help us in our understanding of the Bahian situation. These are as follows:

> First, the perpetuation of the total set of patterns of race relations that developed under slavery and were so damaging to the black man occurred without the whites having had any fear of the probable economic, social, and political consequences of racial equality and open competition with Negroes. For this reason at the root of this phenomenon there can be found no kind of anxiety or restlessness and no sort of intolerance or racial hatred which these two consequences brought to life in the historical stage of action. Therefore, barriers designed to block the vertical mobility of the Negro were never erected, nor were the measures taken to avert the risks which competition with this racial group might have incurred for the white. [27]

Since it is important to understand the socio-economic developments among whites, mulattoes and blacks in Brazil, I would deem it advantageous at this point to quote a section of Fernandes' work dealing with racial heteronomy. Continuing his discussion of the myth of racial democracy, he expounds upon the reasons for class adjustments among the various "races";

> As paradoxical as it may seem, it was the white man's omission rather than his action that redounded in the perpetuation of the *status quo ante*. It seems that the white man put into practice a limited number of the techniques, institutions, and social values inherent in the competitive social order in fairly restricted and confined sectors (in certain kinds of economic activities, legal relationships, and political privileges of the members of the "upper" class). Thus, the field remained open for the survival *en masse* of patterns of social behavior that were often archaic. Along with these patterns there were passed along the norms of the old pattern of race relations, as well as certain social distinctions and prerogatives, the rights and social guarantees, the stereotypes that served to justify such distinctions and prerogatives racially as well as materially and psychologically. From this perspective the historical weaknesses that sur-

---

[27] *Negro in Brazilian Society*, p. 134.

rounded the formation and initial development of the class system were much more decisive for the preservation of a great part of the old order of race relations than the white's tendency to be on guard against the free Negro. The white purely and simply did not confront this kind of historical alternative — as did occur, for example, in a similar situation in the United States.

Second, these circumstances multiplied the dynamic power of the factors of sociocultural inertia. While at the same time that the white did not feel that he had to compete, contend, and struggle against the Negro, the latter tended to passively accept the continuation of old patterns of racial adjustment. Owing to the sociopathic effects of the permanent social disorganization and deficient social integration, whenever the black man managed to overcome his apathy regarding his own fate, he did so only to become attached to a timid and confused conformism. It was inevitable that orientations that were already established and fairly well rooted in conventional behavior should prevail. During the final breakdown of the old order, the ideological and utopian conceptions of the nucleus of landowners almost imperceptibly governed the readjustment of Negroes and whites among themselves and to the new sociohistorical situation.

... ...

The political philosophy of the solution to the Negro problem was based on the old pattern of gradual absorption of black people through the selection and assimilation of those who showed themselves to identify most with the ruling circles of the dominant race and manifest complete loyalty to their interests and social values. Expectations and conceptions of this nature were in unavoidable conflict with the existing social order and could never function as a bridge of understanding between the races in the new socioeconomic and juridical-political context. Nevertheless, these expectations and conceptions prevailed in that historical setting and nourished the illusion that in this way the social peace could be consolidated and the defense of the Negro's interests could be promoted. In the zeal to avoid hypothetical racial tensions and to ensure an effective means of gradually integrating the black population, all doors were closed that could have permitted the Negro and mulatto to receive direct benefits of the process of democratization of social rights and guarantees. The logic underlying this historical standard of social justice is clear: In the name of a perfect equality of the future, the black man was chained to the invisible fetters

THE BAHIAN PEOPLE AND THEIR LANGUAGE 179

of his past, a subhuman existence and a disguised form of perpetual enslavement.[28]

Expounding the facts concerning various social movements among the blacks in Brazil between 1925 and 1948, Fernandes writes the following:

> From 1925 to 1930 the bitterness and dissatisfaction of the black population built up to such a degree that there developed spontaneously several movements representing the Negro's growing awareness of his situation and his criticism and rejection of the difficult destiny to which black men were relegated. By virtue of the very historical situation of the Negro and mulatto, the rebellion did not take on the character of a revolt against the established social order. It was a matter of a deaf and irrepressible insubordination to the greatest shortcomings of the system of race relations that were linked more to the disguised continuation of the old order than to the flagrant injustices of the present order. Thus the Negroes did not pit themselves against the latter. On the contrary, they openly confessed that it satisfied their desires for social security, dignity, and equality and they pleaded only that it be open to them also.
>
> From this perspective the episodes related to these social movements mark the return of the Negro and mulatto to the historical stage of action.
>
> ... ...
>
> In arrogating to themselves the solution of problems ignored or disregarded by the elites in power, the Negro and mulatto delegated to themselves two historical tasks: to begin the modernization of the system of race relations in Brazil; and to prove in a practical way that men must totally and consciously identify with the values that express the chosen legal order.[29]

Present-day Bahia is one of free competition among all members of society regardless of what color their skin may be. Nevertheless, the darker portion of the population has had to face the problem that their parents or grandparents had to begin at the very bottom of society as slaves and that they themselves still carry the physical

---

[28] *Negro in Brazilian Society* pp. 135-137.
[29] *Negro in Brazilian Society*, pp. 187, 188.

traits and low-pay, low-status employments that they were forced into when freed from slavery. Because of this historical background, the conformation of present-day Bahian socio-economic strata displays most of its white membership at the top and the black at the bottom, with the mulatto filling a large gap in the middle.

The presence of a limited degree of racial consciousness in Bahia does not mean that the lower-class blacks are satisfied with what they have, nor does it imply that whites do not consider the Negroes to be socially and culturally inferior.

Marvin Harris, in *Town and Country in Brazil*, has made some excellent observations concerning the white's typical attitude toward the Negro. He writes, in the chapter entitled "Class and Race," the following:

> In most of his evaluation of the Negro as an *abstract type*, the white is inclined to deride and to slander. The mayor's son, addressing a group of friends, declared, "Everybody knows what kind of thing a Negro is. What I want to know is how did this curse ever come into the world in the first place when Adam and Eve were both white!"
>
> "They must be sons of the devil," someone else immediate replied.
>
> Many informants maintained that "the Negro is more like a buzzard than a man."
>
> All such statements, however, vary in the associated emotional tone. They are rarely said with hatred. The mood is generally lighthearted and tempered with earthly appreciation. There is no monotonous, heavy-handed undercurrent of bitterness or of revulsion. To the white and, to a certain extent, to the Negro himself, the Negro is primarily a curious, laughable anomaly. He is looked upon as a sport of nature, as a being with certain substandard and grotesque characteristics which make him rather amusing. A white man will say, "Negro desgraçado. Que bicho feio!" (Miserable Negro. What an ugly creature!), and smile broadly as though he were speaking of some rare, mirthful freak.
>
> The predisposition to laugh at the Negro rather than to hate him and the prevailing mildness of the emotional tone accompanying the comparison between the white and black lead to occasional inconsistencies and seeming ambivalences. [30]

---

[30] (New York, Columbia University Press: 1956), p. 115.

It may be easily recognized, then, that many of the lower class blacks and mulattoes feel that they have been abused and misunderstood. Conversely, the lighter mixed-bloods and even many of the darker mulattoes think highly of the whites and tend to degrade the purer Negro. The high and middle class mulattoes want to identify with whites and so do everything in their power to separate themselves from any African heritage which may still be lingering in their past. This, in many cases, is very difficult to accomplish, since the mulatto, historically being the offspring of a slave, was regarded as a Negro, and so carries this unwanted stigma with him from the past.

The attitude taken by both mulattoes and Negroes who are rising socially and economically is expressed in their lack of interest and their prevalent intolerance toward being associated with the *candomblé*. Since such "primitive practices" (a phrase they themselves use) immediately associate a member with a very low social standing, these Afro-Brazilian social climbers prefer to make and keep the distance between them and the religious cult houses as great as possible.

A substantial number of whites also show contempt toward anything African and claim that they would not attend a *candomblé* ceremony, yet think nothing of eating African foods such as *acarajé* for a mid-afternoon snack. That part of the African culture manifested in the behavior of these upper-class whites has been acquired unconsciously by the slow process of absorption down through the history of Brazil. The entire Bahian society has become partially Africanized in spite of the scattered efforts to preserve its Europeanism.

In the face of all these trends, both for and against the absorption of the western African culture in Bahia, it can be seen that in spite of the comparative friendliness of the Portuguese in his dealings with the black in Brazil, the latter has remained for the most part captive in a degradingly inferior social position. And, since language functions as a symbol of social class, the African tongues, as part of the low-class society, have not had so much influence on the culturally "superior" language of the Portuguese conquerors as they might have had if history had not forced the black man into such a low level on the socio-economic scale.

Taking into account the words of Charles Bally concerning the important role which prestige plays in the influence of one language on another, we can understand why there has not been a larger amount of African linguistic influence on Portuguese, at least as much, for example, as there was in the case of Norman French on English, and why the amount that did filter into Portuguese is slowly being substituted, especially in the high class society, by linguistic elements of Latin origin. Bally states:

> Por lo general sin saberlo, imitamos a todos aquellos que gozan de una autoridad o que ejercen sobre nosotros un ascendiente: parientes, amigos, representantes de una clase superior, de una minoría selecta, etc. . . .
>
> El prestigio del lenguaje de clase es enorme; la manera de hablar de un superior nos parece envidiable menos por su naturaleza propia que como símbolo de una forma de vida aceptada como ideal. Ya hemos visto . . . por qué se repelen instintivamente las innovaciones lingüísticas que vienen de abajo, aun cuando la reflexión pugne por aprobarlas. [31]
>
> (In general, without realizing it, we imitate all those who have authority over us: relatives, friends, members of a higher social class or of a select minority, etc. . . .
>
> The prestige of a high-class language is very great; the manner of speaking of one superior to us seems enviable, not so much because of its own nature, but as a symbol of a form of life which represents an ideal. We have seen . . . why "inferior" linguistic innovations are instinctively repelled, even when logic would fight to retain them.)

Concerning the natural rejection which all languages seem to demonstrate of any innovations coming from a lower social class, Bally explains that, "por razones sociales, extrañas a la lengua, son tabús, porque simbolizan la mentalidad popular, con el cortejo de ideas convencionales que esto supone: ignorancia, falta de educación y de distinción, etc." [32] (for social reasons, not connected to the language itself, they are taboos, because they represent the popular or base mentality, along with all of the conventional ideas suggested by this mentality: ignorance, lack of education and of distinction, etc.) These taboos exist in the African dialects as they relate to the Portuguese language in Brazil.

---

[31] *El lenguaje y la vida* (Buenos Aires, Editorial Losada, S. A.: 1941), p. 206.
[32] *El lenguaje,* p. 202.

One may contrast the influence of the African dialects on Brazilian Portuguese with the influence of French on the English of the eleventh century. The case of English may be seen as the reverse of what happened in Brazil. In England a small number of French invaders established themselves as the ruling class of a large body of English-speaking people. The borrowing of lexical items from the Norman French occurred in those areas of high social prestige, which the French ruling class represented at that time. The results of such socio-linguistic occurrences are evident today in the usage of certain English words. Winfred P. Lehmann, enumerating examples stemming from this English-French contact, writes:

> The difference in social status of the two languages may be illustrated in contrasting words: for a small crime the English "theft" is used, for a serious one the French "larceny."
> Today foods are still commonly said to reflect the social relation between the Norman French and their English subjects. English terms are used for animals in the field: cow, calf, ox, sheep, boar, swine; French for animals on the table: beef, veal, pork, mutton, bacon. Moreover, the humble meal, breakfast, has an English name, the more elegant dinner and supper, at which jelly and pastry may be served, have French names. [33]

In Brazil, African blacks were imported as slaves in large numbers to work for the ruling Portuguese. Here, the spheres of lexical items borrowed from the Africans were largely in the areas of low social prestige, and even today many of them reflect the socio-economic relation between the white Brazilian and his black neighbor.

The categories of the Afro-Brazilian words studied in Chapter IV bear evidence of the relation between many of these classes of vocabulary items and the social environments in which they are used. The category of names of gods, spirits and dignitaries in *candomblé*, for example, contains expressions used only in reference to the religious cult ceremonies and their influence on the religious life of the members who, with very few exceptions, [34] belong to the lower

---

[33] *Historical Linguistics: An Introduction* (New York, Holt, Rinehart, and Winston: 1966), p. 219.

[34] These exceptions are some well-known authors, such as Jorge Amado, Edison Carneiro and Donald Pierson, who became members of Bahian *can-*

classes of society. Words used as articles, shouts, functions, etc. in *candomblé* are likewise of the same low social groups.

Many of the Afro-Brazilian culinary items have become an active part of the vocabularies of all Bahian social classes. This, of course, is due to the large quantity of Negro foods that are publicly sold on the streets every day. As we saw in Chapter IV, Bahia is famous for its African culinary delicacies. Nevertheless, the majority of the terms which were classified as passive vocabulary in this category are not known or used by the upper classes in Bahia.

Before presenting the results of the correlative study done to discover relationships between recognition and usage of African-derived vocabulary items and the various socio-economic levels of Bahian society, the manner in which the native informants were classified into said levels will be discussed. Informants whose yearly income was at least 10,000 dollars, who held very high responsible professional and/or political positions in the society, and who owned large, expensive homes, were placed in what I term the high or upper social class. Those Bahian informants whose annual income ranged from 2,000 to 9,000 dollars, who held lower yet still respectable jobs, such as medical doctors, lawyers, high school and university teachers, some secretaries, etc., and who owned or rented smaller, less expensive, yet comfortable homes or apartments, were classified as belonging to the middle class. The lower class is defined as consisting of those informants who earn less than 2,000 dollars a year, who live in poor housing conditions or in the *favelas* (slums) and who hold menial jobs, such as janitors and day laborers, or who hold no jobs at all.

On all sixty-five questionnaires, the level of formal education corresponded to the amount of income of each informant in that those who earned more had received more education. This was to be expected, however, since in Bahia, only the wealthy can attend secondary school and hope to continue at the university level. The wealthier you are, the greater your chances for receiving a good and extensive education.

---

domblé in order to penetrate its secrets, which are carefully kept from all non-initiates, and so be able to study and write about it. Another exception, of course, is Deoscóredes M. dos Santos, who is a member of the middle class in Bahia. The names of a few of the spirits worshipped in *candomblé*, such as *Iemanjá* and *Oxunmarê*, have become popular with the *baianos* mainly through the works of such authors.

THE BAHIAN PEOPLE AND THEIR LANGUAGE 185

Although it is true that there are more than just three socio-economic classes in Bahian society, I have grouped the informants into three main categories for the purpose of simplification. The most useful criteria for placing the Bahians interviewed into three classes were profession, yearly income and size and location of their houses. I found that recognition among the informants of the vocabulary items was not connected in any way to age, sex, trips, or place of birth of the parents. The first major category of tentatively identified Afro-Bahian lexical items which appears in Chapter IV is that of the names of gods, spirits and dignitaries of the *candomblé*. The breakdown of the identification of these items (words for which meanings were given) among the informants of the three socio-economic classes in Bahia for this first category is the following: [35]

	1	2	3
A	∅	4	16
B	4	6	4
C	17	12	2

The second category was that of articles, shouts, functions, and other miscelaneous words found in the *candomblé*. The identification/socio-economic class correlation for this category is as follows:

---

[35] The letters A, B, C found in the vertical column to the left represent: number of people identifying most of the words, number of people identifying few words, and number of people identifying none of the words, respectively. The numbers 1, 2, and 3 in the horizontal column at the top of the chart represent: high class, middle class, and low class, respectively. These representations are the same for all of the charts so designated.

	1	2	3
A	∅	∅	5
B	∅	∅	6
C	21	22	11

Informants who were affiliated with *candomblé* in Bahia were able to recognize considerably more of the vocabulary items connected with the cult houses. Also, since *candomblé* was brought to Bahia by West African slaves, and since these black slaves remained, for the most part, in the lower socio-economic levels of society, vocabulary terms of African origin pertaining to *candomblé* have filtered into the Portuguese language more among members of the lower class, whether or not they belong to *candomblé,* than among those of the upper social strata.

It may be noted, too, that since most of the middle class informants tend (very strongly) to adhere to social mores established by the upper class, members of this middle socio-economic group responded to the questionnaires in much the same way as did those of the higher brackets, i.e., they did not recognize or identify as many items as members of the lower social echelons.

However, those informants of the middle and high classes of Bahian society associated with *candomblé* (not included among the forty-three) knew anywhere from 50 % to 100 % more words on the list than those of the same socio-economic standing who were not connected with the religious cults. As Melville J. Herskovits so accurately states in his study of cult life in Brazil:

> ... membership in the various African-derived candomble cult-groups is undoubtedly weighted on the lower social-economic levels; nevertheless, the higher strata are by no means unrepresented. For the candombles include in their numbers entrepreneurs who are owners of business establishments and small manufacturing concerns, labor leaders and political figures, skilled operatives and other minor industrial supervisory personnel as well as manual workers and

casual laborers. And when one moves out of the category of active and acknowledged membership, those who have less formal relations with the candomble are found to some degree in all strata. Such relationships are to be seen in the instances where the services of Afrobahian diviners and priests are utilized by persons who belong to the higher social and economic levels, seeking guidance from the powers these specialists are held to control.[36]

The third category of lexical items in Chapter IV is that of food. The identification/socio-economic class correlation for this was the following:

	1	2	3
A	3	4	17
B	8	18	5
C	10	∅	∅

The same general results are found in the category of food as were observed in the other two previously-examined ones; i.e., that informants in the high and middle socio-economic classes were able to identify ostensibly fewer items than those Bahians belonging to the low class. As more categories of word items in Chapter IV were correlated with the three socio-economic classes, similar results were also forthcoming. Verbs and adjectives of African origin showed a much higher frequency of usage among the low socio-economic groups than among the high.

Many of the items in the categories of Afro-Brazilian musical instruments and of components of carnival were recognized only by informants of the low classes. In fact, 96 percent of the poorer people identified the words in these two categories. Very few of the middle or high class informants were able to recognize any of them. Some

---

[36] *The New World Negro* (Bloomington, Indiana University Press: 1966), p. 248.

of the well-to-do whites even had trouble defining the active word *agôgô*.

Items identified as clothing and ornaments worn on the body also showed a high frequency of usage among the lower social levels, and not so among the higher ones. This, of course, would be expected when one examines the contextual environments in which these words are found. They denote the costumes which are identified with either the religious cults or Afro-Brazilian carnival regalia.

In the case of names for animals and plants, many items for which Portuguese had no terms were borrowed from the African tongue into the Portuguese. This, of course, is a common linguistic phenomenon in situations of language contact. Similarly, the names of African languages and tribes, having no Latin or Romance equivalents, were borrowed into Portuguese. Again, all of my informants from low social levels identified these words; yet only 32 % of those from the upper level of society could give suitable definitions for the vocabulary pertaining to African languages and tribal names.

Lexical items falling into the remaining categories demonstrated the same general pattern of lower class cognizance and upper class ignorance.

Reconsidering for a moment the correlation between race/color and membership in one of Bahia's socio-economic classes, we are reminded that, generally, people of a lighter skin and caucasion features belong to the higher brackets and those who have darker complexions and more prominent Negroid features form a part of the lower socio-economic levels. [37] Correlations between race/color and usage of African-derived vocabulary, therefore, were very similar to those for socio-economic class membership and usage of this vocabulary. The following chart gives the results of the answers on the questionnaires concerning race-color and income. Again, as for class divisions, races were divided into three main categories for purposes of simplification:

---

[37] References to studies indicating this race/class correlation are abundant. For example, see Charles Wagley, op. cit., Marvin Harris, *Town and Country in Brazil*, Florestan Fernandes, op. cit., Donald Pierson, op. cit., and Thales de Azevedo, *Cultura e Situação Racial no Brasil* (Rio de Janeiro, Editôra Civilização Brasileira, S. A.: 1966).

THE BAHIAN PEOPLE AND THEIR LANGUAGE

Income, etc.	$10,000 or more	$2,000-9,000	under $2,000
race/color			
black	0	3	18
mulatto	3	7	3
white	18	12	1

There are, certainly, blacks in the higher levels of society, just as there are whites at the very bottom of the scale, for as Marvin Harris so aptly points out in his study, "an individual's rank is determined always by a combination of all four major criteria [economic, occupational, educational and racial] and never by one in isolation." [38] We must also remember that in Bahia, as in all of Brazil, "money whitens," so that it is not impossible for a black to climb socially if he is economically healthy, and, conversely, a poor white person will not be able to mingle in the high social levels simply because his skin happens to be light.

Before any general concluding remarks are made, it should be mentioned at this point that only those people who had either been born and raised or who had spent most of their lives in Bahia, were included in the count of native Bahian informants. Six questionnaires were also given to non-Bahians in order to compare results. Three of these were distributed to Brazilians and three to informants of Portuguese (European) origin. Among the Brazilian non-Bahians, 31 of the 217 words were identified by the first informant, 35 by the second, and 37 by the third. The first of these informants, from São Paulo, admitted that he had learned 7 or 8 of the vocabulary items in Bahia. Of the other two non-Bahians, the second mentioned here was from Pôrto Alegre and the third from Recife. These two did not say they had learned any of the words in Bahia, but that they knew them because they are used in their respective native cities. These

---

[38] *Town and Country*, p. 97.

items recognized by the non-Bahians could have been brought to the other parts of Brazil by the black slaves in earlier centuries, or they could have been disseminated by native Bahians who established themselves in other sections of the country, although the latter of these two alternatives seems less likely.

Among the Portuguese informants, the first, from O Pôrto, recognized 9 words on the list. The second and third, both from Lisbon, recognized 12 and 14, respectively. All three of these informants had lived in Bahia for approximately eight years at the time of the interviews and they all admitted that they had learned the few words they recognized on the questionnaire after having arrived in Bahia from Portugal.

Although the sample of non-Bahians and Portuguese informants in this study is very small, I can state that from personal observations made in a general way, these six cases seem to be indicative of the general knowledge of words of African origin that are used and recognized by non-native Bahians. This conclusion is, of course, a subjective one, and will hopefully induce future studies of a more objective nature in this particular area.

Returning to the discussion of the class/vocabulary usage correlation, it is worthwhile to note here that the lack of penetration of the African-derived lexical elements into the higher classes, as seen in Bahian Portuguese, has been caused by three main factors. The first is that of the automatic rejection by upper class members of any features of language which are associated with ethnolinguistic inferiority. The second goes hand in hand with the first: the lack of enthusiasm on the part of the low classes to inject their speech habits into what they consider a prestigiously superior language. The third has to do with the division and distribution of the blacks, mulattoes and whites among the three social classes in Bahia. Since the lowest class is mainly composed of Negroes and mulattoes, for reasons we have already discussed, a relatively large percentage of African traits would be expected in the speech of these people, and their speech would most probably influence the linguistic conformation of the few whites belonging to the bottom level of the social scale. This low class, then, has its own vocabulary and manners of speaking, which are different from those of the middle and high classes. The differences have developed historically from the African heritage held by the majority of the members in the lower class and find expression in the linguistic elements of this heritage.

Because of these factors and because there is a fundamental lack of social intermingling and intercommunication of the lower class with the middle and high classes, greater possibilities than those which presently exist for linguistic borrowings between socio-economic groups are stunted.

In conclusion, then, some general statements concerning this study can be made at this point. Ever since the middle of the 16th century the black has represented an important and indelible factor in influencing the ethnolinguistic life of the Bahian population. As the Portuguese and African peoples mixed together genetically down through the years when Brazil was being developed, mutual linguistic interchanges were also taking place. Therefore, the Portuguese language was enriched by a considerable number of foreign lexical items which contributed new semantic possibilities. A western African culture had brought to Brazil different and unique manners of expression as it had introduced new cultural elements which broadened and changed the contour of what Portuguese life had been in Europe.

In Bahia, these influences came mainly from the Yoruba, Ewe and Ijesha tribes, and from the peoples of the lower Congo and Angola. These Africans established their own cultural pockets throughout the state of Bahia, where they retained their own languages and ethnic customs. At the same time they spread some of their distinctive ethnolinguistic habits among the Portuguese by means of a mutual development between master and slave of a pidgin language which was necessary for basic communicative purposes. The pockets of African heritage exist today as religious cult organizations and are the only cultural vestiges approximating the pure African elements that were taken to the New World. These *candomblé* sects have also influenced the Portuguese in Bahia, especially by introducing into its culture features of music, dance, a few culinary delicacies, and some types of clothing and jewelry.

Historical connections established in past centuries between Africa and Bahia seem to have been more intimate and more permanent than in most other sections of America. And, at present, the spoken Bahian Portuguese of the lower classes of society shows more traces of African influence than does the language of the upper social levels, because the lower groups contain the majority of the black population.

Today one may also find traces of the African influence in Bahia as it has penetrated all levels of society. Besides the Afro-Brazilian dishes sold in upper-class restaurants, such as the Italian "La Pérgola," the "Hotel da Bahia," and even the French "Chez Susanne," names of *candomblé* saints have been borrowed and used to name hotels: the *Oxunmarê* Hotel, Hotel *Xangô*; modern apartment buildings: *Ogum, Oxum, Nanã*; restaurants: *Dendê*; beauty salons: *Iemanjá, Iansã*; streets: *Nagô, Alaqueto* (part of the Yoruba "nation").

Such ethnolinguistic contributions as these throughout Bahian life have enriched the Portuguese language in this area of Brazil especially, giving it new and varied expressive qualities. The fusion of two very distinct yet compatible cultures and languages, the sub-Saharan African and the European Portuguese, has formed, in a land that was alien to both, a unique environment which has developed into the contemporary city of Salvador da Bahia de Todos os Santos.

APPENDIX I

A SMALL VOCABULARY OF YORUBA, GATHERED IN BAHIA BY DR. OSCAR DE CARVALHO IN 1900

Aláfiouá Bom dia — obrigada (Good day — Thank you)
Atá Pimenta (Pepper)
Acará Pão (Bread)
Aburou Irmão (Brother)
Agouminlê Dá licença nesta casa (Let me in this house)
Ajotó? Sou eu só? (I alone)
Aou Prato (casal) (Plate)
Acou Panela (Pot)
Agou Dá licença, deixe-me passar (Allow me in)
Agê Deus lhe ajude (May God help you)
Aiéucomin Passarinho está cantando (A little bird sings)
Adjôquê Camisa (Shirt)
Adjosalê Saia (Skirt)
Abêjaou Casado (Married)
Aioibí Assucar de branco (White sugar)
Acáraguguê Bolacha (Cookie)
Adiá Galinha (Hen)
Amuónimá Eu sou casado (I am married)

Bábá Pae (Father)
Boujouriadaké Cala a bôca (olho vê bôcca cala) (Be quiet)
Bábálêou Homem rico (Rich man)
Batá Sapato (Shoe)
Bái-nin Assim mesmo (Exactly right)
Babolêmin Meu tio (My uncle)

Didê Ali, neste lugar (There, in that place)
Dúdúm Bonito, bom (Fine)
Didê Levante-se (Get up)

Efúm Farinha (Manioc flour)
Eran Carne (Meat)
Eguê Mentira (Lie)
Emimtemim Eu não (Not I)
Equédé Banana (Banana)
Ecuá Amendoim (Peanut)
Eutááficêlê Flôr que enfeita a casa (Decorative flower)
Eó Mão (Hand)
Exi Cavalo (Horse)
Eué Papel (Paper)
Éúêri Cabêlo (da cabeça) (Hair [on head])

Ilê-boubou? Como vão todos? (How are you all?)
Ilê-imbé Todos vão bem (We are all fine)
Ilê Casa — família (Home — family)
Iaré Sua mãe (Your mother)
Iá Mãe (Mother)
Ipêlú O diabo te carregue (May the devil take you)
Inin Vá saíndo (Get going)
Idiré Outra pessoa — você (Another person)
Ialêmin Minha tia (My aunt)

Jamin Minha mãe (My mother)

Joucou Assente-se (Sit down)
Jôcê Eu faço (I do)

Lêdará Casa bonita (Pretty house)
Laze Pé (Foot)

Mim Meu, minha (My)
Maféirêorêmim Quero bem a você (I love you)
Maféáquêtê Eu quero chapéu (I want a hat)
Môdê Já cheguei (I arrived)
Mafiancan Quero uma coisa (I want something)
Matijoucou Estou sentado (I am seated)
Mididê Já me levantei (I got up)
Môfé Porque não? (Why not?)
Manin-nálê Eu tenho uma môça (I have a girl)
Molú Bói (Ox)
Molúúbri Vaca (Cow)
Maféórórê Gosto de sua língua (I like your language)
Matafiaió Quero farinha (I want manioc flour)

Ougirê Bom dia (Good day)
Oumim Água (Water)
Oucôô Dez réis (Ten pence)
Ou dára Bom, boa (Good)
Ougôje Um vintém (A small amount of money)
Oubirim Mulher (Woman)
Oulêpátápátá Ladrão fino (An expert thief)
Oumon Filho, filha (Son, daughter)
Ogórim Dois vinténs (Two small coins)
Oujarê Me deixe (Let me alone)
Otó Só (Alone)
Oulê Ladrão (Thief)
Oumididê Chuva (Rain)
Ouluou Deus (God)
Ouluouducouajou Somos dominados por Deus (God controls us)
Oxum Nossa Senhora (Our Lady)
Ougem Santo Antônio (Saint Anthony)
Ouxálá Senhor do Bomfim (Christ of Bomfim)

Ou dára Sim, justamente (Yes, exactly)
Oumicoufê Eu quero (I want)
Oudoulá Boa noite, até amanhã (Good night)
Omólêcum-kêkêrê Chave (Key)
Omolêcum Pôrta (Door)
Oujoucoucourou Olhos maiores do que a barriga (Eyes bigger than stomach)
Ouou Dinheiro (Money)
Obé Faca e garfo (talher) (Knife and fork)
Oiboumim Meu senhor (My lord)
Oré mim Meu camarada (My friend)
Ocúdúdúcú Arroz (Rice)
Ômidudú Café (Coffee)
Ômigôná Chá (Tea)
Ôlônuafućluô Deus lhe dê com quê (saúde e dinheiro) (May God give you health and money)
Ôlonúafuôirê Deus lhe favoreça (May God favor you)
Ômiálaiá Prima (Cousin)

Pátápátá Fino, esperto (Expert)

Quêquêrê Pequeno (Small)
Quimafé Que quer? (What do you want?)

Térapadê Até amanhã se Deus quiser (See you tomorrow, if God wills it)
Tulútulú Peru (Turkey)

Uá Venha cá, pode entrar (Come on in)
Umbá Fogo, fósforo (Fire, match)
Uáu-ulê Vá embora (Go away)
Uánibátánilaze Você tem sapato nos pés (You have shoes on your feet)
Ubri Mulher (Woman)
Ubrié? Como vai sua mulher? (How is your wife?)
Unufenon Eu não posso fazer (I cannot do it)
Ubriancó Como vai sua senhora? (How is your wife?)
Umoiáminucurim Meu irmão (My brother)
Umoiaminúbri Minha irmã (My sister)

APPENDIX II

"EWE" MATERIAL

The songs presented in this appendix continue the numbering of "Ewe" songs (1a-6a) begun in Chapter III.

The following song is one which *dã* himself sings:

(7) bwɛsɛmine'wa ɛ ma'jwĩ
"Êle conta o que êle é. Vem da terra dos gêge. Êle diz: eu sou da terra dos gêge."

(He tells what he is. He comes from the land of the Ewe. He says: I am from the land of the Ewe.)

According to my Bahian informant, the word *dã* means "snake." In Ewe, it is *da*, and in the Gɛ̃ dialect, *edã*. I was told that it also refers to the Land of Dan mentioned in the *Bible*, meaning that Dan was the original homeland of the Ewe.[1]

The following five songs are all related to *dã* and are sung in his honor:

(8) o dã isu dã dɔv'rɔ isu dã
"ko'vɛ quer dizer 'fome.' Esta canção nos diz que *dã* está com fome."

(ko'vɛ means "hunger." This song tells us that *dã* is hungry.)

Perhaps the *isu dã* in this song should be *i sudã*, referring to the Sudan? African Ewe tradition places

---

[1] The *Old Testament* mentions two places called Dan. One is in the lowlands of Canaan north of Judah and the other is a city in the most northerly part of Palestine.

their origin on the Niger River, to the northeast of their present location.

Note that the word [ko'vɛ], which the informant translates, does not appear in the song.

Ewe has *dɔwuamɛ,* "hunger."

(9)   bogã ɛu'a bogã vi da'lɔ ɛ'tã
ma'yõ mi'wa

Mãe V. explained this song by translating three words:

gã "chave" (key)
a'lɔ "mão" (hand)
a'basa "sala" (livingroom) which does not appear in the song.

The word *gã* appears as *bogã* when sung. According to the informant, *bogã* cannot be separated into *bo gã* when in the song. Likewise, *a'lɔ*, when sung, must be *da'lɔ*. Mãe V. was not able to tell me the reasons behind such changes.

When *dã* wishes to enter the *terreiro,* he sings:

(10)   ɛro'bwa hoh'wɛ sumɛnu bɛ'sẽ
ɛro'bwa hoh'wɛ

followed by:

(11)   sɛu jãɛmay ada kay'a

"Está pedindo licença."

(He is asking for permission)

Another song *dã* uses when he wants entrance into the ceremony, is:

(12)   ɛdɛjũ'sɔ ɛdɛlɔy'ã aɛ ɛɛ
ba'fonu de'ka dɛloyan ayɛ

"Êle está pedindo licença quando chega na casa."

(He is asking for permission [to enter] when he arrives at the house.)

Finally, as a homage to *dã,* this song is sung:

(13)   aj'a jwɛ'rɛ mo'kã fɛbi'ɔ

The word *mo'kã* was translated as "bracelete," indicating that these few words could refer to the jewelry or garments which *dã* wears.

The next two songs honor *Ogã*. This spirit is described by Carneiro as "protector civil do candomblé, escolhido pelos orixás e 'confirmado' por meio de festa pública, com a função de prestigiar e fornecer dinheiro para as festas sagradas."[2] (civil protector of the *candomblé*, chosen by the spirits and 'confirmed' by means of a public ceremony, with the task of upgrading and providing money for the sacred festivals.) In the *Gũ* dialect of Ewe, we find *ogá̃*, "chief or elder."

The first song is called *a salva de Ogã*:

(14)   ofɛrɛ'rɛ moydagwa'rɛ ogã

"Ogã salvando os outros."

(*Ogã* saving the others)

The second one for *Ogã*:

(15)   korɛ'dã a'ɛ a mina'dã a'ɛɛ vo'dũ
         'kaka bonu 'kaka mɛji'tɔ nu'jũ dɔ'si

Mãe V. was unable to give any translation for this particular chant. She said, however, that there is a shout that accompanies the song, which is:

(16)   aobo'boy

"Viva!" (Long live [the god]!)

Cf. Ewe *abóbo*, "to cry out."

The following seven songs are supposed to be directed to Daomé, the West African land of the Ewe.

The *canto a Daomé* (song for Dahomey) is:

(17)   li lɛ gwɛa'ba hwɛna'do mɛrɛ
         vo'dũ ɛ'zo

---

[2] *Candomblés*, p. 188.

"Quando a pessoa se veste bem para saír à sala."

(When the person dresses well to enter the room.)

This song may be used in conjunction with the first one which was transcribed. It tells of the elaborate costumes which the initiates wear when dancing in the *terreiro*.

The next song of Dahomey is one which only a native of the land can sing:

(18) ho'o ho'o daho'mɛ javalɛ'si
vodũ si daho'mɛ

"Eu sou um santo da terra do Daomé."

(I am a saint from the land of Dahomey.)

When there is a false saint present, the following song is heard:

(19) ma'wa ma'wa vodũ si'dɛ
ma'wa bona'jɛ nu vu'ɛ

"É pessoa mentirosa, isto é que está fingindo o santo."

(This is a person who tells lies; he is pretending to be a saint.)

The utterance *nu vu'ɛ* means "pessoa está mentindo" (a person is telling lies). We may compare the western interior dialect of Ewe, which has *nu*, "to speak," and the Gɛ̃ dialect, which has *vuɛ̃*, "bad, wrong, evil."

The following two songs are for the departure of the spirit to Dahomey:

(20) mayo kwɛ bo'a naji'vĩ

"Êle se vai despedindo porque vai para casa dêle."

"kwɛ é casa."

(He is saying good-bye because he is going home. kwɛ is "home.")

(21) ja hwala bweje'mi la'de
mo'kwe jɛ'vɔ

"A despedida do santo."

(The farewell of the saint.)

APPENDIX 199

This song is usually sung by one person only until the others shout mɛ'rɛ, which means "everyone," and then everyone joins in singing. The *Gũ* dialect of Ewe has *mɛdé*, "anyone."

The last two Dahomey songs are quite common in Ewe *candomblés*. The first one is:

(22)   ɛmɛ'wɛ dodo hũsɔa'dɛ
       ɛmɛ'wɛ dodo hũsɔa'dɛ

"Cadê a mãe pequena?"³

(Where is the little mother [second in command]?)

The expression *hũsɔa'dɛ* means *mãe pequena* (little mother). The second is:

(23)   mɛkɛji kɔjɛ mi'lu to'jũ mɛrɛ
       mõ'joru hũ'damɛ sa'lɛ na sa'lɛ
       hu'ɛ na hu'ɛ

"O santo está chamando."

(The saint is calling.)

The following song is entitled *Canto para Ogã maior* (A song for the great *Ogã*). *Mãe* V. was unable to render a translation of it:

(24)   tanumbɛ'lɛ tanumbɛ'lɛ hũtɔ tanudɛ'wa
       bafonu dɛ'wa ata'kã madah'wa o'je o'je

The Ewe ceremony often ends with more songs in honor of *dã*. Two such songs are the following:

The first is called *Canto de Dã*:

(25)   'ire 'mire ko'we be'sẽ
       dawirɛko'wɛ

"Quando eu cheguei, todo o mundo está me vendo."

(Everyone saw me when I arrived.)

The second has neither title nor translation:

(26)   kɛrɛ'bɔ ma'jwɛ to'rɛ jwen'du bɛsɛ jweto'rɛ jwen'du

---

³ The *mãe pequena*, according to Edison Carneiro, is the immediate substitute for the *mãe*.

Appendix III

"YORUBA" MATERIAL

The numbering of Yoruba songs and expressions in this appendix continues the sequence (1b-6b) begun in Chapter III.

Oxósse appears and the initiates sing the following:

(7) ao'ro ε'bε odεba'nu
     sambu'ra

"Oxósse está caçando e botando os bichos no samburá (no mocó)." [1]

(*Oxósse* is hunting and putting the animals in the sack.)

When *Iansã* becomes hungry, she asks for some *acará*: [2]

(8) a'go oy'a εa aka'ra o a
     ñi bo'ε a'go ɔy'a

"Iansã pede acará para comer."

(*Iansã* asks for *acará* to eat.)

When comparing this to modern Yoruba, we can recognize the forms *àgò*, "give way or permission," and *àkàrà*, "cake."

Before many of the ceremonies, some type of small animal, such as a chicken, a dove or a goat, is killed and the blood is used to

---

[1] *Samburá* or *mocó* is a wicker basket.
[2] *Acará*, according to Renato Mendonça, *A Influência*, p. 103, is "bolos de feijão, fritos em azeite de dendê com pimenta malagueta." (cakes of black beans, fried in *dendê* oil with pepper.)

appease the saints. One of the songs, sung when a chicken is killed, is the following:

(9) olo'o ɔki'kɔ o'ju mamãe
ɔki'kɔ o lɛ lɛ o

"Está chamando porque está na hora da matança."

(He is calling because it is time for the sacrifice.)

In this song, [olo'o] could be Yoruba òlórun, "someone who oversees, i.e., god"; [o'ju], ojú, "eyes or a dear one (that you would take care of as if he or she were your own eyes)"; and [ɔki'kɔ], àkùkọ́, "cock."

My Brazilian informant told me that, in this chant, "ɔki'kɔ é galinha; olo'o é zelador de santo" (ɔki'kɔ is a chicken; olo'o is the caretaker of the saint.) The word mamãe is Portuguese.

A song which accompanies the killing of a four-legged animal is:

(10) ɛmafori kã ɛ'lɛ ko'tã

"É cantiga para matança de bicho de quatro pés. Cantam isso na hora que mata."

(This is a song sung for the killing of a four-legged animal. They sing this at the time of the sacrifice.)

My Nigerian informant recognized the following in this chant:

emá f'orí kan, meaning "do not use your head to touch (something)." Emá is "do not," f'orí, "use head to," and kan, "touch." He also recognized the word ẹlẹ́, which means "owner of." The whole chant could mean something to the effect that "the owner or pai de santo does not use his head to touch the animal that they are going to kill or sacrifice."

The mãe de santo calls all the initiates together to pay homage to the animal being sacrificed, in this manner:

(11) ɛma fo karī'ño
(No translation.)

Certain elements present in modern Yoruba were recognized here: emá, "do not," fo, "to jump or fly into," and o kari, "enough to go around."

A candle is lit when the time comes for the spirits to appear and bestow blessings upon the initiates. As this is done, the following is sung:

>(12)   bɔ'kɛ bɔ'kɛ iai'a
>   imia 'mia 'mia
>   bɔ'kɛ bo'a soboa'ju
>   bɔ'kɛ bo'a
>   ki'mī kilɔ'fɛ

> "A hora que a gente acende a luz para o santo vir tomar a bênção. Quando toma a bênção, cantam ki'mī kilɔ'fɛ."

> (The hour in which the people light the candle for the saint to come and receive the blessing, they sing ki'mī kilɔ'fɛ.)

The only part of this chant recognizable to my Nigerian informant was the line [kimī kilɔ'fɛ], which, in modern Yoruba, would be *kini kilofẹ́*, meaning "What is it?" or "What do you want?" *Kini* is "What is it?" and *kilofẹ́* is "What do you want?"

A song devoted to the minor spirit *Abaluaé*:

>(13)   a'go a'go nana'wɛ
>   ɛ'ma da'go
> (No translation.)

As discussed earlier, the name of the god *Abaluaé* is a shortened form of the Nigerian expression *ọbaolúwayé*, meaning "appeal to the king of the gods." In modern Yoruba, *Oba* is "king," *olúwa* is "god," and *yé* is "please." In the song itself, we may recognize Yoruba *yàgò*, abbreviated *àgò*, meaning "give way or permission."

When *Xangô*, one of the most important spirits, appears, the following is sung:

>(14)   aoriša ɛ'lo kiɛ'do
>   a'bɛ nio'mā bakotoa'ro

> "Xangô está dançando, agradecendo."

> (Xangô is dancing and giving thanks.)

In this song, two elements were recognized as being Yoruba: [ori'ša], which is *òrìṣà*, "anything worshipped," and [a'bɛ], which is *ẹ̀bẹ̀*, "to beg."

APPENDIX

Xangô in his happiness sings:

(15)   aira kɛmikɛ šo'ro olu'a
         mi so mãe,
         mãe celeste
         aira aira'e

"Xangô está satisfeito com a festa que a gente lhe deu."

(*Xangô* is happy with the celebration that the people gave him.)

The words *mãe* and *celeste* are Portuguese.

According to my Nigerian informant, this chant sounded very similar to the Yoruba sentence *ará t'emí sòrò olúwa mi so pé*, meaning "my people that are celebrating the god, says that." The expression in Bahia could mean, then, "Someone says that my people are celebrating my god." In Yoruba, *ará* is "my people," *t'emí*, "that are," *sòrò*, "celebrating," *olúwa*, "god," *mi*, "my," *so*, "says," and *pé*, "that."

Santa Bárbara, who is the Catholic counterpart of *Iansã*, has a song sung in her honor:

(16)   ɛrɔy'a miako'a

"É a cantiga de Santa Bárbara."

(This is the song for Saint Barbara.)

An utterance similar to [ɛrɔy'a] in modern Yoruba is *èrò yà*, meaning "crowd, give way."

Iansã, or Saint Barbara, proud of her crown, dances alone and sings:

(17)   ɛ ko'ro ko'ro a ko'ro

"A santa coroada. Santa Bárbara está mostrando a coroa. Já foi feita." [3]

(The saint is crowned. Saint Barbara is showing off her crown. She has been "made.")

---

[3] The expression *foi feita* refers to the fact that the *filha de santo* has passed from the novice stage into that of a full-fledged *orixá*, and as such can receive the spirit of her own particular saint, in this case, *Iansã*.

The word *ko'ro* souds like the Portuguese *coroa*, "crown."

As more spirits appear in the *terreiro*, the *mãe de santo* notices that *Xangô* has disappeared. An appropriate song is begun to entice him to return:

(18) ago'le mošupa ale agole'le

"É de *Xangô*; chamando êle."

(A song for *Xangô*; calling him.)

The following expressions, having no connection with *candomblé*, are ordinary conversational items:

(19) i'lɛyjo'ko a po'či
nu i'lɛ

"Chegou na pôrta, entrou, e sentou."

(He came to the door, came in, and sat down.)

My Nigerian informant recognized the following elements in this phrase: *ilé*, "house," *ìjókó*, "sitting place," *apotí*, "stool," *inú-ilé*, "in the house," or possibly *inú-ilẹ̀*, "in the ground." The Yoruba word *ilẹ̀*, "ground," is phonetically closer to [i'lɛ], but *ilé*, "house," fits the translation given by the Brazilian informant.

(20) i'lɛ "casa" (house)
Yoruba: *ilé*, "house."

(21) yjo'ko "entrou" (entered)
Yoruba: *ìjókó*, "sitting place"

(22) apu'či "banco" (bench)
Yoruba: *apotí*, "stool"

(23) ada'ba "Eu já vou" (I am going)
Yoruba: *ódà-bọ̀*, "I am going"

(24) ɔ'kɔ "homem" (man)
Yoruba: *ọkọ* "husband" and *akọ*, "male"

(25) ɛfi'mi "mulher" (woman)

(26) ǰi'jina "terra" (land, earth)
Yoruba: *ìjìnlẹ̀*, "indigenous"

APPENDIX

(27) olo'rũ "Que Deus lhe aumente. Se diz a uma pessoa quando esta lhe dá algo." (May God increase your well-being. This is said to a person when he gives you something.)
Yoruba: Ọlọ́run, "God."

(28) i'ɔ "sal" (salt)
Yoruba: iyọ̀, "salt"

(29) ɛ'po "azeite" (oil)
Yoruba: épó, "cooking oil"

(30) ɛ'fũ "farinha" (flour)
Yoruba: láfún, "cassava flour." ẹfun, "chalk, lime."

(31) o'o "dinheiro" (money)
Yoruba: owó, "money"

(32) oko'sĩ im'bɛ "Não tem um tostão e está pedindo." (He has no money and is begging.)
Yoruba: òkò sí nìbè, "you are not there."

(33) milɔnga "caneco; copo" (cup)
Kimbundu: ma'lɔŋga, "plates, dishes."

(34) milɔŋ'giña "prato" (plate)

(35) 'mazi "água" (water)
Cf. Kikongo: 'maza, "water." Also, the Ewe verb ná tsi, "to water."

(36) o'mi dõ'dũ "café" (coffee)
Yoruba: ómi dúdú, "black water"

(37) mi de'i ũ a'šɔ "roupa" (clothing)
Yoruba: mi, "my"; aṣọ, "clothing"

(38) ɔ'bɛ "faca" (knife)
Yoruba: òbẹ, "knife"

(39) ɔbɛ ki'ñi "garfo" (fork)
Yoruba: kiní, "first"

(40) ñi ɔ'bɛ "colher" (spoon)
Yoruba: ọbè, "soup"
"Spoon" in modern Yoruba is ṣibi.

(41) fili'mĩ "Vem cá." (Come here.)
Yoruba: *tèle mi,* "follow me."

(42) o'mi "água" (water)
Yoruba: *ómí,* "water"

(43) meapučĩ'ni "banco pequeno" (small bench)
Yoruba: *àpotí,* "stool"

(44) ε'rã "carne de sertão" (meat from the backlands)
Yoruba: *eran,* "meat"

(45) εrã jie'lu "carne de boi" (ox meat)
Yoruba: *eran,* "meat" and *màlù,* "ox"

(46) zambi na kwate'sa "Deus que esteja com a gente tôda." (May God be with all His people.)
Kimbundu: *'nzambi,* "god"
Kikongo: *ina,* "to be"
Kimbundu: *akua dì'bata mba sa'nzala,* "people"

(47) aki'kɔ "galinha" (hen)
Yoruba: *àkùkọ́,* "cock"

(48) e'tu "com quem" (with whom)

(49) pepe'e "pato" (duck)
Yoruba: *pẹ́pẹ́yẹ,* "duck"

(50) i'lε "pombo" (pidgeon)
Yoruba: *ẹiyẹ-lé,* "house dove"

(51) ašε'gε "porco" (pig)
Yoruba: *ẹlẹ́dẹ̀,* "pig"

(52) u'ke "gritar" (to shout)
Yoruba: *iké,* "to shout"
My Nigerian informant told me that the form *iké* is rarely used in Nigeria today. It usually only appears in the expression *iké-de,* meaning "a public announcement." *Íké* is "announcement" and *odé,* "public."

(53) age'de nafilimi
muši'ba nia keke're
bejõku no'lɔ

(An obscene utterance which *mãe* C. refused to translate.)
Yoruba: *kekere*, "small."

Unfortunately, I was able to obtain a translation for only one of the following chants (recorded in the interview with the *pai de santo*, because these songs are considered to be so sacred that to disclose their meaning would destroy their magic powers. The eleven songs given to me are the following:

(54)   ε ka bo ki lε gi hi
           e das kɔbra kani'ña
           kaboku jimã sam'bira hε
           pasči'e na ībū'rã

My Nigerian informant recognized the following: *ekabò*, "welcome," and *ki ilè ji*, "let the atmosphere be lively."

(55)   ka'bota jianɔbey'es
           kaitumba
           ka'bota zya'nɔba ay'εs
           kaitumba

Yoruba: *ki ábọ́ si ità*, which in contracted form is *k'ábọ́ s'ità*, which, in spoken form becomes more contracted or shortened, and is *k'ábọtà*, which means "let us go out." Also, Yoruba *kátúbá*, meaning "to pay homage to," is phonetically similar to [kaitumba].

(56)   ababa mifayɔ ji'dε
           akwεwa'rã amana'kε oro
           'manda'kε 'manda'ji
           olεni'jε aka tami mbɔdε
           ni'ša anεpakata oži'dε

Yoruba: *bàbá mi f'ayò jidé*, "my father resurrects with joy." *Bàbá*, "father," *mí*, "my," *f'ayò*, "with joy," and *jidé*, "resurrects." Yoruba: *mádàke mádàji*, "not to be quiet, then to speak later." Here, *má* is "do not," the long form of which is *máse*. The word *orò* is "a type of deity." Edward Esan also told me that the last line of this utterance sounded very much like Yoruba, but that he was unable to recognize any words.

(57)   akwε'ra mana jε 'okɔ
           a zi de 'kosimi

```
ašakɔ'lɛ
'kɔsidi'dɛ akwɛ'ra
mana jɛ
ababa mifa 'oži'de
a gu azɔ'ani 'jibo'si
kɛlɛwi jɛ kwãmã jɛ
```

Elements of modern Yoruba recognized here are: *ǫkǫ* "husband," *aṣákó-ilè̩*, "desert," *bàbá mi f'ayò jidé*, "my father resurrects with joy," and *kilẹwi*, "What do you (plural) see?"

(58)
```
ta ta kemalɛmba
ay o'gũ ɛy
ta ta kemalɛmba
```

"Ai senhor Ogúm, pela vossa coroa, não me deixa à tôa."

(Please, *Ogúm*, don't abandon me, for your crown's sake.) Yoruba: *Ògún*, "god of iron."

(59)
```
o'gũ ɔya ɛžimini
tam'ba la'si bɛnu
tamba laju
tam'ba la'si bɛbu
tamba laju
a'e ku sinu tamba laju
```

Certain elements were recognized in the first line of this utterance only: *Òyà*, "the River Niger," *éjin*, "more than beautiful," and *ní*, "it is."

(60)
```
y'a dɛ'na akwɛ'rã
amana mɛšɛ kɔta mi
dao dide
```

Yoruba: *iyá*, "mother," *dènà*, "to waylay," and *dìde*, "to stand up."

(61)
```
y'a koi'jɛ
```
Yoruba: *iyá kòiti jẹ*, "mother has not eaten."

(62)
```
ɔba lori'ša ɔbalua'e
ɔba lori'ša ɔbalua'e
a'to'to
```

Yoruba: *ǫba olórìṣà*, "god of idol worshippers," and *ǫbaolúwayé*, "appeal to the king of the gods."

(63)   ɔma luta na ku'ɛra
        di su'dã
        e'lo e'lo e'jo
        šɛrɛgɛ'dɛ

Yoruba: *ẹlo ẹlo ẹjọ̃*, "go away, please," and *sẹgede*, "mumps." The song is no doubt one sung to cure the mumps.

(64)   a'go a'go lo'na e
        dide ma da'go a'go
        le le le

Yoruba: *yàgò lọ́nà*, "give way," *ẹ*, "you people" (abbreviated form), and *dìdé*, "get up."

Some examples taken from Deoscóredes M. dos Santos' book *Yorubá Tal Qual se Fala* are:

(65)   Ôdun kan   "um ano" (a year)
        Ôdun tó kójó   "o ano passado" (last year)
        Ôdun tó mbó   "o próximo ano" (next year)
        Ôxu kan   "um mes" (a month)
        Ósé kan   "uma semana" (a week)
        Ójó kan   "um dia" (a day)
        Wakati kan   "uma hora" (an hour)
        Abó wakati   "meia hora" [4] (a half hour)

Three songs dedicated to *Yemanjá*: [5]

(66)   eeman'ja lãgo'oλa
        epe ɛfulo ɛbumi
        eman'ja ɛle manja're

(No translation)
Yoruba: *iyemọja*, "mermaid," *ẹbùn mi*, "you give me."

(67)   eman'ja so'ba
        eman'ja so'ba mirere
        so'ba mirere o

---

[4] See Deoscóredes M. dos Santos, *Yorubá Tal Qual Se Fala* (Bahia, Tipografia Moderna: 1950), p. 6.

[5] *Yemanjá*, according to Edison Carneiro, *Candomblés*, p. 81, is "a mãe d'água, se identifica com a Senhora da Conceição e é festejada a 8 de dezembro." (the water-sprite, [who] is identified with Our Lady of Conception and is celebrated on the 8th of December.)

(No translation)
Yoruba: ṣoba, "becomes king," mi, "me," ní, "in," and rere, "good." This chant could mean, then, "Yemanjá made a good king for me."

(68)   eman'ja io'do manja're

"Yemanjá fica pedindo comida."

(*Yemanjá* is asking for food.) Cf. Kikongo: *iuda*, "light food."

In the following three, *Ogúm* is the guest of honor:

(69)   o'gũ apro'rī olo'rī
         mɛ'rɛ mɛ'rɛ o
         o'gũ a olo'rī olɛ'rɛ
         olɛ'rũ o

É o pai de todos nós. Ogúm é o dono da cabeça, de quem fôr de dentro do candomblé." (He is the father of us all. *Ogúm* is the owner of the entire lot, of whoever belongs to the *candomblé*.)

Yoruba: *olori*, "head of or owner of."
Ewe: *mɛdé*, "anyone."

(70)   o'gũ ɔ'dɛ ma'fa
         siɔ'tɔ
         o'gũ a o'gu ɔ'dɛ
         o'gũ kari'dɛ jiaŋ'ga

"Ogúm é guerreiro, homem sério, homem tímido, homem que toma conta de tôdas as estradas." (*Ogúm* is a warrior, a serious man, a feared man, who controls all of the roads.)

Yoruba: *Ògún*, "god of iron," and *ọdẹ*, "hunter."

(71)   o'gũ ɛrɛ'rɛ ɛma'sa
         fi'otu bi'ɔ mo'lu

"Divindade dos caçadores; é simbolizado por arco e flecha." (A divinity of the hunter; he is symbolized by the bow and arrow.)

Yoruba: *ẹmása* "do not run away."

Oxósse and *Ogúm* share the next song:

(72) ɔ'šɔsi ɔdɛ ɛma fasi'otu
o'gũ o'gũ ɔ'dɛ

"Oxósse e Ogúm, sincretizados como São Jorge. Suas contas são azul e celeste. Seu dia é quinta-feira." (*Oxósse* and *Ogúm*, in the person of Saint George. Their beads [colors] are blue and sky blue. Their day is Thursday.)

Yoruba: *emá*, "group of people," *fàsi*, "pull to," *ọtún*, "right hand," and *ọde*, "hunter."

The final song in *Nagô* is a request for a brief pause in the ceremony, during which the participants clap their hands:

(73) kɔ'dɛ lu'na ba'ba
kɔ'dɛ lu'na
o'kũ ba'ba kɔ'dɛ 'luna

"É pedindo misericórdia aos filhos do terreiro, pedindo que parem e pedindo macó."[6] (He is asking for mercy from the members of the *terreiro*, asking them to stop and clap their hands.)

Yoruba: *okú*, "something dead."
Yoruba: *baba*, "father."
Ewe: *tɔ dé* (*tsítrè*), "to stop."

---

[6] *Macó* is a clapping of hands of all present at the ceremony in honor of any particular saint. Cf. Kimbundu: *maku*, "to clap hands."

Appendix IV

"IJESHA," "ANGOLA" AND PORTUGUESE MATERIAL

Mãe Z. supplied me with a relatively long passage in *"Ijexá."* [1] It speaks about the spirit *Exu*:

(1) e'šu a'na e'šu a'na 'mõči're lɔ'dɛ ale'bara prɔ'ni e'šu a'na tey'o ɛlɛ'bara parane'e e'šu a'na ke 'nãu e'šu ba'ra ũ'ko e'šu ka'ra ka'ra bɛ'bɛ e'šu ala'beo e'ke 'mõči ba'ra eɔ'pa'a ma'kɔ e'šu kalaru'e kã ēifo'ro e'šu kalaru'e

The translation of the above passage, as given to me by *mãe* Z. is the following:

> Exu, mensageiro dos orixás, chamado familiarmente como um compadre, mas é rebôlo e é fàcilmente irritado. É simbolizado por motivo de terra, na qual estão confiados ferro e lanças devido ao seu caráter de mau. Em condições de mensageiro dos outros orixás recebe o seu sacrifício por primeiro, quer dizer que os sacrifícios são a comida; recebe primeiramente para poder dar a comida aos orixás; são os santos, os encantados. É êrradamente sincretizado como o diabo, bem tratado, trabalha para o bem, e seu dia é segunda-feira.

> (*Exu*, messenger of the spirits, more commonly called godfather, is irritable and easily upset. He is symbolized by land, in which iron and weapons are confided because of his evil character. As messenger of the other spirits, he receives his sacrifice first; the sacrifices being food; he receives it first in order to give it to the other spirits, which are the saints or ghosts. He is erroneously believed to be the devil,

---

[1] *"Ijexá"* is a dialect of Yoruba.

[but actually] he works to promote good things, and his day is Monday.)

The only word recognized by my Nigerian informant was [a'na], which could be Yoruba ọ̀nà, "road."

The following African words may be compared to the "Ijesha":

Yoruba: àna, "relatives by marriage," godfather (?) for a'na.
Yoruba: ẹlẹ́gbára, "god of mischief, Satan," for ɛlɛ'bara.
Yoruba: purọ́, "to tell a lie," and ni, "to say" for prɔ'ni.
Yoruba: bara, "the devil," for bara.

The utterance 'nãu e'šu ba'ra ũ'ko may be a combination of the Portuguese word não, and Yoruba èṣù, bara, and ùn-hún and ko, which mean "not, not so." It may mean, then, that èṣù is not the devil. This would agree with the translation given to me by the mãe de santo.

Yoruba: èké, "lie, untruth," for e'ke.
Yoruba: eyọ́, "an edible viscous herb," for eɔ.
Kimbundu: maku, "to clap hands," for ma'kɔ.
Kikongo: kala o luuete, "well-being," for kalaru'e.

The Portuguese version of the "Ijesha" is more of a paraphrase with some added frills rather than a translation, showing again the amount of African language that has been lost, for even if the Ijesha words have been retained, the exact meaning of them has been completely forgotten.

Some songs in "Ijesha" employed during candomblé were also obtained from mãe Z. The first one mentions a drink:

(2) bibiriti'šɛ mai'ɔ
     bibiriti'šɛ lɛ byo'ro

Mãe Z. was able to translate only two words of this song:

bibiriti'šɛ "bebida" (drink)
mai'ɔ "maior" (larger)

The word mai'ɔ is probably the Portuguese word maior which has replaced an Ijesha equivalent, although the possibility of its being a chance similarity cannot altogether be disregarded. In modern Yoruba, *mayò* means "rejoice" and *máyò* means "do not rejoice."

The second Ijesha song calls on *Exu*:

(3) e'šu jɛ'lu jɛ'lu le le
 ju'ara ɛlɛ 'bara ke're
 ɛ'šu je'šu jɛ'lu le le
 ju'ara

"É chamando o diabo." [2]

(This song calls on the devil.)

Interestingly enough, the Yoruba word *èṣù* means "devil," and the word *ará*, "thunder," is one used by the Ijesha people to pronounce a curse on someone.

Again we recognize the names *èṣù* and *ẹlégbára*.

The third song calls *Exu* to drink blood:

(4) ɛ'šu kã laɔ'rɛ
 ɛ'šu kã ĩ jo'ro

"É chamando êle para beber sangue; *jo'ro é* sangue."

(They are calling him to drink blood; *jo'ro* is blood.)

We may compare Yoruba *kán*, "to drop, as any liquid drops." Also Yoruba *lá*, "to lap up with the tongue."

The following songs were sung in what *mãe* Z. described as *Angola*. If she was referring to the geographical area of Africa as the point of origin, it is possible that the language is a member of the Benue-Congo group.

The first song calls on and praises *Bombomjira*, the Devil:

(5) ora'ra ore're
 bõbõ'jira ja'kũ jã jo
 ora'ra ore're

---

[2] *Exu*, in Bahia, is not the devil, but is erroneously taken to be so in many cult houses in Bahia. *Mãe* Z. contradicts herself during the interview, for in the Portuguese version of the first passage in "Ijesha," she stated that *Exu* "é êrradamente sincretizado como o diabo..." (is erroneously thought to be the devil...) *Exu*, as found in Bahia, evidently changed in meaning from the original Yoruba, for as we have seen, *èṣù* in modern Yoruba is "devil."

APPENDIX

"É chamando êle e louvando êle."

(They are calling him and praising him.)

The second song has the same purpose as the first:

(6)   kĩdã kĩdã bõbõ'jira
           jĩdã i'ɔ i'e

(No translation.)

The third one makes an offering to the spirit:

(7)   tɔ ma'la zɛ kũ zɛ
           kɔy'a zɛ kuri'ɔ

"Está oferecendo a êle."

(They are offering [gifts] to him.)

The utterance *kuri'ɔ* may be Kimbundu *kuria*, "food."

The following songs were recorded in a *terreiro* in the Plataforma area of Bahia. They are sung in Portuguese and represent songs which were heard in all of the cult houses visited. They are but a small example of the wide-spread usage of Portuguese among Bahian *candomblés*.

The first is dedicated to *Yemanjá*. Its chorus is in *Nagô*:

(8)   Dona Janaína,[3] princêsa que é
           Filha das águas, lá d'Abaeté,[4]
           ke na na'e
           ke na na'e'o

(Janaína, princess, daughter of the waters of Abaeté.)
(No translation.)

The second has its title in "Yoruba," but the remaining part in Portuguese:

(9)   dini ja na'in (title)
           Êle é do rio,

---

[3] *Janaína* is another name for *Yemanjá*.

[4] *Abaeté* is a lake just outside the city of Salvador. The word comes from Tupi *abaeté*, meaning "a man of worth."

>   êle é do mar,
>   traga ouro, traga prata
>   para a seréia vadear.

(No translation.)

(He comes from the river, he comes from the sea, bringing gold, bringing silver so that the mermaid may cross the sea.)

The utterance *ja na'in* is probably Janaína.
The third has no title and is entirely in Portuguese:

(10)   Tem morador, de certo tem morador,
        no lugar que o galo canta,
        de certo tem morador.

(Someone certainly lives where there is a rooster singing.)

Mãe Z. was able to give me only two expressions in "Yoruba" which are commonly used around the house and have no connection with *candomblé*. They are:

(11)   ko'lɔ ko'lɔ ji
        ɛ da'i ɔ ma da'i
        ɛ da'i

"O pirão está pronto ou não?" "Está pronto."

(Is the manioc mush ready yet? It is ready.)

(12)   o mĩ dũ'dũ

"Café."

(Coffee.)

Yoruba: *ómi dúdú*, "black water."

Appendix V

ADDITIONAL WORDS RECORDED AS PART
OF THE PASSIVE VOCABULARY IN BAHIA

The following are names of minor spirits:

1 Alabês
2 Arárun
3 Axé de Kétu
4 Axogum
5 Ayabás
6 Baniáni
7 Beji
8 Dalé Xangô
9 Erê
10 Euá
11 Iyá
12 Iyá Kalá
13 Iyamasê
14 Iyá Oxalá
15 Kubá
16 Nambu
17 Obaluagê
18 Obará
19 Obá Sãiyá
20 Obatalá
21 Odô
22 Osanhi
23 Osi Dagan
24 Otim

The following are shouts used in the *candomblé*:

25 Aiaiá
26 Balué
27 Epa Rei
28 Erã Paterê
29 Ierê
30 Iyawô
31 Mariô
32 Olelé
33 Opaxorô

A SELECTED BIBLIOGRAPHY

A Dictionary of the Yoruba Language. London: Oxford University Press, 1956.
Abraham, R. C. *A Dictionary of the Tiv Language*. London: the Government of Nigeria, 1968.
———. *Dictionary of Modern Yoruba*. London: University of London Press, 1958.
———. *The Principles of Tiv*. Hertford: Stephen Austin and Sons, 1968.
Ajayi, J. F. Ade, and Robert Smith. *Yoruba Warfare in the Nineteenth Century*. Cambridge: Cambridge University Press, 1964.
Alves, P. Albino. *Dicionário Etimológico Bundo-Português*. (2 vols.). Lisboa: Centro Tip. Colonial, 1951.
Amado, Jorge. *Bahia de Todos os Santos*. São Paulo: Livraria Martins Editôra, 1946.
Armstrong, Robert G. *A Comparative Wordlist of Five Igbo Dialects*. Ibadan: Institute of African Studies, 1967.
———. *The Study of West African Languages*. Ibadan: Ibadan University Press, 1964.
Arrázola, Roberto. *Palenque, primer pueblo libre de América*. Cartagena, Colombia: Ediciones Hernández, 1970.
Ashton, E. O., et al. *A Luganda Grammar*. London: Longmans, Green and Co., 1954.
———. *Notes on Form and Structure in Bantu Speech*. London: Oxford University Press, 1945.
Avermaet, E. Van. *Dictionnaire Kiluba-Français*. Tervuren: Commission de Linguistique Africaine, 1954.
Ayrosa, Plínio. *Têrmos Tupis no Português do Brasil*. São Paulo: Emprêsa Gráfica da "Revista dos Tribunais," 1937.
Azevedo, Fernando de. *Brazilian Culture*. New York: New World, 1950.
Azevedo, Thales de. *As Elites de Cor; um Estudo de Asenção Social*. São Paulo: Companhia Editôra Nacional, 1955 (Série V, Vol. 282).
———. *Cultura e Situação Racial no Brasil*. Rio de Janeiro: Editôra Civilização Brasileira, S. A., 1966.
———. "Índios, Brancos e Prêtos no Brasil Colonial." *América Indígena*, 13, No. 2 (April 1953).
Bally, Charles. *El lenguaje y la vida*. Buenos Aires: Editorial Losada, S. A., 1941.
Bamgboṣe, Ayol. *A Grammar of Yoruba* (West African Monographs 5). Cambridge: Cambridge University Press, 1966.

A SELECTED BIBLIOGRAPHY

Bartels, F. L. and J. A. Annobil. *Mfantse Nkasafua Dwumadzi* (A Fante Grammar of Function). London: Methodist Book Depot, 1946.

Bascom, William R. "Afro-Americains," *Memoires de l'Institut Français d'Afrique Noire*, No. 27. Dakar, Africa. n.d.

———. "The Focus of Cuban Santeria," *Southwestern Journal of Anthropology*, 6, No. 1 (Spring 1950). The University of New Mexico Press.

———. "Two Forms of Afro-Cuban Divination," *Acculturation in the Americas*, II. Proceedings of the 29th International Congress of Americanists (1952). The University of Chicago Press.

———. *Ifa Divination*. Bloomington: Indiana University Press, 1969.

———. "The Sociological Role of the Yoruba Cult Group," *American Anthropologist*, 46, No. 1, Part 2 (January 1944).

———. *The Sociological Role of the Yoruba Cult-Group*. Menasha: American Anthropological Association, 1944.

Basset, André. *La Langue Berbère*. London: Oxford University Press, 1952.

Bastide, Roger. *Les Religions Africaines au Brésil*. Paris: Presses Universitaires, 1960.

Benedict, Ruth. *Race and Racism*. London: The Scientific Book Club, 1943.

Benson, T. G. *Kikuyu-English Dictionary*. London: Oxford University Press, 1964.

Bentley, W. H., Rev. *Dictionary and Grammar of the Kongo Language* (As spoken at San Salvador, the Ancient Capital of the Old Kongo Empire, West Africa). London: Trüber and Co., 1886.

Berry, J. *English, Twi, Asante, Fante Dictionary*. London: Macmillan and Co. Ltd., 1960.

———. *The Pronunciation of Ewe*. Cambridge: Heffer, n.d.

Birnie, J. R. and G. Ansre, eds. *Proceedings of the Conference on The Study of Ghanaian Languages*. Legon: Ghana Publishing Corp., 1969.

Bluteau, Rafael. *Vocabulário Português e Latino*. Coimbra: Colégio das Artes da Companhia de Jesus, 1712.

Bowen, T. J. *A Grammar and Dictionary of the Yoruba Language*. Smithsonian Institution, May, 1858, Smithsonian *Contributions to Knowledge*, Washington, 1858.

Boxer, C. R. *Portuguese Society in the Tropics: The Municipal Councils of Goa, Macao, Bahia, and Luanda, 1510-1800*. Madison: the University of Wisconsin Press, 1965.

———. "Negro Slavery in Brazil." *Race, the Journal of the Institute of Race Relations*, 5, No. 3 (1964).

Brandão, Adelino. *Recortes de Folklore*. São Paulo: Araçatuba, n.d.

Brandão, Darwin. *A Cozinha Baiana*. Rio de Janeiro: Tecnoprint Gráfica, S. A., 1967.

Bryan, M. A. *The Bantu Languages of Africa*. London: Oxford University Press, 1959.

Bueno, Francisco da Silveira. "Tratado de Semântica Geral Aplicada à Língua Portuguêsa." *Filologia e Lingua Portuguêsa*, No. 1, Boletim LXXXIII, São Paulo: Universidade de São Paulo, 1947.

Bunche, Ralph J. *A World View of Race*. Port Washington, New York: Kennikat Press, Inc., 1968.

Burns, Sir Alan. *History of Nigeria*. London: Unwin Brothers Ltd., 1969.

Burton, Richard. *Explorations in the Highlands of Brazil*. London: Tinsley Brothers, 1896.

Cabrera, Lydia. *El monte*. Eastchester, New York: Eliseo Torres, 1954.

Cabrera, Lydia. *Anagó*. Eastchester, New York: Eliseo Torres, 1957.

———. *Otan Iyebibe. Las piedras preciosas*. Eastchester, New York: Eliseo Torres, 1969.

Cannecattim, Fr. Bernardo Maria de. *Collecção de Observações Grammaticaes sobre A Lingua Bunda ou Angolense e Diccionario Abreviado da Lingua Congueza*. Lisboa: Imprensa Nacional, 1859.

Carneiro, Edison. *Antologia do Negro Brasileiro*. Rio de Janeiro: Tecnoprint Gráfica, 1967.

———. *Candomblés da Bahia*. Rio de Janeiro: Tecnoprint Gráfica, S. A., 1961.

———. *A Lingua Popular da Bahia*. Salvador: Publicações do Museu do Estado, 1951.

———. *Religiões Negras*. Rio de Janeiro: Civilização Brasileira, S. A., 1936.

Carneiro, Sousa. *Os Mitos Africanos no Brasil*. Rio de Janeiro: Ciência do Folk-lore Companhia Editôra Nacional, 1937.

Carvalho, Oscar de. "Pequeno Vocabulário de Língua Nagô," 1900, unpublished.

Carvalho, Rodrigues de. "Aspectos da Influência Africana na Formação Social do Brasil." *Novos Estudos Afro-Brasileiros*. Rio de Janeiro: Civilização Brasileira, 1937.

Cascudo, Luis da Câmara. *Dicionário do Folklore Brasileiro*. Rio de Janeiro: Instituto Nacional do Livro, 1962.

Castelanau, Francis de. *Renseignements sur l'Afrique Centrale et sur une nation d'hommes à guerre qui s'y trouverait d'après le rapport des Négres du Soudain esclaves à Bahia*. Paris: P. Bertrand, 1851.

Castro, Guilherme de Sousa and Yêda Pessoa de Castro. "Estudo da Língua Portuguêsa numa Comunidade Brasileira em Lagos, Nigeria." *Afro-Asia* (Salvador: Centro de Estudos Afro-Orientais da Universidade Federal da Bahia), No. 1 (December 1965).

Castro, Yêda Pessoa de. "As Línguas Africanas na Bahia." *A Tarde*, Sábado, 30 de maio, 1968.

Chatelain, Heli, *Kimbundu Grammar (Grammática Elementar do Kimbundu ou Lingua de Angola)*. Genebra: Typ. de Charles Schuchardt, 1888-89.

Christaller, Johann Gottlieb. *A Dictionary of the Asante and Fante Language Called Tshi*. Basel: Basel Evangelical Missionary Society, 1881.

———. *A Grammar of the Asante and Fante Language Called Tshi*. Basel: Basel Evangelical Missionary Society, 1875.

Cole, D. T. *Bantu Linguistic Studies in South Africa*. Johannesburg: Witwatersrand University Press, 1957.

Couto de Magalhães, General. *O Selvagem*. São Paulo: Companhia Editôra Nacional, 1940.

Crabb, D. W. *Ekoid Bantu Languages of Ogoja, Eastern Nigeria* (Part 1). Cambridge: Cambridge University Press, 1965.

Crowther, Samuel A. *A Vocabulary of the Yoruba Language* (Parts 1 and 2). London: Church Missionary Society, 1843.

———. *A Grammar and Vocabulary of the Yoruba Language*. London: Seeleys, 1852.

Curtin, Philip D. *Africa Remembered: Narratives by West Africans from the Era of the Slave Trade*. Madison: University of Wisconsin Press, 1967.

———. *The Atlantic Slave Trade: A Census*. Madison: University of Wisconsin Press, 1969.

A SELECTED BIBLIOGRAPHY 221

Dard, Jean. *Dictionnaire Français-Wolof et Français-Bambara, suivi du Dictionnaire Wolof-Français*. Paris: n.p.,[1] 1825.

Da Silva Neto, Serafim. *Introdução ao Estudo da Língua Portuguêsa no Brasil*. Rio de Janeiro: Departamento de Imprensa Nacional, 1951.

———. *Introdução ao Estudo da Língua Portuguêsa no Brasil*. Rio de Janeiro: Instituto Nacional do Livro, Ministério de Educação e Cultura, 1963.

De Guiraudon, T. G. *Manuel de la Langue Foule*. Paris: n.p., 1894.

De Jonghe, E., director. *Le Plus Ancien Dictionnaire Bantu*. Louvin: Imprimerie J. Kuyl-Otto, 1928.

Delafosse, Maurice. *Les langues du monde*. Paris: Payot et Cie., 1922.

———. *Manuel Dahoméen*. Paris: Ernst Leroux, éditeur, 1894.

Dennett, Richard E. *Nigerian Studies*. London: Frank Cass and Co. Ltd., 1968.

Dicionário Cinyanja-Português by the Missionários da Companhia de Jesus. Lisboa: Junta de Investigações do Ultramar, 1963.

Doke, C. M. *The Southern Bantu Languages*. London: Oxford University Press, 1954.

Do Nascimento, Abdias, ed. *O Negro Revoltado*. Rio de Janeiro: Edições GRD, 1968.

Dos Santos, Deoscóredes M. *Axé Ôpô Afonjá*. Rio de Janeiro: Instituto Brasileiro de Estudos Afro-Asiáticos, 1962.

———. *Contos de Nagô*. Rio de Janeiro: Edições GRD, 1963.

———. *Contos Negros da Bahia*. Rio de Janeiro: Edições GRD, 1961.

———. *Iorubá Tal Qual se Fala*. Bahia: Tipografia Moderna, 1950.

——— and Juana Elbein. "West African Sacred Art and Rituals in Brazil." Monograph, Institute of African Studies, University of Ibadan, Nigeria, 1967.

Dos Santos, Pe Luís Feliciano. *Dicionário Português-Chope e Chope-Português*. Moçambique: n.p., 1949.

Dozier, Edward. "Two Examples of Linguistic Acculturation: The Yaqui of Sonora and Arizona and the Tewa of New Mexico." *Language*, 32 (1956).

Dunstan, Elizabeth. *Twelve Nigerian Languages*. London: Longmans, Green and Co., Ltd., 1969.

Echegaray, Carlos G. *Estudios Guineos*. Madrid: n.p., 1964.

Edelweiss, Frederico G. *Estudos Tupis e Tupi-Guaranis*. Rio de Janeiro: Livraria Brasiliana Editôra, 1969.

Elia, Sílvio. *O Problema da Língua Brasileira*. Rio de Janeiro: Irmãos Pongetti Editôres, 1940.

Ellis, Alfred B. *The Ewe-Speaking Peoples of the Slave Coast of West Africa*. London: Chapman and Hall, 1890.

———. *Raça de Gigantes*. Fifth edition. São Paulo: Editôra Nacional, 1948.

———. *The Tshi-Speaking Peoples of the Gold Coast of West Africa*. Chicago: Benin Press, Ltd., 1964.

———. *The Yoruba-Speaking Peoples of the Slave Coast of West Africa*. Chicago: Benin Press, Ltd., 1964.

Escalante, Aquiles. *El negro en Colombia*. Bogotá: Universidad Nacional, 1964.

Fadipẹ, N. A. *The Sociology of the Yoruba*. Ibadan: Ibadan University Press, 1970.

---

[1] n.p. — name of publisher not available.

Faidherbe, Le Général. *Langues Sénégalaises, Wolof, Arabe-Hassania, Soninké, Sérère.* Paris: Ernest Leroux, 1887.

———. *Grammaire et Vocabulaire de la Langue Poul* (à l'usage des voyageurs dans le Soudan). 2nd ed. Paris: n.p., 1882.

Fernandes, Florestan. *A Integração do Negro à Sociedade de Classes.* São Paulo: Faculdade de Filosofia, Ciências e Letras da Universidade de São Paulo, 1964.

———. *The Negro in Brazilian Society* (Translated by Jacqueline D. Skiles, A. Brunel, and Arthur Rothwell.) Phyllis B. Eveleth, ed. New York: Columbia University Press, 1969.

Fernández, P. L. *Diccionario Español-Kômbè.* Madrid: Instituto de Estudios Africanos, 1951.

Forde, Daryll, ed. *Efik Traders of Old Calabar.* London: Oxford University Press, 1956.

——— and G. I. Jones. *The Ibo and Ibibio-Speaking Peoples of South-Eastern Nigeria.* London: Oxford University Press, 1950.

——— and P. M. Kaberry, eds. *West African Kingdoms in the Nineteenth Century.* Oxford: Oxford University Press, 1967.

Foucauld, P. de. *Dictionnaire Abrégé Touareg-Français.* Paris: Larose, 1940.

Franco, José Luciano. *Présence Africaine au Nouveau Monde.* Dakar: Centre de Hautes Études Afro-Ibero-Americaines, n.d.

Frazier, E. Franklin. *Race and Culture Contacts in the Modern World.* Boston: Beacon Press, 1968.

Freire, Gilberto. *Casa Grande e Senzala.* Second edition. Rio de Janeiro: Schmidt Editôra, 1936.

———. *The Masters and the Slaves.* New York: Alfred A. Knopf, 1956.

Gaden, Henri. *Le Poular: Dialecte Peul du Fouta Senegalais.* Tome Second: Lexique Poular-Français. Paris: Ernest Leroux, 1914.

Gamble, David Percy. *The Wolof of Senegambia...* London: International African Institute, 1957.

Gardner, George. *Travels in the Interior of Brazil, 1836-1841.* London: Reeve, Bentham, and Reeve, 1849.

Gleason, H. A., Jr. *An Introduction to Descriptive Linguistics* (Revised Edition). New York, Chicago, San Francisco, Toronto, London: Holt Rinehart, and Winston, 1965.

Góes, Jayme de Farias. *Festas Tradicionais da Bahia.* Bahia: Livraria Progrêsso Editôra, 1961.

Goldie, Hugh, Rev. *Dictionary of the Efik Language.* Ridgewood, New Jersey: Gregg Press, Inc., 1964.

Greenberg, Joseph H. *The Languages of Africa.* The Hague, The Netherlands: Mouton and Co., 1963. In *International Journal of American Linguistics*, 29, No. 1 (January 1963).

Gregory, John W. *The Menace of Colour.* Philadelphia: J. B. Lippincott Co., 1925.

Guthrie, Malcolm. *The Bantu Languages of Western Equatorial Africa.* London: Oxford University Press, 1953.

———. *The Classification of the Bantu Languages.* London: Dawsons of Pall Mall, 1967.

Hall, Robert A., Jr. *Pidgin and Creole Languages.* Ithaca and London: Cornell University Press, 1969.

Hama, Boubou. *L'Histoire Traditionnelle d'un Peuple, Les Zarma-Songhay.* Paris: Présence Africaine, 1967.

A SELECTED BIBLIOGRAPHY

Harris, Marvin. *Patterns of Race in the Americas.* New York: Walker and Co., 1964.
———. "Racial Identity in Brazil." *Luso-Brazilian Review,* No. 1 (1964).
———. *Town and Country in Brazil.* New York: Columbia University Press, 1956.
——— and Conrad Kottak. "The Structural Significance of Brazilian Racial Categories." *Sociologia,* 25 (1963).
Henrici, Ernst. *Lehrbuch der Ephe-Sprache.* Stuttgart und Berlin: W. Spemann, 1891.
Herskovits, Melville J. *The American Negro (A Study in Racial Crossing).* New York: Alfred A. Knopf, 1928.
———. *Dahomey, An Ancient West African Kingdom* (2 vols.). New York: J. J. Augustine, 1938.
———. *Estudos Etnológicos na Bahia.* Bahia: Museu do Estado, 1942.
———. *Life in a Haitian Valley.* New York: Alfred A. Knopf, 1937.
———. "An Outline of Dahomean Religious Belief." *Memoirs of the American Anthropological Association.* Menasha, Wisconsin: Collegiate Press, 1933.
———. *The Myth of the Negro Past.* New York: Harper and Brothers, 1941.
———. "The Negro in Bahia, Brazil: A Problem in Method." *American Sociological Review,* 8, No. 4 (1943).
———. "The New World Negro." *Selected Papers in Afro-American Studies.* Bloomington: Indiana.
———. "Problem, Method and Theory in Afroamerican Studies." *Afroamerica,* 1 (1945).
——— and F. S. Herskovits. *Rebel Destiny Among the Bush Negroes of Dutch Guiana.* New York: Whittlesey House, 1934.
———. *Suriname Folklore.* New York: Columbia University Press, 1936.
———. *Dahomean Narrative.* Evanston, Illinois: Northwestern University Press, 1958.
Homburger, Lilias. *The Negro-African Languages.* London: Routledge and K. Paul, 1949.
Hovelacque, Abel. *La Linguistique.* Paris: Reinwald, 1878.
Howeidy, A. *Concise Hausa Grammar.* London: George Ronald, 1959.
Huyghe, P. G. Le. *Dictionnaire Chaouia-Arabe-Kabyle et Français.* Alger: Typographie Adolphe Jourdan, 1907.
Hymes, Dell. *Pidginization and Creolization of Languages.* Cambridge: Cambridge University Press, 1971.
Jaubert, P. Amédée. *Grammaire et Dictionnaire Abrégés de la Langue Berbère.* Paris: Imprimerie Royal, 1845.
Johnson, Samuel, Rev. *The History of the Yorubas.* London: Lowe and Brydone, 1956.
Johnston, Harry H., Sir. *A Comparative Study of the Bantu and semi-Bantu Languages.* London: Oxford University Press, 1919-22.
———. *The Negro in the New World.* London: Methuen and Co., Ltd., 1910.
———. *Pioneers in West Africa.* London: Blackie and Son, Ltd., 1912.
Jover Peralta, Anselmo and Tomás Osuna. *Diccionario Guaraní-Español y Español-Guaraní.* Buenos Aires: Editorial Tupã, 1950.
Klingenheben, August. *Die Sprache Der Ful* (Dialekt von Adamaua). Hamburg: n.p., 1963.

Knight, Franklin W. *Slave Society in Cuba During the Nineteenth Century.* Madison: University of Wisconsin Press, 1970.
Kottak, Conrad. "Race Relations in a Bahian Fishing Village." *Luso-Brazilian Review,* No. 4 (1967).
Krapf-Askari, Eva. *Yoruba Towns and Cities.* Oxford: Clarendon Press, 1969.
Ladefoged, Peter. *A Phonetic Study of West African Languages.* Cambridge: Cambridge University Press, 1968.
Language Guide (Ewe Edition). Bureau of Ghana Languages, 1961.
Lecomte, E., P^e, and P^e J. Sutter and coordinated by P^e Domingos Vieira Baião. *Dicionário Ganguela-Português.* Lisboa: Centro de Estudos Filológicos, n.d.
Lehmann, Winfred P. *Historical Linguistics: An Introduction.* New York, Chicago, San Francisco, Toronto, London: Holt, Rinehart, and Winston, 1966.
Leite, Solidónio. *A Língua Portuguêsa no Brasil.* Rio de Janeiro: Editôres J. Leite e Cia., 1922.
Lemos Barbosa, P^e A. *Pequeno Vocabulário Tupi-Português.* Rio de Janeiro: Dept. de Imprensa Nacional, 1967.
Lemos, Virgílio de. *A Língua Portuguêsa no Brasil.* Bahia: Imprensa Oficial do Estado, 1916.
Le Page, R. B., ed. *Jamaican Creole.* London: Macmillan and Co., Ltd., 1960.
Lloyd, Peter C. *The Political Development of Yoruba Kingdoms in the Eighteenth and Nineteenth Centuries.* London: William Clowes and Sons, Ltd., 1971.
———. *Yoruba Land Law.* London: Oxford University Press, 1962.
Lopes Gama, Miguel do Sacramento, Padre. *O Carapuceiro.* Recife: n.p., 1832.
Lucas, J. Olumide, Archdeacon. *The Religion of the Yorubas....* Lagos: C.M.S. Bookshop, 1948.
Machado, José Pedro. *Dicionário Etimológico da Língua Portuguêsa,* 1ª edição. Lisboa: Editôra Confluência, 1952. 2 vols.
Maia, António da Silva. *Dicionário Complementar Português-Kimbundu, Kikongo.* Cucujães: Tipografia das Missões, 1962.
———. *Dicionário Elementar Português-Omumbuim-Mussele* (Dialectos do Kimbundu e Mbundu). Cucujães: Tipografia das Missões, 1955.
———. *Lições de Gramática de Quimbundo.* Cucujães: Escola Tipográfica das Missões, n.d.
Marroquim, Mário. *A Língua do Nordeste.* São Paulo: Editôra Nacional, 1945.
McGregor, Pedro. *The Moon and Two Mountains.* London: Souvenir Press, 1966.
Mello, Octaviano. *Dicionário Tupi Português e Vice-Versa.* São Paulo: Editor Folco Masucci, 1967.
Melo, Gladstone Chaves de. *A Língua do Brasil.* Rio de Janeiro: Livraria AGIR Editôra, 1946.
Mendonça, Renato. *A Influência Africana no Português do Brasil.* Pôrto: Livraria Figueirinhas, 1948.
———. *O Português do Brasil.* Rio de Janeiro: Civilização Brasileira, S. A., Editôra, 1936.

Mezzera, Baltasar Luis. *Idioma español y habla criolla.* Montevideo: Editorial Solange, 1968.
Migeod, F. W. H. *The Languages of West Africa.* London: Kegan Paul and Co., 1911.
———. *The Mende Language.* London: Kegan Paul, Trench, Trübner and Co., Ltd., 1908.
Murphy, John D. and Harry Goff. *A Bibliography of African Languages and Linguistics.* Catholic University Press, 1969.
Nascentes, Antenor. *A Gíria Brasileira.* Rio de Janeiro: Livraria Acadêmica, 1953.
———. *Tesouro da Fraseologia Brasileira.* São Paulo: Livraria Editôra Freitas Bastos, 1945.
Neiva, Arthur. *Estudos da Língua Nacional.* São Paulo: Cia. Editôra Nacional, 1940.
Ojo, G. J. Afolabi. *Yoruba Culture.* London: Hazell Watson and Viney, Ltd., 1966.
Oliveira Lima, Manuel de. *João VI no Brasil.* Rio de Janeiro: Vol. III, Livraria José Olympio Editôra, 1945.
Olmsted, David L. "Comparative Notes on Yoruba and Lucumí." *Language,* 29, No. 2 (1953).
———. "The Phonemes of Yoruba." *Word,* 7, No. 3 (1951).
Ortiz, Fernando. *Hampa afrocubana. Los negros esclavos.* Havana: Editorial América, 1916.
———. *La africanía de la música folklórica de Cuba.* Havana: Publicaciones del Ministerio de Educación, 1950.
———. *Los bailes y el teatro de los negros en el folklore de Cuba.* Havana: Publicaciones del Ministerio de Educación, 1951.
———. "Los negros curros." *Archivos del Folklore Cubano.* Havana: Ediciones de Cultura, S. A., 3, No. 1 (1927).
———. "Un catuaro de cubanismos." *Revista Bimestre Cubana,* 18 (1923).
———. "Los cabildos afrocubanos." (Folleto), Havana: n.p., 1923.
———. *Glosario de afronegrismos.* Havana: Imprenta "El Siglo XX," 1924.
———. "El cocoricamo y otros conceptos teoplasmiscos del folklore afrocubano." (Conferencia), Havana, 1930.
———. *De la música afrocubana.* Havana: n.p., 1935.
———. *La clave xilofónica de la música cubana.* Havana: Molina, 1935.
———. "La poesía mulata." *Revista Bimestre Cubana* (1934, 1935, 1936).
———. "La música sagrada de los Negros Yoruba en Cuba." *Revista Estudios Afrocubanos* (1938).
Ott, Carlos B. *Formação e Evolução Etnica da Cidade do Salvador: O Folklore Baiano.* Salvador: Tipografia Mann Editôra Ltda., 1955.
Pádua, Ciro T. de. "O Dialeto Brasileiro" (Ensaio de filologia e sociologia sôbrea língua falada no Brasil). São Paulo: Editôra Guaíra, Ltda., 1942.
Pierson, Donald. *Negroes in Brazil.* Chicago: University of Chicago Press, 1942.
———. "Race Relations in Portuguese America." *Race Relations in World Perspective* (ed. by Andrew W. Lind). Honolulu: University of Hawaii Press, 1955.
Querino, Manuel. *O Colono Prêto como Fator da Civilização Brasileira.* Bahia: Imprensa Oficial do Estado, 1918.
Quintão, José Luís. *Dicionários Xironga-Português e Português-Xironga.* Lisboa: Agência Geral das Colônias, 1951.

Raimundo, Jacques. *A Língua Portuguêsa no Brasil.* Rio de Janeiro: Renascença Editôra, n.d.
──────. *A Língua Portuguêsa no Brasil.* Rio de Janeiro: Imprensa Nacional, 1941.
──────. *O Elemento Afro-Negro na Língua Portuguêsa.* Rio de Janeiro: Renascença Editôra, 1933.
Rambaud, M. J.-B. *La Langue Mandé.* Paris: Imprimerie Nationale, 1896.
Ramos, Arthur. *A Aculturação Negra no Brasil.* São Paulo: Companhia Editôra Nacional, 1942.
────── et al. *O Negro no Brasil.* (Trabalhos apresentados ao 2° Congresso Afro-Brasileiro [Bahia]). Rio de Janeiro: Biblioteca de Divulgação Scientífica, Civilização Brasileira, S. A., Editôra, 1940.
──────. *As Culturas Negras no Nôvo Mundo.* Rio de Janeiro: Civilização Brasileira, S. A., Editôra, 1937.
──────. *O Folklore Negro do Brasil.* Second edition. Rio de Janeiro: Civilização Brasileira, 1954.
Rechenbach, Charles W. *Swahili-English Dictionary.* Washington, D. C.: n.p., 1967.
Redden, J. E., et al. *Twi, Basic Course.* Washington: Department of State, 1963.
Ribeiro, João. *O Elemento Negro.* Rio de Janeiro: Record, 1934.
──────. *O Folklore.* Rio de Janeiro: Yacintha Ribeira dos Santos, Livraria Editôra, 1919.
Robinson, Charles H. *Dictionary of the Hausa Language,* I. Cambridge: Cambridge University Press, 1925.
Rodney, Walter. *West Africa and the Atlantic Slave-Trade.* Nairobi: East African Publishing House, 1967.
Rodrigues, Nina. *Os Africanos no Brasil.* São Paulo: Cia. Editôra Nacional, 1932.
Romero, Sílvio. *Cantos Populares do Brasil.* Rio de Janeiro: Livraria José Olympio Editôra, 1954.
Rossi, Nelson. *Aspectos do Léxico da Bahia.* Salvador: Comunicação ao IV Colóquio Internacional de Estudos Luso-Brasileiros, 1958.
Ruiz de Montoya, Antonio. *Gramática y Diccionarios* (Arte, Vocabulario y Tesoro) *de la lengua tupí o guaraní.* Paris: Faesy y Frick, 1876.
Saint-Hilaire, Augustin François. *Viagens ao Rio Grande do Sul.* Rio de Janeiro: Editôra Nacional, 1820.
Samarin, William J. *A Grammar of Sango.* Paris: Mouton and Co., 1967.
Schlenker, C. F., Rev. *A Collection of Temne Traditions, Fables and Proverbs.* Stuttgart: J. F. Steinkopf, 1861.
Schlichthorst, Henrich. *O Rio de Janeiro como é.* Rio de Janeiro: Editôra Nacional, 1826.
Schneider, Gilbert D. *Preliminary Glossary, English > Pidgin-English (Wes-Kos).* Athens: Ohio University Press, 1965.
Scott, David Clement, Rev. *A Cyclopaedic Dictionary of the Mang'anja Language Spoken in British Central Africa.* Edinburgh: Lutterworth Press, 1892.
──────. *Dictionary of the Nyanja Language.* London: Lutterworth Press, 1957.
Sebeok, Thomas A. *Current Trends in Linguistics.* Vol. 7, *Linguistics in Sub-Saharan Africa.* The Hague, The Netherlands: Mouton, 1971.

Seidel, A. *Lehrbuch der Ewhe-Sprache in Togo*. Heidelberg: Julius Groos, Verlag, 1906.
Senna, Nelson de. *Africanos no Brasil*. Belo Horizonte: Oficinas Gráficas Queiroz Breyner, Ltda., 1938.
Senghor, Léopold Sedar. *Latinité et Négritude*. Dakar: Centre de Hautes Études Afro-Ibero-Americaines, n.d.
Silveira, Luis. *Temas Lusíadas*. Lisboa: Agência Geral das Colónias, 1945.
———. "Exéquias no Bôgum de Salvador." *O Mundo Português*, 10 (1942).
Silveira Bueno, Francisco da. *Grande Dicionário Etimológico-Prosódico da Língua Portuguêsa*. São Paulo: Edição Saraiva, 1963.
Smith, Robert. *Kingdoms of the Yoruba*. London: McPruen and Co., Ltd.,, 1969.
Taylor, F. W. *A Fulani-English Dictionary*. Oxford: Clarendon Press, 1932.
Temas Lusíadas: Obra Nova de Lingua Geral de Mina de Antônio da Costa Peixoto. Manuscrito da Biblioteca de Évora e da Biblioteca Nacional de Lisboa, Publicado e apresentado por Luis Silveira. Lisboa: Agência Geral das Colónias, 1945.
Thomas, J. J. *The Theory and Practice of Creole Grammar*. London: New Beacon, Ltd., 1969.
Torrend, Jules. *A Comparative Grammar of the South African Bantu Languages....* London: K. Paul, French, Trübner and Co., Ltd., 1891.
Valente, P. José Francisco. *Gramática Umbundu, A Língua do Centro de Angola*. Lisboa: Junta de Investigações do Ultramar, 1964.
Valente, Waldemar. *Sincretismo Religioso Afro-Brasileiro*. São Paulo, 1955.
———. *Sobrevivências Daomeanas dos Grupos-de-Culto Afronordestinos*. Recife: Ministério Joaquim Nabuco de Pesquisas Sociais, 1964.
Valkhoff, Marius F. *Studies in Portuguese and Creole*. Johannesburg: Witwatersrand University Press, 1966.
Van Sambeek, J. *A Bemba Grammar*. Cape Town: Longmans, 1955.
Van Wing, J. and C. Penders S. J., eds. *Le Plus Ancien Dictionnaire Bantu*. Bibliothèque Congo: Directeur: E. De Jonghe; Vocabularium - P. Georgii Gelensis. Louvain: Kuyl-Otto, 1928.
Verger, Pierre. *Flux et Reflux de la Traite des Nègres entre le Golfe de Bénin et Bahia de Todos os Santos du XVIIe au XIXe Siècle*. Paris: Mouton and Co., 1968.
———. *Formação de uma Sociedade Brasileira no Golfo de Benim no Século XIX*. Dakar: Centre de Hautes Études Afro-Ibero-Americaines, n.d.
———. "Notes sur le culte des Orisa et Vodun à Bahia, la baie de tous les saints, au Brésil et à l'ancienne Coté des Esclaves en Afrique." Dakar: Memoire 51 de l'Institute Français de l'Afrique, Moires, 1957.
———. *O Fumo da Bahia e o Tráfico dos Escravos do Gôlfo de Benim*. Salvador: Fundação Gonçalo Moniz, Publicação do Centro de Estudos Afro-Orientais, Universidade Federal da Bahia, 1966.
Viana, Hélio. *Contribuição à História*. Rio de Janeiro: Imprensa Brasileira, 1945.
Viana, Hildegardes. *A Cozinha Baiana: Seu Folclore, Suas Receitas*. Bahia: Fundação Gonçalo Moniz, 1955.
———. *A Cozinha Baiana*. Bahia: Imprensa Oficial do Estado, 1955.
Vianna Filho, Luis. *O Negro na Bahia*. São Paulo: Livraria José Olympio Editôra, 1946.
Vieira Baião, P[e] Domingos. *Dicionário Ganguela-Português*. Lisboa: Centro de Estudos Filológicos, 1940.

Von Den Steinen, Karl. *O Brasil Central.* São Paulo: Companhia Editôra Nacional, 1942.
Von Schlegel, Friedrich. *Ueber die Sprache und Weisheit der Indier.* 1808 (no publication).
Wagley, Charles. *An Introduction to Brazil.* New York: Columbia University Press, 1963.
――――, ed. *Race and Class in Brazil.* Paris: UNESCO, 1952.
Warburton, Irene, et al. *Ewe Basic Course.* Bloomington: Indiana University Press, 1968.
Welmers, William E. *A Descriptive Grammar of Fanti.* Philadelphia: University of Pennsylvania, 1945.
―――― and Beatrice F. Welmers. *Igbo: A Learner's Dictionary.* Los Angeles: University of California Press, 1968.
Westermann, Diedrich. *Gbesela Yeye or English-Ewe Dictionary.* Berlin: Dietrich Reimer (Ernst Vohsen), 1930.
――――. *Grammatik der Ewe-Sprache.* Berlin: Reimer, 1907.
――――. *A Study of the Ewe Language.* London: translated from the German by A. L. Bickford-Smith, Oxford University Press, 1930.
――――. *Die Ewe-Sprache in Togo, Eine Praktische Einführung.* Berlin: Walter de Gruyter and Co., 1961.
―――― and M. A. Bryan, *The Languages of West Africa. Handbook of African Languages.* London: Oxford University Press, 1952, Part II.
―――― and M. A. Bryan. *The Languages of West Africa.* Folkestone: Dawsons of Pall Mall, 1970.
――――. *Wörterbuch der Ewe-Sprache.* Berlin: Akademie-Verlag, 1954.
―――― and Ida C. Ward. *Practical Phonetics for Students of African Languages.* London: Oxford University Press, 1949.
Winks, Robin W. *Slavery: A Comparative Perspective.* New York: New York University Press, 1972.
Wolff, Hans. *A Comparative Vocabulary of Abuan Dialects.* Evanston: Northwestern University Press, 1969.

The following manuscript sources were also utilized:

Obituaries of the Santa Casa de Misericórdia do Salvador
Obituaries of the Câmara Ecclesiástica do Salvador
Inventories of the Public Archives of the City of Salvador.
Sales Contracts of the Municipal Archives of Salvador.

The native informants were:

Edward Esan (Nigeria) — Yoruba
Bernard Malandila Ngwayan Pangulula (Congo) — Kikongo, Lingala
Kwadwo Oduro (Ghana) — Akan (Fanti-Asante)
Hassan Izzeldin (Sudan) — Arabic, Hausa
Victor Matimba (Rhodesia) — Shona, Chewa, Zulu
Onyango Peter Obado (Kenya) — Swahili, Luo, Dholuo

A LIST OF BAHIAN WORDS OF AFRICAN ORIGIN DEFINED IN CHAPTER IV

(Portuguese words are placed in parentheses. Numbers indicate word order in the chapter.)

abiã 11
abó 12
abô 148
abombar 93
acaçás 75
acarajé 76
acucó 13
afoxé 139
agô 1
agôgô 41
agolêlê 2
alabê 42
alufá 14
amalá 3
angu 77
assarapantar 109
atabaque 130
atôtô 44
axé 45
axêxê 46

babá ifá 15
bamba 177
bambambã 171
bambo 109
bangolar 94
banguela 110
batucada 140
beiju 78
bengala 211
berimbau 131
bimba 202
binga 169
bingar 95

boboca 111
bocó 112
bôlo 79
bori 154
briquitar 96
bunda 203
burucutu 144
búzio 47
buzuntão 113

cabala 212
cabinda 165
cachaça 80
cachimbo 213
caçúa 199
cacula 81
caçula 208
cafanga 180
cafifa 214
cafua 191
cafuçu 173
cafuinha 192
cafunga 114
cafungar 97
cafurna 193
cambaio 115
cambar 98
cambondo 215
candonga 181
canjerê 48
canzuá ∽ ganzuá 49
caolho 186
capangas 200
capêta 189

capiango 176
carcunda 116; 187
cassange 117; 166
(catar) cafuné 99
catende 149
caxinguêlê 150; 177
caxinje ∽ caxixe 216
caxixi 132
chicana 182
comboça 170
congado 141
congo 142
cubata 161
cufar 100
cuíca 133
cumba 16; 118
curau 82
curiar 101
cutuba 119

Dahomey 4
(dar) dobalé 50
(dar o) iká otum iká osi 51
dendê 155
dengoso 120
dunga 121

ebó 52
eiru 53
eleda 17
empalamado 122
engangento 123
engoio 217

engoma 134
Exu onã 18

(fazer o) osé 54
(feixe de) atori 55
filá 56
fiota 179
fuã 194
fubá 83
fulo 218
fuzué 195

gã 5
ganga 58
ganzá 136
garapa 84
gonga 201
gongá 59
gunga 206
gungunar 102

iá ô 19
Iansã 33
ijexá 167
inganja 183
inhame 85
ixê 60
ixés 219
iyalaxé ôpô afonjá 20
iyalorixá 21
iyá nasó 22

jimbo 204

kelé (also spelled quelé) 151

mabaça 209
maconha 156
mandinga 61
mangalaço 124
mangar 103
mangôlô 174
manzanza 175
marufu 86

mataca 220
mironga 62; 196
missanga 145
mixe 125
mocotó 87
molongó 126
mondrongo 188
mucama 210
mulungu 63; 137; 157
munganga 184
mutamba 158
muxinga 197
muzenza 23

nagô 168
Nanã 34

obá 24
obá orum 25
ôbí 64
odi 26
ogã 27
Ogum 6
ôlubajé 65
omi xum 28
Omolu 35
oquicó 7
oriki 66
orixá 8
ôrôbô 67
ossé 68
Ossi iyalaxé 29
Otum iyalaxé 30
Oxagiyan 31
Oxalufan 32
Oxóssi 36
Oxunmarê 37

padê 69
peji 70
peji gã 71
pepeyé 152

quenga 88; 171
quêrêrêquêxê 138

quiba 127
quilombo 162
quisila 185
quitanda 221
quitute 89

rôko (also spelled rôco) 159
rum, rumpi, lé 72

samba 143
sangangu 198
senzala 163
soba 207

tanga 146
tata 164
titica 222
tungar 104
tutu 205

umulucu 90

vodum 9

Xangô 39
xará 223
xaxará 10
xerés 74
ximxim 91
xingar 105
xokotós 147
xôxo 128
xuxu (also spelled chuchu) 92

Yemanjá 38

zanzar 106
zanzo 160
zimbo 153
zombar 107
zumbi 190
zurrar 108

NORTH CAROLINA STUDIES IN THE ROMANCE LANGUAGES AND LITERATURES

I.S.B.N. Prefix 0-8078-

Recent Titles

THE HISPANO-PORTUGUESE CANCIONERO OF THE HISPANIC SOCIETY OF AMERICA, by Arthur Askins. 1974. (No. 144). *-944-8.*

HISTORIA Y BIBLIOGRAFÍA DE LA CRÍTICA SOBRE EL "POEMA DE MÍO CID" (1750-1971), por Miguel Magnotta. 1976. (No. 145). *-945-6.*

LES ENCHANTEMENZ DE BRETAIGNE. AN EXTRACT FROM A THIRTEENTH CENTURY PROSE ROMANCE "LA SUITE DU MERLIN", edited by Patrick C. Smith. 1977. (No. 146). *-9146-0.*

THE DRAMATIC WORKS OF ÁLVARO CUBILLO DE ARAGÓN, by Shirley B. Whitaker. 1975. (No. 149). *-949-9.*

A CONCORDANCE TO THE "ROMAN DE LA ROSE" OF GUILLAUME DE LORRIS, by Joseph R. Danos. 1976. (No. 156). *0-88438-403-9.*

POETRY AND ANTIPOETRY: A STUDY OF SELECTED ASPECTS OF MAX JACOB'S POETIC STYLE, by Annette Thau. 1976. (No. 158). *-005-X.*

FRANCIS PETRARCH, SIX CENTURIES LATER, by Aldo Scaglione. 1975. (No. 159).

STYLE AND STRUCTURE IN GRACIÁN'S "EL CRITICÓN", by Marcia L. Welles, 1976. (No. 160). *-007-6.*

MOLIERE: TRADITIONS IN CRITICISM, by Laurence Romero. 1974 (Essays, No. 1). *-001-7.*

CHRÉTIEN'S JEWISH GRAIL. A NEW INVESTIGATION OF THE IMAGERY AND SIGNIFICANCE OF CHRÉTIEN DE TROYES'S GRAIL EPISODE BASED UPON MEDIEVAL HEBRAIC SOURCES, by Eugene J. Weinraub. 1976. (Essays, No. 2). *-002-5.*

STUDIES IN TIRSO, I, by Ruth Lee Kennedy. 1974. (Essays, No. 3). *-003-3.*

VOLTAIRE AND THE FRENCH ACADEMY, by Karlis Racevskis. 1975. (Essays, No. 4). *-004-1.*

THE NOVELS OF MME RICCOBONI, by Joan Hinde Stewart. 1976. (Essays, No. 8). *-008-4.*

FIRE AND ICE: THE POETRY OF XAVIER VILLAURRUTIA, by Merlin H. Forster. 1976. (Essays, No. 11). *-011-4.*

THE THEATER OF ARTHUR ADAMOV, by John J. McCann. 1975. (Essays, No. 13). *-013-0.*

AN ANATOMY OF POESIS: THE PROSE POEMS OF STÉPHANE MALLARMÉ, by Ursula Franklin. 1976. (Essays, No. 16). *-016-5.*

LAS MEMORIAS DE GONZALO FERNÁNDEZ DE OVIEDO, Vols. I and II, by Juan Bautista Avalle-Arce. 1974. (Texts, Textual Studies, and Translations, Nos. 1 and 2). *-401-2; 402-0.*

GIACOMO LEOPARDI: THE WAR OF THE MICE AND THE CRABS, translated, introduced and annotated by Ernesto G. Caserta. 1976. (Texts, Textual Studies, and Translations, No. 4). *-404-7.*

LUIS VÉLEZ DE GUEVARA: A CRITICAL BIBLIOGRAPHY, by Mary G. Hauer. 1975. (Texts, Textual Studies, and Translations, No. 5). *-405-5.*

UN TRÍPTICO DEL PERÚ VIRREINAL: "EL VIRREY AMAT, EL MARQUÉS DE SOTO FLORIDO Y LA PERRICHOLI". EL "DRAMA DE DOS PALANGANAS" Y SU CIRCUNSTANCIA, estudio preliminar, reedición y notas por Guillermo Lohmann Villena. 1976. (Texts, Textual Studies, and Translation, No. 15). *-415-2.*

LOS NARRADORES HISPANOAMERICANOS DE HOY, edited by Juan Bautista Avalle-Arce. 1973. (Symposia, No. 1). *-951-0.*

ESTUDIOS DE LITERATURA HISPANOAMERICANA EN HONOR A JOSÉ J. ARROM, edited by Andrew P. Debicki and Enrique Pupo-Walker. 1975. (Symposia, No. 2). *-952-9.*

When ordering please cite the *ISBN Prefix* plus the last four digits for each title.

Send orders to: University of North Carolina Press
 Chapel Hill
 North Carolina 27514
 U. S. A.

NORTH CAROLINA STUDIES IN THE ROMANCE LANGUAGES AND LITERATURES

I.S.B.N. Prefix 0-8078-

Recent Titles

MEDIEVAL MANUSCRIPTS AND TEXTUAL CRITICISM, edited by Christopher Kleinhenz. 1976. (Symposia, No. 4). -954-5.
SAMUEL BECKETT. THE ART OF RHETORIC. edited by Edouard Morot-Sir, Howard Harper, and Dougald McMillan III. 1976. (Symposia, No. 5). -955-3.
DELIE. CONCORDANCE, by Jerry Nash. 1976. 2 Volumes. (No. 174).
FIGURES OF REPETITION IN THE OLD PROVENÇAL LYRIC: A STUDY IN THE STYLE OF THE TROUBADOURS, by Nathaniel B. Smith. 1976. (No. 176). -9176-2.
A CRITICAL EDITION OF LE REGIME TRESUTILE ET TRESPROUFITABLE POUR CONSERVER ET GARDER LA SANTE DU CORPS HUMAIN, by Patricia Willett Cummins. 1977. (No. 177).
THE DRAMA OF SELF IN GUILLAUME APOLLINAIRE'S "ALCOOLS", by Richard Howard Stamelman. 1976. (No. 178). -9178-9.
A CRITICAL EDITION OF "LA PASSION NOSTRE SEIGNEUR" FROM MANUSCRIPT 1131 FROM THE BIBLIOTHEQUE SAINTE-GENEVIEVE, PARIS, by Edward J. Gallagher. 1976. (No. 179). -9179-7.
A QUANTITATIVE AND COMPARATIVE STUDY OF THE VOCALISM OF THE LATIN INSCRIPTIONS OF NORTH AFRICA, BRITAIN, DALMATIA, AND THE BALKANS, by Stephen William Omeltchenko. 1977. (No. 180). -9180-0.
OCTAVIEN DE SAINT-GELAIS "LE SEJOUR D'HONNEUR", edited by Joseph A. James. 1977. (No. 181). -9181-9.
A STUDY OF NOMINAL INFLECTION IN LATIN INSCRIPTIONS, by Paul A. Gaeng. 1977. (No. 182). -9182-7.
THE LIFE AND WORKS OF LUIS CARLOS LÓPEZ, by Martha S. Bazik. 1977. (No. 183). -9183-5.
"THE CORT D'AMOR". A THIRTEENTH-CENTURY ALLEGORICAL ART OF LOVE, by Lowanne E. Jones. 1977. (No. 185). -9185-1.
PHYTONYMIC DERIVATIONAL SYSTEMS IN THE ROMANCE LANGUAGES: STUDIES IN THEIR ORIGIN AND DEVELOPMENT, by Walter E. Geiger. 1978. (No. 187). -9187-8.
LANGUAGE IN GIOVANNI VERGA'S EARLY NOVELS, by Nicholas Patruno. 1977. (No. 188). -9188-6.
BLAS DE OTERO EN SU POESÍA, by Moraima de Semprún Donahue. 1977. (No. 189). -9189-4.
LA ANATOMÍA DE "EL DIABLO COJUELO": DESLINDES DEL GÉNERO ANATOMÍSTICO, por C. George Peale. 1977. (No. 191). -9191-6.
RICHARD SANS PEUR, EDITED FROM "LE ROMANT DE RICHART" AND FROM GILLES CORROZET'S "RICHART SANS PAOUR", by Denis Joseph Conlon. 1977. (No. 192). -9192-4.
MARCEL PROUST'S GRASSET PROOFS. Commentary and Variants, by Douglas Alden. 1978. (No. 193). -9193-2.
MONTAIGNE AND FEMINISM, by Cecile Insdorf. 1977. (No. 194). -9194-0.
SANTIAGO F. PUGLIA, AN EARLY PHILADELPHIA PROPAGANDIST FOR SPANISH AMERICAN INDEPENDENCE, by Merle S. Simmons. 1977. (No. 195). -9195-9.
BAROQUE FICTION-MAKING. A STUDY OF GOMBERVILLE'S "POLEXANDRE", by Edward Baron Turk. 1978. (No. 196). -9196-7.
THE TRAGIC FALL: DON ÁLVARO DE LUNA AND OTHER FAVORITES IN SPANISH GOLDEN AGE DRAMA, by Raymond R. MacCurdy. 1978. (No. 197). -9197-5.
A BAHIAN HERITAGE. An Ethnolinguistic Study of African Influences on Bahian Portuguese, by William W. Megenney. 1978. (No. 198). -9198-3.
TWO AGAINST TIME. A Study of the very present worlds of Paul Claudel and Charles Péguy, by Joy Nachod Humes. 1978. (No. 200). -9200-9.

When ordering please cite the ISBN Prefix plus the last four digits for each title.

Send orders to: University of North Carolina Press
Chapel Hill
North Carolina 27514
U. S. A.

The Department of Romance Studies Digital Arts and Collaboration Lab at the University of North Carolina at Chapel Hill is proud to support the digitization of the North Carolina Studies in the Romance Languages and Literatures series.

www.ingramcontent.com/pod-product-compliance
Lightning Source LLC
Chambersburg PA
CBHW022013220426
43663CB00007B/1063